Electric Power Transmission and Distribution

AUTHOR

Dr. Sudhir Sharma

Associate Professor and Head of Department,
Electrical Engineering Department,
DAV Institute of Engineering and Technology,
Jalandhar

REVIEWER

Dr. V.S.K.V. Harish

Assistant Professor,
Instrumentation and Control Engineering,
Netaji Subash University of Technology, New Delhi

KHANNA BOOK PUBLISHING CO. (P) Ltd.
4C/4344, Ansari Road, Darya Ganj,
New Delhi, India

All India Council for Technical Education
Nelson Mandela Marg, Vasant Kunj,
New Delhi, India

Dear Readers,

To prevent the piracy, this book is secured with HIGH SECURITY HOLOGRAM on the front title cover. In case you don't find the hologram on the front cover title, please write us to at contact@khannabooks.com or whatsapp us at +91-99109 09320 and avail special gift voucher for yourself.

Specimen of Hologram on front Cover title:

Moreover, there is a SPECIAL DISCOUNT COUPON for you with EVERY HOLOGRAM.

How to avail this SPECIAL DISCOUNT:

Step 1: Scratch the hologram

Step 2: Under the scratch area, your "coupon code" is available

Step 3: Logon to www.khannabooks.com

Step 4: Use your "coupon code" in the shopping cart and get your copy at a special discount

Step 5: Enjoy your reading!

ISBN: 978-93-5538-590-1

Book Code: DIP472EN

Electric Power Transmission and Distribution

by Dr. Sudhir Sharma

First Edition: 2025

Originally Published by:

All India Council for Technical Education, Ministry of Education, GOI

Exclusively Published & Distributed by:

Khanna Book Publishing Co. (P) Ltd.
4C/4344, Ansari Road, Daryaganj,
New Delhi (INDIA)

Visit us at: **www.khannabooks.com**
Write us at: **contact@khannabooks.com**

To view complete list of books, Please scan the QR Code: KPH

Printed in Bharat.

प्रो. टी. जी. सीताराम
अध्यक्ष
Prof. T. G. Sitharam
Chairman

सत्यमेव जयते

आज़ादी का अमृत महोत्सव

अखिल भारतीय तकनीकी शिक्षा परिषद्
(भारत सरकार का एक सांविधिक निकाय)
(शिक्षा मंत्रालय, भारत सरकार)
नेल्सन मंडेला मार्ग, वसंत कुंज, नई दिल्ली-110070
दूरभाष : 011-26131498
ई-मेल : chairman@aicte-india.org

ALL INDIA COUNCIL FOR TECHNICAL EDUCATION
(A STATUTORY BODY OF THE GOVT. OF INDIA)
(Ministry of Education, Govt. of India)
Nelson Mandela Marg, Vasant Kunj, New Delhi-110070
Phone : 011-26131498
E-mail : chairman@aicte-india.org

FOREWORD

Engineers are the backbone of any modern society. They are the ones responsible for the marvels as well as the improved quality of life across the world. Engineers have driven humanity towards greater heights in a more evolved and unprecedented manner.

The All India Council for Technical Education (AICTE), have spared no efforts towards the strengthening of the technical education in the country. AICTE is always committed towards promoting quality Technical Education to make India a modern developed nation emphasizing on the overall welfare of mankind.

An array of initiatives has been taken by AICTE in last decade which have been accelerated now by the National Education Policy (NEP) 2020. The implementation of NEP under the visionary leadership of Hon'ble Prime Minister of India envisages the provision for education in regional languages to all, thereby ensuring that every graduate becomes competent enough and is in a position to contribute towards the national growth and development through innovation & entrepreneurship.

One of the spheres where AICTE had been relentlessly working since past couple of years is providing high quality original technical contents at Under Graduate & Diploma level prepared and translated by eminent educators in various Indian languages to its aspirants. For students pursuing 2nd year of their Engineering education, AICTE has identified 87 books, which shall be translated into 12 Indian languages - Hindi, Tamil, Gujarati, Odia, Bengali, Kannada, Urdu, Punjabi, Telugu, Marathi, Assamese & Malayalam. In addition to the English medium, books in different Indian Languages are going to support the students to understand the concepts in their respective mother tongue.

On behalf of AICTE, I express sincere gratitude to all distinguished authors, reviewers and translators from the renowned institutions of high repute for their admirable contribution in a record span of time.

AICTE is confident that these outcomes based original contents shall help aspirants to master the subject with comprehension and greater ease.

(Prof. T. G. Sitharam)

Prof. T. G. Sitharam
Chairman

ALL INDIA COUNCIL FOR TECHNICAL EDUCATION
Nelson Mandela Marg, Vasant Kunj, New Delhi-110070
E-mail: chairman@aicte-india.org

FOREWORD

Engineers are the backbone of any modern society. They are the ones responsible for the marvels as well as the improved quality of life across the world. Engineers have driven humanity towards greater heights in a more evolved and unprecedented manner.

The All India Council for Technical Education (AICTE), have spared no efforts towards the strengthening of the technical education in the country. AICTE is always committed towards promoting quality Technical Education to make India a modern developed nation emphasizing on the overall welfare of mankind.

An array of initiatives has been taken by AICTE in last decade which have been accelerated now by the National Education Policy (NEP) 2020. The implementation of NEP under the visionary leadership of Hon'ble Prime Minister of India envisages the provision for education in regional languages to all, thereby ensuring that every student becomes competent enough and is in a position to contribute towards the national growth and development through innovation & entrepreneurship.

One of the spheres where AICTE had been relentlessly working since past couple of years is providing high quality original technical contents at Under Graduate & Diploma level prepared and translated by eminent educators in various Indian languages to its aspirants. For students pursuing 2nd year of their Engineering education, AICTE has identified [illegible] Books, which shall be translated into 12 Indian languages - Hindi, Tamil, Gujarati, Odia, Bengali, Kannada, Urdu, Punjabi, Telugu, Marathi, Assamese & Malayalam. In addition to the English medium book, [illegible] Indian Languages are going to support the students to understand the concepts in their respective mother tongue.

On behalf of AICTE, I express sincere gratitude to all distinguished authors, reviewers and translators from the renowned institutions of high repute for their admirable contribution in a record span of time.

AICTE is confident that these outcomes based original contents shall help aspirants to master the subject with comprehension and greater ease.

(Prof. T. G. Sitharam)

ACKNOWLEDGEMENT

The author is grateful to the authorities of AICTE, particularly Prof. T. G. Sitharam, Chairman; Dr. Abhay Jere, Vice-Chairman; Prof. Rajive Kumar, Member-Secretary; Dr. Ramesh Unnikrishnan, Advisor-II and Dr. Sunil Luthra, Director, Training and Learning Bureau, for their planning to publish the books on Electric Power Transmission and Distribution. I sincerely acknowledge the valuable contributions of the reviewer of the book, Dr. VSKV Harish, Assistant Professor, Instrumentation and Control Engineering, Netaji Subash University of Technology, New Delhi, for making it reader-friendly and giving it a better shape in an artistic manner.

Furthermore, I would like to express my gratitude to Sh. Rahul Sharma, assistant professor at the IKG Punjab Technical University in Kapurthala, for his significant input into the writing of this book. I also want to thank my wife, Seema Sharma, for giving me the encouragement and emotional support I needed to write this book.

This book is the outcome of various suggestions from AICTE members, experts, and authors who shared their opinions and thoughts on how to further develop engineering education in our country. Acknowledgements are due to the contributors and different workers in this field whose published books, review articles, papers, photographs, footnotes, references, and other valuable information enriched us at the time of writing the book.

Dr. Sudhir Sharma

PREFACE

This book is intended for diploma students studying electrical engineering and provides the students with a solid foundation in the theory and practice of electric power transmission and distribution." Electric Power Transmission and Distribution" is an important subject for Diploma Engineering students. The purpose of this book is to give students a thorough understanding of the fundamental concepts, technologies, and practices associated with electric power transmission and distribution.

The book begins with an introduction to the fundamental principles of electric power transmission and distribution, such as power transmission from generation plants, various types of transmission and distribution systems, and the key components and equipment used in these systems.

The technical aspects of transmission and distribution are covered in greater detail as the book goes on, with chapters on transmission line parameters and performance, extra-high voltage transmission, ac distribution systems, etc. The components of transmission and distribution and transmission and distribution network design and planning are among the other topics discussed in this book.

We have also included a variety of examples, multiple-choice questions, and practice problems to help the students understand the concepts better and relate the theories to practical applications. We hope that this book will serve as a valuable resource for students as they continue to learn about transmission and distribution systems.

I hold a genuine aspiration that this book will serve as a wellspring of inspiration for students, igniting their curiosity to delve into and deliberate upon the fundamental concepts underpinning the transmission and distribution of electric power. Moreover, I am confident that this work will play a pivotal role in establishing a robust bedrock of understanding in this field.

We extend our heartfelt appreciation for any valuable insights, comments, or suggestions that may contribute to enhancing future editions of this book. The opportunity to entrust this book into the hands of both educators and students fills us with immense joy. The journey of crafting the diverse spectrum of topics encompassed within the pages of this book has undeniably been a gratifying endeavor.

Dr. Sudhir Sharma

OUTCOME BASED EDUCATION

For the implementation of an outcome-based education the first requirement is to develop an outcome-based curriculum and incorporate an outcome-based assessment in the education system. By going through outcome-based assessments, evaluators will be able to evaluate whether the students have achieved the outlined standard, specific and measurable outcomes. With the proper incorporation of outcome-based education there will be a definite commitment to achieve a minimum standard for all learners without giving up at any level. At the end of the programme running with the aid of outcome-based education, a student will be able to arrive at the following outcomes:

Programme Outcomes (POs) are statements that describe what students are expected to know and be able to do upon graduating from the program. These relate to the skills, knowledge, analytical ability attitude and behaviour that students acquire through the program. The POs essentially indicate what the students can do from subject-wise knowledge acquired by them during the program. As such, POs define the professional profile of an engineering diploma graduate.

National Board of Accreditation (NBA) has defined the following seven POs for an Engineering diploma graduate:

PO-1: Basic and Discipline specific knowledge: Apply knowledge of basic mathematics, science and engineering fundamentals and engineering specialization to solve the engineering problems.

PO-2: Problem analysis: Identify and analyses well-defined engineering problems using codified standard methods.

PO-3: Design/development of solutions: Design solutions for well-defined technical problems and assist with the design of systems components or processes to meet specified needs.

PO-4: Engineering Tools, Experimentation and Testing: Apply modern engineering tools and appropriate technique to conduct standard tests and measurements.

PO-5: Engineering practices for society, sustainability and environment: Apply appropriate technology in context of society, sustainability, environment and ethical practices.

PO-6: Project Management: Use engineering management principles individually, as a team member or a leader to manage projects and effectively communicate about well-defined engineering activities.

PO-7: Life-long Learning: Ability to analyse individual needs and engage in updating in the context of technological changes.

COURSE OUTCOMES (CO)

The theory, practical experiences and relevant soft skills associated with this course are to be taught and implemented, so that the student demonstrates the following industry-oriented COs associated with the above-mentioned competency: By the end of the course the students are expected to learn:

CO-1: Interpret the normal operation of the electric transmission and distribution systems.

CO-2: Maintain the functioning of the medium and high voltage transmission system.

CO-3: Interpret the parameters of the extra high voltage transmission system

CO-4: Maintain the functioning of the low voltage AC distribution system.

CO-5: Maintain the components of the transmission and distribution lines.

Mapping of Course Outcomes with Programme Outcomes to be done according to the matrix given below:

Course Outcomes	EXPECTED MAPPING WITH PROGRAMME OUTCOMES (1- Weak Correlation; 2- Medium correlation; 3- Strong Correlation)						
	PO-1	PO-2	PO-3	PO-4	PO-5	PO-6	PO-7
CO-1	3	3	3	3	1	1	3
CO-2	3	2	2	2	1	1	3
CO-3	3	2	2	2	1	1	3
CO-4	3	2	2	3	1	1	3
CO-5	3	3	3	3	1	1	3

GUIDELINES FOR TEACHERS

To implement Outcome Based Education (OBE) knowledge level and skill set of the students should be enhanced. Teachers should take a major responsibility for the proper implementation of OBE. Some of the responsibilities (not limited to) for the teachers in OBE system may be as follows:

- Within reasonable constraint, they should manoeuvre time to the best advantage of all students.
- They should assess the students only upon certain defined criterion without considering any other potential ineligibility to discriminate them.
- They should try to grow the learning abilities of the students to a certain level before they leave the institute.
- They should try to ensure that all the students are equipped with the quality knowledge as well as competence after they finish their education.
- They should always encourage the students to develop their ultimate performance capabilities.
- They should facilitate and encourage group work and team work to consolidate newer approach.
- They should follow Blooms taxonomy in every part of the assessment.

Bloom's Taxonomy

Level	Teacher should Check	Student should be able to	Possible Mode of Assessment
Creating	Students ability to create	Design or Create	Mini project
Evaluating	Students ability to Justify	Argue or Defend	Assignment
Analysing	Students ability to distinguish	Differentiate or Distinguish	Project/Lab Methodology
Applying	Students ability to use information	Operate or Demonstrate	Technical Presentation/ Demonstration
Understanding	Students ability to explain the ideas	Explain or Classify	Presentation/Seminar
Remembering	Students ability to recall (or remember)	Define or Recall	Quiz

GUIDELINES FOR STUDENTS

Students should take equal responsibility for implementing the OBE. Some of the responsibilities (not limited to) for the students in OBE system are as follows:

- Students should be well aware of each UO before the start of a unit in each and every course.
- Students should be well aware of each CO before the start of the course.
- Students should be well aware of each PO before the start of the programme.
- Students should think critically and reasonably with proper reflection and action.
- Learning of the students should be connected and integrated with practical and real-life consequences.
- Students should be well aware of their competency at every level of OBE.

ABBREVIATIONS AND SYMBOLS

List of Abbreviations

General Terms			
Abbreviations	**Full form**	**Abbreviations**	**Full form**
AC	Alternating current	R	Resistance
DC	Direct current	L	Inductance
kV	Kilo volts	C	Capacitance
HVDC	High voltage direct current	G	Conductance
HVAC	High voltage alternating current	H	Henry
H.T.	High tension	p.d.	Potential difference
HV	High voltage	F	Farad
LV	Low voltage	Q	Charge
cos- / p.f.	Power factor	V.R.	Voltage regulation
kWh	kilowatt hour	VS	Sending end voltage
GMR	Geometrical mean radius	VR	Receiving end voltage
kW	kilo Watt	XL	Inductive reactance
KVA	kilo Volt Ampere	P	Power
ROW	Right of way	Zo	Surge Impedance
V	Voltage	Hk	Field strength
I	Current	Bk	Flux density
VP	Phase voltage	UHV	Ultra-high voltage
IP	Phase current	X	Equivalent reactance
VL	Line voltage	SIL	Surge impedance loading
IL	Line current	rms	root mean square
km	kilometre	mm	millimetre
cm	centimetre	dB	decibel
Q	Charge	RI	Radio Interference
ACSR	Aluminium conductor steel reinforced	FACTS	Flexible AC transmission system
		XC	Capacitive reactance
Hz	Hertz	+ve	positive
CT	Current transformer	-ve	negative
PT	Potential transformer	RFID	Radio frequency identification

SF6	Sulphur Hexafluoride	EV	Electric Vehicles
Q	Reactive power	VAr	Volt ampere reactive
V	Valve	SCR	silicon controlled rectifier
E	Electrode	f	Frequency
T	Converter transformer	ACB	Air circuit breaker
IEEE	Institute of Electrical and Electronics Engineers	OCB	Oil circuit breaker
		HRC	High rupturing capacity
R	Red	RCC	Reinforced cement concrete
Y	Yellow	VIR	Vulcanized Indian rubber
B	Blue	TPIC	Triple pole iron clad
i.e.	That is	IER	Indian electricity rules
e.g.	Example		
SLD	Single line diagram		
GOS	Gang operating switch		

List of Units and Symbols

Symbols	Description	Symbols	Description
ϕ	Phase	ψ	Flux linkage
ρ	Resistivity	μ_o	Absolute permeability
μ	micro	μ_r	Relative permeability
Ω	ohm	δ	Load angle
η	efficiency	Δ	Delta
°C	Degree Celsius	Y	Star
η_T	Transmission efficiency		

LIST OF FIGURES

CONTENTS

1 Basics of Transmission and Distribution

UNIT SPECIFICS

Through this unit we will discuss the following aspects:

- What is the need to transfer power and why in the form of electric power?
- What are the various components of an electric supply system?
- How transmission lines are classified based on voltage and other parameters.
- What are the standard voltage levels in India and basis of choosing voltage level for a transmission line?
- Steps to construct an electric transmission and distribution supply system.

The theory topics are correlated with practical applications to invoke critical and innovative thinking amongst the readers.

Unit highlights are given at the end of the chapter to facilitate the quick revision of the unit contents. The exercise questions are designed keeping in view the HOTs and LOTs orders of revised bloom's taxonomy. Multiple choice questions, true false options and fill-in-the blanks are given for the practice of the students. Material/links/references for further reading about the topics is given under the heading "know more" and "references" are also provided. The QR codes provided in the different sections can be easily scanned for quick reference about the related topics.

The practical related to the unit has been painstakingly planned to give a clear understanding of the topics covered in unit 1. Solved Numerical Problems, formula summery and unsolved numerical problems are given for reference and practice of the users of this book. Finally, a basic understanding about transmission and distribution supply systems is developed relating the subject matter with our day-to-day life or/and industrial applications.

RATIONALE

This fundamental unit on electric transmission and distribution systems helps readers to get a primary idea about the electric supply system (transmission and distribution) along with its various components. Significance of transmission of power, in electrical form, has been explained. It explains the classification of transmission and distribution system on the basis of type of voltage i.e. AC or DC, voltage levels, length of transmission lines etc. All these points are discussed to understand why the voltage levels of transmission lines are kept at higher levels.

Electric power is generated in bulk at a generating station, and this bulk power at high voltage is transmitted via transmission lines from a generating station to an electric substation. Whereas, the distribution of power is done at low voltage levels, so the power received at the distribution substation is stepped down for further distribution and used by domestic, commercial, public, and industrial customers. The steps taken in building electric power transmission and distribution networks are explained to the reader in this unit. This unit includes comprehensive details on voltage levels used for transmission and distribution in India; detailed descriptions supported by solved examples; and figures that enable the students to envisage the components of transmission supply systems.

PRE-REQUISITES

Basic subject of electrical power systems. No prerequisite is required.

UNIT OUTCOMES

The students will be able to:

U1-O1: Interpret single-line diagrams of transmission and distribution supply systems.

U1-O2: Classify transmission lines based on various parameters.

U1-O3: Differentiate between transmission and distribution system

U1-O4: Infer methods of construction of electric supply transmission and distribution system

Unit-1 Outcome	EXPECTED MAPPING WITH COURSE OUTCOMES (1 - Weak Correlation; 2 - Medium Correlation; 3 - Strong Correlation)				
	CO-1	CO-2	CO-3	CO-4	CO-5
U1-O1	3	1	1	1	2
U1-O2	1	3	3	2	2
U1-O3	3	3	2	3	3
U1-O4	2	2	3	2	3

1.1 INTRODUCTION

Today's modern society can't be imagined without electricity. The per capita consumption of electrical power reflects the living standards and prosperity of a nation. Any shortage of energy will hamper economic growth and the progress of the country. The electric power generating stations are generally located at faraway places from the load centres, such as hydroelectric plants, which are generally located in hilly areas; thermal power plants, which are preferably located near coal mines; and nuclear power plants, which are also constructed away from densely populated areas. Whereas load centres such as large industries, commercial centres, institutions, and domestic consumers are located in big cities and villages. In order to transfer bulk power from one location to another, the most efficient and economical method is to transfer in the form of electric power. The advantages of transferring power in the form of electric power include the easy conversion of electric power into other forms such as heat, mechanical power, light, etc. Once the transmission lines are installed and start functioning, the transportation of electricity becomes very easy. Transmission lines have a lifespan measured in years, with little or no maintenance required. Human life has changed by the invention of electricity. We cannot assume that any sector of today's modern society can work without electricity. When compared to other fuels, the efficiency of systems increase when they use electricity. The need for electricity further increases with the use of electricity in railway transportation and with the increasing share of electric vehicles.

Bulk electric power is generated at power plants. This is transmitted to power receiving substations through transmission lines. These receiving power substations then distribute it to end-users through distribution lines. The combination of this transmission and distribution network is known as the electric power grid. In India, it is called the National Grid. Electrical power transmission is done at high voltage, in a range of 33 kV to 765 kV, to minimize transmission losses. Then this voltage is stepped down and distributed to end-users by using step-down transformers. These transformers reduce the voltage from high voltage to 415 V/220 V. In India, most of the domestic electrical equipment works at this voltage. Transmission and distribution of electrical power can be performed either via AC or DC systems, but generally, in India, a 3-phase, 3-wire system is used for large power transmission and a 3-phase 4-wire system is used for distribution of electrical power. For long distances, High voltage direct current (HVDC) transmission lines are more economical and efficient than high-voltage AC (HVAC) transmission lines. A few HVDC transmission lines are also operational in India.

1.2 COMPONENTS OF SUPPLY SYSTEM

A large network of conductors and cables is required to transmit electrical power from generating stations to end users. This large network of conductors and cables is generally divided into two sections, namely the power transmission system and the distribution supply system.

The typical outline of an ac transmission and distribution supply system is shown in figure 1.1. The single line diagram shows all the subsections of transmission and distribution supply systems; however, it isn't fixed that all supply systems incorporate all stages, i.e., primary and secondary supply systems. In some cases, the power supply system may not have secondary power transmission, and in another situation, the power supply system might be little to the point that there is, as it were, only secondary distribution and no primary distribution, or vice versa.

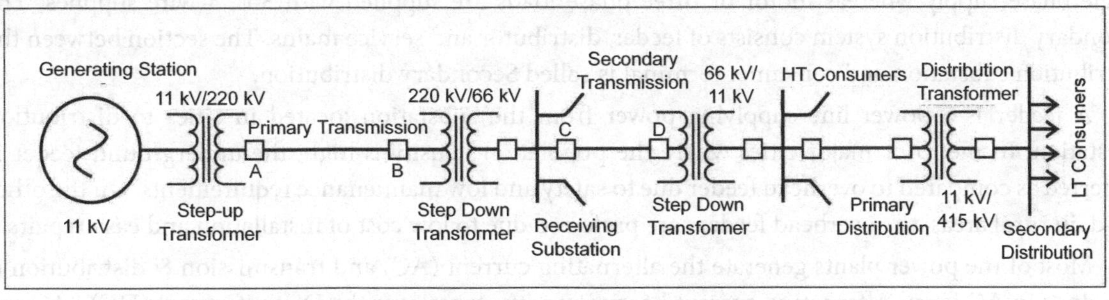

Fig. 1.1: Typical outline of an ac transmission and distribution supply system

The generating station shown in figure 1.1 may be of any type, such as hydroelectric, thermal, nuclear, or any other renewable source. Generally, three-phase alternators are used for generating electrical power. The generating voltage is generally 11 or higher, but in some cases, it may be as high as 6.6 kV or 33 kV. It is economical to generate voltages at lower voltages simultaneously, and it is economical to transmit power at higher voltages. This generated voltage is stepped up to 132, 220 kV, or a higher value at the substation station using step-up power transformers. High voltages are used for transmission because of various advantages, such as high transmission efficiency and the saving of conductor material. However, the transmission voltages can only be increased to certain limits. Higher voltages in transmission systems cause insulation problems. The switchgear and transformer costs also increase with an increase in transmission voltage levels. Therefore, voltage levels for a transmission line should be selected considering technical and economical constraints. Voltage levels for transmission of electric power in India are generally 66 kV, 132 kV, 220 kV, 400 kV, and 765 kV in the case of AC transmission systems.

Primary transmission: The bulk transmission of electric power from the generating station to a substation in the surrounding area of cities or load centres is called the primary transmission system. In Fig. 1.1, the section shown between points A and B is called the primary transmission system. The power is transferred by a 3-ϕ three-wire overhead transmission system. The voltage levels are stepped down at the receiving substations for secondary transmission.

Secondary transmission: The secondary transmission system includes power transmission via 3-ϕ three-wire overhead transmission lines from the receiving substation located in the surrounding area of the city or load centers to the substations located at various points near the consumers in the city. The section marked between points C and D in Fig. 1.1 shows the secondary transmission system. The voltage levels are further stepped down to 33 kV or 11 3-ϕ three-wire at these substations.

Primary distribution: From the substation located in the city, power is supplied to large H.T. consumers via 3-ϕ three-wire overhead or underground system. The power is further stepped down by these large consumers at their own premises to 415/220 V, 3-ϕ four-wire for further uses by the large consumers in their premises. The section of the supply system between substations and large consumers supplied at 11, 33 kV via 3-ϕ three-wire overhead is called the primary distribution system.

Secondary Distribution: The electric power from the primary distribution lines is delivered to pole-mounted transformer located near the residential localities. The distributed line voltage is stepped down to 415/220 V, 3- four-wire for secondary distribution. Residential consumers are supplied with single phase supply whereas motor or three phase loads are supplied with 3-ϕ, 4 wire supplies. The secondary distribution system consists of feeder, distributor and service mains. The section between the distribution substation and consumer terminal is called Secondary distribution.

A feeder is a power line supplying power from the substation located in cities to distribution substation. In metro or major cities where the population density is high, the underground feeder is preferred as compared to overhead feeder due to safety and low maintenance requirements. On the other hand, in rural areas, the overhead feeders are preferred due to low cost of installation and easy repairs.

Most of the power plants generate the alternating current (AC) and transmission & distribution is also done in AC form. Alternating current has many advantages over the Direct Current (DC). AC can easily be stepped down or stepped-up using transformers as compared to DC. Therefore, AC is an easy and economical option to generate and distribute the electric power. For the household use of current, the power utility companies supply the alternating current. Most of the electronic instruments use DC to operate therefore, each instrument contains a converter to convert the supplied AC to usable DC at houses. The transmission system can be classified based on various parameters:

1. **Type of voltage:**
   (a) A.C. Transmission line
   (b) D.C Transmission line
2. **Type of system:**
   (a) Overhead transmission
   (b) Underground transmission
3. **Length of power transmission line system:**
   (a) Long power transmission line
   (b) Medium power transmission line
   (c) Short power transmission line
4. **Classification on the basis of voltage level**
   Standard voltage limits for Transmission Lines as per Indian Grid code are given in the table1.1. The operating grid voltages are always kept within the specified values.

Table 1.1: Standard voltage limits for Transmission Lines

Sr. No.	Nominal System line Voltage (kV)	Maximum line Voltage (kV)	Minimum line Voltage (kV)
1.	765	800	728
2.	400	420	380
3.	220	245	198
4.	132	145	122
5.	110	121	99
6.	66	72	60
7.	33	36	30

The standard voltage level for distribution lines is 66/33 kV level. Therefore, the voltage levels in the distribution network are 66 kV, 33 kV, 22 kV, 11 kV and 400/230 volts, and sometimes 6.6 kV, 3.3 kV and 2.2 kV. The amount of distribution power and the line distance over which power is to be delivered decides the voltage level of the transmission lines. Other major distribution devices include HV and LV voltage lines, distribution transformers, substations, switchgear, shunt capacitors, line conductors and energy meters. voltage lines deliver electricity to bulk consumers while LV lines supply residential purchasers.

1.3 A.C. AND D.C. TRANSMISSION

The electrical power can be transferred via A.C. or D.C. transmission systems. Each system has its own advantages and disadvantages. The transmission systems are generally compared on a technical and economical basis. With the developments of technology particularly in the field of power electronics; use of dc for long distance transmission is also increasing. However, to compare these two systems we must know their advantages and disadvantages. The following section gives a comparison between AC and DC transmission systems.

1.3.1 AC Transmission

Most of the electrical power generated these days is AC due to its many advantages. The biggest advantages of AC voltage is that it can be easily stepped up and stepped down with the help of transformers. It is economical to transmit power at higher voltages which can be done easily in AC systems. The electrical power is generated at higher voltages such as 11/6.6/33 kV. The maintenance of equipment used in AC substations is easy and economical as compared to DC. In contrast, it is more difficult to construct AC transmission lines than DC ones. The number of conductors required in ac transmission lines is 3 (in case of 3-ϕ, 3-wire power transmission system) line supports and conductor costs are more. We need to compensate for the effects of capacitances and inductances which inherently appear in ac transmission lines resulting in power loss.

1.3.2 DC Transmission

The first ever transmission line was a DC transmission line constructed in lower Manhattan USA in 1882. DC has numerous advantages, one of which is that it requires only two conductors for transmission of power, hence conductor costs are low as compared to AC 3-wire systems. Also, there is no effect of capacitance and inductance in DC lines and in the absence of any capacitive and inductive reactance the voltage drop in DC lines is less as compared to AC transmission lines. In contrast to AC transmission lines, DC transmission lines do not experience the Skin effect since the whole cross section of the line conductor is used to carry current. This results in lower resistance. In case of power transmission through cables there are no dielectric losses because of the absence of capacitance. DC transmission lines are also free from synchronising and stability problems. The insulation stress on insulators is low in DC transmission as compared to AC transmission.

But generating DC power at high voltages is limited due to the commutation problem in DC generators. The switchgear and circuit breakers used in the DC transmission system also have their own limitations. The stepping up or stepping down of DC voltage is not as easy as in case of AC Transmission Systems. The transmission of electric power by DC lines for long distances is getting dynamic consideration by engineers because of its various benefits and latest developments in the field of power electronics.

1.4 CLASSIFICATION OF VOLTAGE LEVELS

Voltage levels vary widely in various sections of the electric power supply system. The voltage levels in different sections of power supply system are summarized in table 1.2

Table 1.2: Voltage levels in different sections of power supply system

Section of power supply system	Voltages
Generation voltages	11 kV and 33 kV
Primary transmission voltages	132 kV, 220 kV and 400 kV, 765kV
Secondary transmission voltages	33 kV and 66 kV
Primary distribution voltages	6.6 kV, 11 kV
Secondary distribution voltages	415 V (3-ϕ) and 220 V (1-ϕ)

1.5 ADVANTAGES AND DISADVANTAGES OF HIGH VOLTAGE TRANSMISSION

Due to the following advantages, electrical energy transmission takes place at high voltage:

(a) Reduced conductor size: The size of the conductor is reduced for transferring the same amount of power to the same distance when higher voltages are used. Let us consider a 3-ϕ, 3-wire power transmission line:

Amount of Power transmitted	= P watt
Line voltage	= V volts
Length of transmission line	= l meters
Resistance of conductor	= R ohms
Power factor	= cos f
Resistivity (ρ) of transmission line conductor material	= ρ
Transmission line conductor cross-sectional area	= a
Line load current, I	= $P/\sqrt{3}V\ Cos\phi$ Ampers
Resistance(R) of each line conductor	= $\frac{\rho\, l}{a}$

The total power loss in three phase transmission line given by

$$W = 3I2R = 3\ (P/\sqrt{3}V\ Cos\ \phi)^2 \times \rho\, l / a$$

or cross-sectional area 'a' = P 2 ρ l / W V 2cos 2

Total volume of line conductor material required = 2 a l

= 3(P 2 ρ l / W V 2cos 2)…….1.1

From Equation 1.1 it is clear that the required volume of conductive material for line conductors is inversely proportional to V^2 if all other parameters are held constant. Therefore, high-voltage transmission lines require thin conductors, saving conductive material.

(a) It improves the voltage regulation and reduces the voltage drop.

(b) It reduces the power losses (especially the line losses).

(c) As the voltage increases, the efficiency of the transmission line also improves.

The above discussion concludes that it is prudent to note the highest conceivable voltage for power transmission in order to save the transmission line conductor material and cost of the support structure (steel towers). However, there are certain limitations that limit the use of very high voltages for transmission lines. The limitations of using high voltage for transmission lines are given below:

(a) High initial cost of installation due to increased cost of protective devices (such as transformers, switchgear, overhead components, etc).

(b) A high length tower is needed that creates more clearance in between conductors and the ground.

(c) More insulations are required

So, the choice of voltage level for transmission lines is based on technical and economic factors. Economic choice of conductor and voltage is discussed in later sections in this unit.

1.6 DIFFERENT SYSTEMS OF TRANSMISSION OF ELECTRICAL POWER

Generally, 3-ϕ three-wire AC transmission systems are used for power transmission of electric power and 3-ϕ four-wire AC systems are used for distribution of electric power to end consumers. However the below mentioned other systems can also be used for transmission and distribution of electric power. The different systems of power transmission are:

1. **DC Systems:**
   (a) 2-wire DC power system
   (b) DC power system with earthed mid-point using a 2-wire configuration
   (c) 3-wire DC power system
2. **Single-Phase AC Systems:**
   (a) 1-ϕ, 2-wire AC power system
   (b) Single-phase, 2-wire AC power system with a grounded midpoint.
   (c) 1-ϕ, 3-wire AC power system
3. **Two-Phase AC Systems:**
   (a) 2-ϕ, 3-wire AC power system
   (b) 2-ϕ, 4-wire AC power system
4. **Three-phase AC systems:**
   (a) 3-ϕ, 3-wire AC power system
   (b) 3-ϕ, 4-wire AC power system

Since in a transmission system the cost of the material used for conductors represents a significant portion of the total cost of the transmission line, the best electrical power transmission systems are those for which the required volume of conductor material is minimal.

Table 1.3 gives the comparison of conductor material required in various systems of transmission with 2 wire DC transmission systems taken as the basis for comparison. The volume required for conductor material in a two-wire dc system will be taken as the basic quantity.

$$V = \frac{4.\ P^2.\rho.l^2}{V^2.W} = Q$$

Table 1.3: Comparison of conductor material

Systems	Comparison of volume of conductor material required for transmission line	
	Overhead transmission system (same maximum voltage between conductor and earth)	Underground transmission using cables (same maximum voltage between any two conductor)
A. DC Systems:		

(a) DC two-wire system	1	1
(b) DC power system with earthed mid-point using a 2-wire configuration.	0.25	1
(c) DC three-wire system	0.3125	1.25
B. Single-Phase AC Systems:		
(a) 1-ϕ two-wire system	$\frac{2}{\cos^2\phi}$	$\frac{2}{\cos^2\phi}$
(b) Single-phase, 2-wire AC power system with a grounded midpoint.	$\frac{0.5}{\cos^2\phi}$	$\frac{2}{\cos^2\phi}$
(c) 1-ϕ three-wire system	$\frac{0.625}{\cos^2\phi}$	$\frac{2.5}{\cos^2\phi}$
C. Two-Phase AC Systems:		
(a) 2-ϕ three-wire system	$\frac{1.457}{\cos^2\phi}$	$\frac{2.914}{\cos^2\phi}$
(b) 2-ϕ four-wire system	$\frac{0.5}{\cos^2\phi}$	$\frac{2}{\cos^2\phi}$
D. Three-phase AC systems:		
(a) 3-ϕ three-wire system	$\frac{0.5}{\cos^2\phi}$	$\frac{1.5}{\cos^2\phi}$
(b) 3-ϕ four-wire system	$\frac{0.583}{\cos^2\phi}$	$\frac{1.75}{\cos^2\phi}$

From the above table it is clear that saving in the conductor material can be achieved by adopting a DC over AC system however, due to technical challenges, DC transmission is not used in power transmission and distribution. The three phase AC system is more suitable for transmission due to considerable savings in the conductive material as compared to other systems of AC transmission.

1.7 COMPONENTS OF AN OVERHEAD POWER TRANSMISSION LINE

The main components of a power transmission line are given below:

(a) Line conductors: The line conductors used in transmission lines are generally made of aluminium conductor steel reinforced (ACSR). The number of conductors for a single circuit 3-ϕ line are usually three and six for 3-ϕ double circuit lines.

(b) **Transformers:** A transformer is a static device and is used to increase or decrease the voltage levels. A step-up transformer is provided at the generation end of the transmission line and a step-down transformer is used at the receiving end of the transmission line to lower the voltage level.

(c) **Lines Supports:** lines supports (generally steel towers) used to support and provide necessary clearance from the ground level in case of overhead transmission lines.

(d) **Line insulators:** Insulators are used to hold the conductors with line supports and to isolate the live line conductors from the steel towers and ground.

(e) **Protective Switchgear:** Protective Switchgear is used to protect the lines from different types of faults. A protective device includes relays, circuit breakers, lightning arrestors, ground wires to provide required protection to transmission lines.

(f) **Control Switchgear:** This includes voltage regulators, devices switching devices to keep the voltage information limits and for switching on and off transmission lines respectively.

1.8 CHOICE OF CONDUCTOR SIZE:

The major part of the capital cost of a transmission line is the cost of the conductor material used for transmission of electrical power. Hence, for economical design of transmission line proper choice of conductor size is very important. According to Kelvin's law the most economical area of the conductor size is that at which the total annual cost of the transmission line is minimum. The yearly costs associated with a transmission can be categorized into two main components: the annual capital charges for erecting the transmission line and the annual energy loss costs incurred during power transmission across that line.

(a) **Annual charges on capital cost:** This cost includes annual interest and depreciation charges on the capital cost of construction of transmission line. This includes the cost of line supports, conductors, insulators and other material used in the construction of transmission line. For an overhead line the cost of insulators is fixed for a particular voltage level. The cost of the motor is proportional to the size of the conductor used in a transmission line where the cost of line supports is partially constant and partially proportional to the size of the conductor. Therefore, annual charges in capital cost can be expressed as:

$$\text{Annual charges} = K_1 + K_2 a \qquad \text{... (1.2)}$$

In equation 1.2 K_1 and K_2 are constants and "a" is the area of cross section of conductor i.e. the size of the conductor.

(b) **Annual cost of energy wasted in transmission line:** Energy loss occurs in transmission line because of I^2R loss. Since current flowing through the conductor remains almost constant throughout the year the energy losses are mainly dependent upon the resistance of the transmission line and the resistance of the transmission line is inversely proportional to the area of cross section of the conductor.

$$\text{Annual Cost of energy lost in transmission line} = K_3/a \qquad \text{... (1.3)}$$

where K_3 is constant

$$\text{Total annual cost } C = K_1 + K_2 a + K_3/a \qquad \text{... (1.4)}$$

The annual minimum cost can be calculated by differentiating equation 1.3 w.r.t. 'a' and equating it equal to zero.

$$d/da(C) = 0$$

$$d/da\,(K_1+K_2a+K_3/a) = 0$$
$$K_2-K_3/a^2 = 0$$
$$K_2 = K_3/a^2$$
$$K_2a = K_3/a$$

Variable part of annual charges on capital cost = Annual Cost of energy wasted in transmission line.

Therefore, the most economical conductor size is which at Variable part of annual charges on capital cost becomes equal to annual Cost of energy wasted in transmission line.

1.9 ECONOMIC CHOICE OF TRANSMISSION VOLTAGE

The most important factor to consider when designing a transmission line is the capital cost and the operational cost of the transmission line. In the previous section we saw that there are many advantages to transmitting electrical power at higher voltage levels. But at the same time, use of higher voltages levels for transmission has some limitations. The cost of conductor material and line supports are reduced when high voltage levels are used for transmission, and the efficiency of the transmission line will be high as reduced line current results in low copper loss. However, the cost of transformers, isolators, switchgear, etc. increase at the same time. Hence choosing a correct voltage level for transmitting power from one place to another is very important. When the cost savings in conductor materials, support structure are offset by the additional costs of transformers, switchgear, insulators, etc., beyond this point there are no cost benefits of further increasing the voltage levels. An economical transmission voltage is one that minimizes the total cost of conductor materials, support structure, transformers, switchgear, insulators, and other equipment.

For calculating the most economical voltage level for a transmission line for transferring a given amount to a particular distance cost are calculated for various voltage levels. Standard voltage levels are used for calculation and the cost of conductor material, support structure, transformers and switchgears are calculated. Subsequently, a graph is charted to illustrate the total transmission cost in relation to different transmission voltage levels, depicted in figure 1.2. The lowest point on the curve reveals the most cost-effective transmission voltage level. In fig 1.2, the lowest point, designated as point Q, aligns with the optimal transmission voltage denoted by OJ.

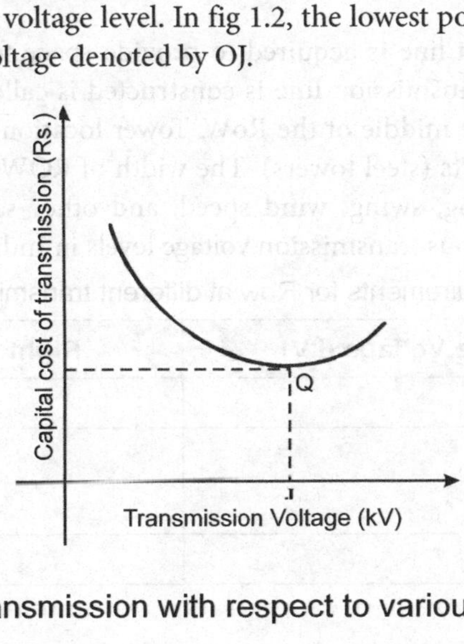

Fig. 1.2: Total cost of transmission with respect to various transmission voltages

The above method of finding the most economical transmission voltage level for a transmission line is not commonly used as it is difficult to pre-determine the costs of various equipment required for erection of transmission line. Instead of using the above method, it is general practice to use an empirical formula. As per this formula, the optimal transmission voltage for a 3-phase AC system is expressed as follows:

$$V_L = 5.5\sqrt{(km/1.6)+(load\ in\ kVA/150)} \quad \text{...(1.5)}$$

or

$$V_L = 5.5\sqrt{(l/1.6)+(3P/100)} \quad \text{...(1.6)}$$

Where, V = line voltage in kV

P = maximum power per phase (in kW) to be delivered over single circuit

L = distance of transmission in km

Moreover, the selection of the transmission voltage level is also contingent upon the amount of power proposed for transmission and the length of the transmission line. If the power to be transmitted is large, cost per kW of switchgear used in erection of transmission line is reduced. On the other hand, for longer transmission distances, increasing the transmission voltage can significantly increase the savings in conductor material.

1.10 TRANSMISSION LINE CONSTRUCTION:

Construction of overhead transmission lines involves the following activities:

(a) Site Preparation
(b) Construction of foundation for line supports
(c) Construction of line supports (Steel towers)
(d) Wire-Stringing Operations

1.10.1 Site Preparation

Land for erection of transmission line is acquired to provide space for construction of transmission line. A strip of land where the transmission line is constructed is called the right of way (RoW). The transmission line is erected in the middle of the RoW. Tower locations are cleared of vegetation prior to construction of the line supports (steel towers). The width of ROW depends upon the voltage level of transmission, tower design, sag, swing, wind speed, and other safety considerations. The space requirements for RoW as per various transmission voltage levels in India are given below:

Table 1.4: Space requirements for Row at different transmission voltage levels

Transmission Line Voltage (kV)	Right of Way (Meters)
11	7
33	15
66	18
110	22

Transmission Line Voltage (kV)	Right of Way (Meters)
132	27
220	35
400	46
765	64
± 500 kV (HVDC)	52
± 800 kV (HVDC)	69

Enhancements to existing approach roads or the creation of new roads might be necessary to facilitate the movement of construction vehicles and equipment, enabling access to each tower site.

1.10.2 Construction of Foundation for Line Supports

The majority of electrical tower structures are built upon concrete foundations. The size and type of the foundation depends on the type of soil, type of steel tower and the terrain. Construction of the foundation begins with the digging pits or holes for laying concrete footings (four for lattice steel towers and one for tubular steel poles. Regardless of the structure type, foundations typically have a slight projection above the ground.

After the footing holes are excavated, they are reinforced with steel and then concrete is poured into the holes. Construction of the actual structure can start once the concrete has fully hardened.

1.10.3 Construction of Line Supports (Steel Towers)

The various types of line supports (poles or towers) are used for providing mechanical support for the overhead conductors or wires. The line supports are used to support the conductors over the ground level maintaining the required ground clearance and to keep the proper spacing between the conductors. The clearance between the conductors and ground depends upon the voltage level and other electrical and mechanical considerations. The line supports are generally made up of wood (rarely used these days), concrete pole, steel or aluminium pole/towers. Line supports are mainly classified into two categories;

1. Pole structure
2. Tower structure

Generally steel lattice towers are used in high voltage transmission lines. However, for lower voltages electrical poles are used. Steel tower structures are very large and generally built from the ground up at the construction site of the transmission line. Steel structures are manufactured in parts in factories, transported to tower sites and parts are assembled near the new tower location. Tower erection is usually performed by cranes. Cranes are used to lift heavy parts and place these parts. Different parts are then bolted or riveted together. But the areas inaccessible or having difficult terrain helicopters are used for tower construction.

Whereas, electrical poles are assembled near the tower location and then erected at once, or are assembled in sections at the site. terrain and the space that is available adjacent to the construction site of the structure.

1.10.4 Wire-Stringing

Wire stringing is the process of fixing the earth wire and line conductors onto the transmission line structures. The different steps involved in the installation of line conductors, earth/ground wires, insulator strings, stringing sheaves (rollers or travellers), dampeners, weights, suspensions, and dead-end assemblies for the complete length of the transmission line are given below. Wire stringing can be divided into the following four steps:

(a) Insulator strings are fixed with transmission tower arms to insulate the live from tower and ground. The number of discs in the insulator string are decided by the voltage level of the transmission line.

(b) **Stringing the pilot wire:** A light-weight pulling rope/cable is installed from tower to tower using rope/cable puller machines or helicopters. threading ropes/cables through pulleys/ rollers attached to the lower part of the insulator strings on each tower structure. A camlock device secures the rope/cable to the pulley/ rollers.

(c) **Conductor Wire Pulling:** The tow rope/cable is attached to the conductor wire that is connected to the wire tensioner machine. Subsequently, a pulling machine is employed to draw the conductor wire. The puller and tensioner collaborate throughout the pulling procedure to guarantee consistent maintenance of appropriate ground clearance and sag for the conductor.

(d) **Sagging and dead ending:** While the conductor is being drawn along the entire length of the line, a tensioner is employed to accurately apply the necessary tension and sag to the conductor. Conductors undergo expansion and contraction in response to temperature fluctuations. At high temperature the conductor expands and with the decrease in temperature sag is reduced but tension is increased. Therefore, it must be installed with proper tension and sag so that it does not sag too much at maximum temperatures and required ground clearance is maintained.

(e) **Splicing:** Once the wires (conductors) are pulled in through the rollers/ pulleys and the proper tension and sag limits of the conductors are reached any temporary pulling splices are replaced with permanent splices/ connectors. After proper splicing and sagging, conductors are affixed to dead-end towers.

The above method/ steps are generally common for 110 kV, 220 kV, 400 kV transmission lines. However, conductor size, the type and size of steel towers and line insulator strings will differ depending upon the voltage level, length of transmission line, power to be transmitted and the terrain.

1.11 DISTRIBUTION SYSTEM

The section of electric supply distribution systems between distribution substation and end consumers is called distribution system. A distribution system generally consists of three subsections i.e., feeder, distributor, and service mains. Feeder is that section of the line which connects the distribution substation to the area where the supply is to be distributed. The design of the feeder is determined by its ability to carry current.

The distributor is that section of the distribution system from which tappings are taken to supply the electric power to consumers. The distributor is designed keeping in view the voltage drops along its length and it should remain within the limits specified by Indian standards. The current in the distributor is not the same as tapping is taken throughout its length. The current throughout the feeder remains the same as no tappings are taken from the feeder. Initially the distribution system was built to cater to urban areas having domestic and commercial loads. With the increase of rural electrification agriculture pump load was increased. The distribution system is required to be designed keeping in view the minimum loss, availability of supply, easy maintenance and voltage at the consumer terminals should be well within range specified in Indian grid code.

A distribution system broadly divided into two types i.e. radial distribution and network distribution. A radial system has only one path for power flow from distribution substation to the load. Whereas, a network distribution system power can flow via more than one simultaneous path. Both these two types of distribution systems can be further subdivided into a number of systems. Figure 1.3 shows different feeder arrangements such as tie, loop, radial and parallel feeders. The following sections describe the features and characteristics of the above feeder arrangements.

1.11.1 Tie Feeder

In this system a tie feeder is used to connect two sources of power supply to supply load as shown in fig 1.3 (a). This system provides service continuity as the load is supplied from either of the two different sources.

1.11.2 Ring Main Feeder

A ring main feeder forms a closed loop supplied from different sources and feeding different sections of loads. Its primary purpose is to supply multiple load points with electricity from distinct sources. This type of system is generally used in cities. Every load point has the flexibility to receive power from either direction, enabling the disconnection of any section of the system from operation without disrupting power supply to other load points.

1.11.3 Radial Feeder

A radial feeder provides a connection between a source and a load point; one or more loads can be supplied by each radial feeder. Since load is supplied from the substation in one direction only hence each load point can be supplied from one direction only. In this type of feeder, it is difficult to maintain supply continuity in case of feeder maintenance or faults. Radial feeders are most widely used in agriculture load, residential load in villages because of the simple circuits, easy to protect, and low in cost.

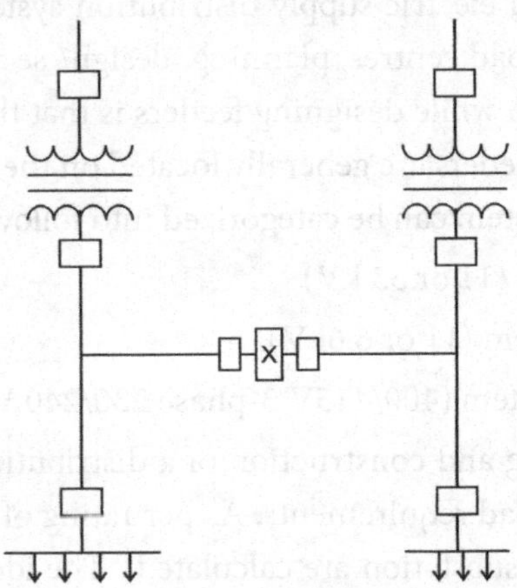

(a) Tie feeder

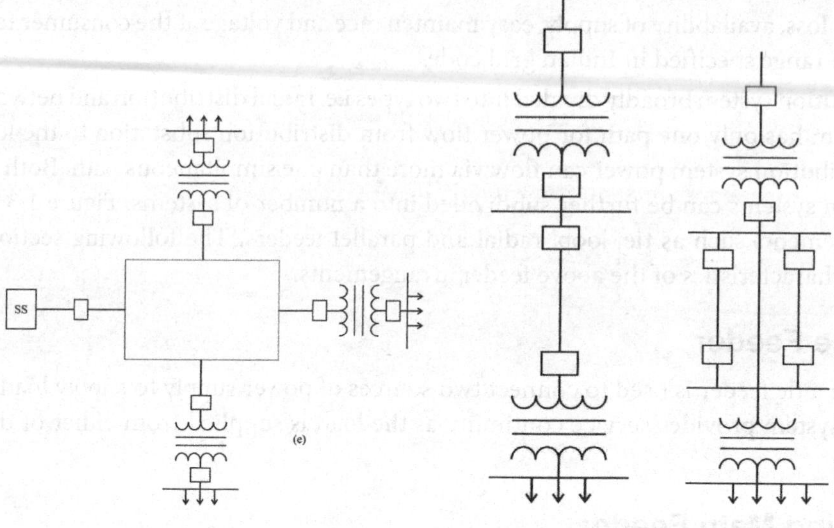

(b)- Ring main feeder (c) - Radial feeder (d) - Parallel feeder

Fig 1.3: (a, b, c, d) - Different feeder arrangements

1.11.4 Parallel Feeder

In this case, parallel radial feeders connect the distribution substation and the consumers or localities. This type of arrangement provides the ability to supply power to the load through one or any number of parallel feeders. Parallel arrangement makes maintenance easier as the load can be supplied from other parallel feeders. Maintenance is easy as can be done without interrupting the other consumers. It's easy to restore the supply to load in case of failure of one feeder.

1.12 METHOD / STEPS OF CONSTRUCTION

Method / steps of construction of electric supply distribution systems includes selecting locations for distribution substation near the load centres, planning, design/ section of feeders depending upon the type load. The main consideration while designing feeders is that the length of feeder and voltage drop in feeder should be minimum. Feeders are generally located on the road side for easy maintenance and repair. The distribution supply system can be categorized into following three categories:

1. Primary distribution system (11 or 33 kV)
2. Secondary distribution system (11 or 6.6kV)
3. Low voltage distribution system (400/415V 3-phase 230/240 V Single phase)

The primary task in planning and construction of a distribution system is to calculate the rating of the feeders as per consumers load requirements. As per rating of feeder the ratings of the switchgear to be installed at the distribution substation are calculated. The ideal way of locating the substation is to have it at the centre of the load centre so that feeders can be directly connected along its radial lines.

Unit Summary

In this chapter the main features of the electric supply system i.e., various types of Transmission Systems, its classification, main components, based on various types of transmission systems are discussed. The main features of a distribution supply system, such as type, methods of construction and the types of feeders are discussed. The various design considerations and the methods of construction of transmission and distribution supply systems for various voltage levels are also presented in this unit.

Unit Highlights

1. **Power system:** The generation (11 kV), transmission (132 kV or above) and distribution (415V / 220V) of electrical power is known as power system.

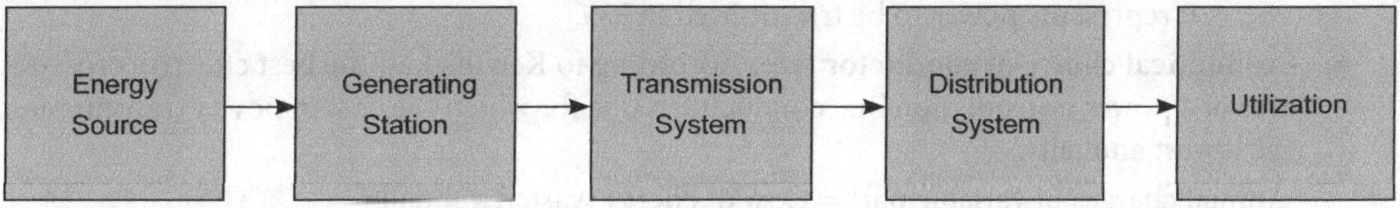

2. **Layout of Electrical System:** The connection scheme which represents the generation (11 kV), transmission (132 kV or above) and distribution (415V / 220V) of electrical power.
   (a) **Generating station:** In this, the electrical power is generated by 3-ϕ alternators. The generating voltage is generally 11kV but in some cases it may be 6.6/ 9.9/ 13.2 kV.
   (b) (i) **Primary Transmission:** In this system, the power from the generating station to a substation in the outskirts of load centres is transmitted at 400 kV, 200 kV or 132 kV. This power is transferred by a 3-ϕ, 3-wire overhead transmission system.
   (ii) **Secondary transmission:** In this system, the voltage levels of primary transmission are stepped down at the substation for secondary transmission. The system includes power transmission via 3-ϕ, 3-wire overhead transmission from the substation which is located at the suburbs of the city to the various substations near the load centres, generally at 33kV.
   (c) (i) **Primary distribution:** The section of the supply system between substations to large consumers supplied at 11 kV 3-phase three wire is called **Primary distribution.**
   ii) **Secondary distribution:** This includes substation feeder, distribution lines and service mains. The section between substation to consumer terminal is called **Secondary distribution.** The voltage is stepped down to 415/220 volts 3-ϕ, 4-wire for secondary distribution. Residential consumers are supplied with single phase supply whereas motor or three phase loads are supplied with 3 phase 4 wire supplies.
3. **Advantages of HVAC:**
   (a) increases in transmission efficiency
   (b) reduces the line voltage drop
   (c) reduces the cost of conductor material required
   (d) increase in transmission capacity of line
4. **Limitations of HVAC:**
   (a) Corona loss increases (But to reduce the corona loss, bundled conductors are used)

(b) Height of tower has to be increased (between earth and conductor)

(c) Design of circuit breakers, PT's, CTs become complicated.

(d) Insulators in the transmission system have to be increased. Thus, overall cost increases.

5. **Empirical formula for the selection of transmission voltage:**

$$V_L = 5.5\sqrt{(km/1.6)+(load\ in\ kVA/150)}$$

or

$$V_L = 5.5\sqrt{(l/1.6)+(3P/100)}$$

where, V_L represents line voltage in kV,

represents length of line in km and

P represents power to be transmitted in kW.

6. **Economical choice of conductor size:** According to Kelvin's law, the best effective cross-sectional area of a power transmission line conductor is one for which the cost of power transmission line is the lowest annually.

   Annual charges of variable part = Cost of energy wasted annually

   The total yearly costs of the power transmission line is divided two parts:

   (a) Capital outlay on annual charges

   (b) Cost of energy wasted annually

   Therefore, Annual cost = $K_1 + K_2 . a + (K_3 / a)$

7. **Limitations of Kelvin law:**

   (a) The conductor's X-sectional area calculated from Kelvin's law may be too weak from a mechanical aspect. Therefore, to increase the breaking stress (in case of aluminium conductor) diameter of conductor has to be increased keeping the economy aside.

   (b) Based on the assumption, the supporting structure's cost i.e. insulator, cross arm & tower is fixed and independent of the conductor's X-sectional area. This assertion is inaccurate, as the cost of the supporting structure is influenced in part by the cross-sectional area of the transmission line conductor.

Exercise

1. Compare the advantages of HVDC and HVAC systems.
2. Draw the single line diagram of a power system between generating station and end consumer of electric power.
3. Make a cost comparison between d.c. system, 1-ϕ, a.c. transmission system and 3-ϕ, three-wire transmission system, considering the voltage between earth and one conductor is maximum.
4. Make a cost comparison between d.c. system, 1-ϕ, a.c. transmission system and 3-ϕ, three-wire transmission system, considering the voltage between any two outgoing conductors is maximum.
5. How does increase of voltage affect the efficiency of transmission lines and weight of conductor material?
6. What do you mean by an economical transmission voltage? How can it be roughly calculated?

7. The current trend is 'direct current (d.c.) for transmission and alternating current (a.c.) for generation and distribution'. Discuss.
8. Explain the application of Kelvin's law taking into account the practical limitations for economical size of the line conductor.
9. Considering the required volume of conductor, which system (d.c./ a.c.) is better.
10. Distinguishing between a feeder and a distributor. Make a single line diag. representing elements of the transmission system.

Multiple Choice Questions

1. A 3-ϕ, 4-wire system is mostly used for
   (a) Secondary distribution (b) Primary distribution
   (c) Secondary transmission (d) Primary transmission
2. Which among the following is not the voltage used in generation?
   (a) 13.2 kilovolts (b) 220 kilovolts
   (c) 6.6 kilovolts (d) 11 kilovolts
3. The major drawback of over-head system over under-ground system is
   (a) Higher charging current
   (b) High initial cost
   (c) Surge problem
   (d) Under-ground system is more flexible than over-head system
4. If the voltage level of the transmission line has doubled of its actual value, for the same amount of power transfer the line loss will become.
   (a) One-fourth of actual value
   (b) Half of actual value
   (c) Equal to actual value
   (d) Double the actual value
5. For an ac power transmission line the volume of conductor material used is inversely proportional to
   (a) Voltage (V) (b) Current (I)
   (c) Power factor (cos-ϕ) (d) Both (a) and (c)
6. The rated voltage of a 3-ϕ, transmission line is given as
   (a) $V_{(L\text{-}L)\ rms}$ (rms line to line voltage) (b) $V_{(L\text{-}L)\ peak}$ (peak line to line voltage)
   (c) $V_{(p)\ rms}$ (rms phase voltage) (d) $V_{(p)\ peak}$ (peak phase voltage)
7. Why for long distance transfer of electric power high voltage levels are used
   (a) Increase in system reliability (b) Reduction in time of transmission
   (c) Reduction in transmission losses (d) None of the above
8. Highest a.c. transmission voltage used in country India is
   (a) 765 kilovolts (b) 132 kilovolts
   (c) 220 kilovolts (d) 400 kilovolts

9. The best economical cross-sectional area of conductor is one for which the cost of transmission line is the lowest annually. The statement is defined as
   (a) Ohm's law (b) Faraday's law
   (c) Kelvin's law (d) Lenz's law
10. An increase in the temperature of line conductors results in
    (a) Increase in tension
    (b) Increase in length
    (c) Increase in length and decrease in tension
    (d) Decrease in length and increase in tension

ANSWERS															
1.	(a)	2.	(b)	3.	(c)	4.	(a)	5.	(d)	6.	(a)	7.	(c)	8.	(a)
9.	(c)	10.	(c)												

Fill in the Blanks

1. For high voltage levels of the transmission voltage, the requirement of volume of conductor is.........................
2. Cost of conductor material used in transmission lines is proportional to .... of conductor.
3. The best method for electric power generation and distribution is .... system while for transmission is .... system.
4. The prime reason for using high voltage for long distance transmission of electrical power is ....
5. For an a.c. transmission line, the requirement of volume of conductor in a transmission line is inversely proportional to .... & ....

ANSWERS							
1.	lesser	2.	area of cross section	3.	a.c., d.c.	4.	reduction in transmission losses
5.	voltage, power factor						

True or False

1. System through which the electrical power is supplied from substations to various consumers is called a power system.
2. Secondary distribution is done by a 3-ϕ, 4-wire alternating current (a.c.) system.
3. For a transmission line, the annual charges can be expressed as (P_3 / a).
4. With the decrease in voltage of transmission, the line support cost reduces.
5. Mostly the high voltage transmission is carried out by underground systems due to low cost.

ANSWERS									
1.	False	2.	True	3.	False	4.	True	5.	False

Short and Long Answer Type Questions

1. List advantage of DC supply system over AC supply system.

Ans. DC supply system has the following advantage over AC supply system: (a) No Skin effect (b) saving in conductor material (c) Better voltage regulation (d) Less Corona loss (e) no phase displacement, inductance, surge problem and capacitance.

2. What is the effect of voltage on transmission efficiency?

Ans. With increase in transmission voltage, the transmission efficiency increases.

3. State the empirical formula for determining the system voltage of the transmission linc.

Ans. Approximate economical voltage for transmission in kV

$$5.5\sqrt{(km/1.6)+(load\ in\ kVA/150)}$$

4. How does increase of voltage affect efficiency in transmission and weight of conductor material?

Ans. (a) Reduces the Conductor Cost:

If at a line voltage V volt, P be power to be transmitted in kW, and power factor cos ϕ, then.

$$P = \sqrt{3}.V.I.\cos\phi$$

or $I = \dfrac{P}{\sqrt{3}.V.\cos\phi}$, it is clear that for constant power, current I is inversely proportional to the voltage and power factor (cos ϕ), thus with the increase in voltage, the line current reduces. Since conductor area is proportional to the current, therefore the X-sectional area decreases. Similarly, the volume is proportional to the X-sectional area and will also reduce, therefore the cost of the conductor material will automatically reduce.

(b) Transmission Efficiency Increases:

$I = \dfrac{P}{\sqrt{3}.V.\cos\phi}$, as per formula, with the increase in voltage, the line current reduces i.e. copper loss (W) is directly proportional ($\propto$) to square of current ($W = I_2 R$, i.e. $W \propto I_2$, if R is constant) and will result in the improvement of transmission efficiency.

5. State any two drawbacks of Kelvin's law.

Ans. Ideally Kelvin's law stands good but in actual working conditions it has various drawbacks.

The cross-sectional area of the transmission line conductor calculated from Kelvin's law may be too weak from a mechanical aspect. Therefore, to increase the breaking stress (in case of aluminium conductor) diameter of conductor has to be increased keeping the economy aside.

According to Kelvin's law, the cost of various structures like insulator, cross-arm and tower is fixed and independent of the cross-sectional area of the transmission line conductor. But the cost of the above said structures depends partly on the cross-sectional area of the transmission line conductor.

6. Mention the factors to be considered while Designing of Feeders.

Ans. Following are the factors which is to be considered while designing of feeders:

(a) Type of conductor

(b) Current carrying capacity

(c) Distance and cost

7. What is the impact of selection of high voltage on the transmission line conductor area?

Ans. Let

(i) Power = P

(ii) Length of line = l

(iii) Line losses = W

ac power is given as,

$$P = \sqrt{3} . V.I. \cos \phi$$

$$\text{Line Current } I = \frac{P}{\sqrt{3}.V.\cos\phi},$$

$$\text{Resistance of conductor is } R = \rho . \frac{l}{a}$$

$$\text{Copper loss } W = 3 I^2 R$$

$$= 3.\frac{P}{\sqrt{3}.V.\cos\phi}.\frac{P}{\sqrt{3}.V.\cos\phi}.\rho.\frac{l}{a}$$

$$= \frac{P^2 . \phi . l}{V^2 . a.\cos^2\phi}$$

Area of X-section of the transmission line conductor:

$$a = \frac{P^2 . \rho . l}{V^2 . W . \cos^2\phi} \quad \text{... (i)}$$

Here, 'a' represents the area of X-section of the transmission line conductor.

It's evident that the cross-sectional area of the transmission line conductor exhibits an inverse relationship with the transmission line voltage, while keeping other factors constant. In simpler terms, as the transmission voltage increases, the required cross-sectional area decreases.

8. What are the difficulties in adoption of HVAC transmission systems?

Ans. (a) Corona loss increases (But to reduce the corona loss, bundled conductors are used)

(b) Height of tower has to be increased (between earth and conductor)

(c) Design of circuit breakers, PT's, CT's become complicated

(c) Insulators in the transmission system have to be increased. Thus overall cost increases.

Numerical Problems

Formula used:

1. Resistance $R = \rho . \frac{l}{a}$

[R = Resistance, ρ = resistivity, l = length, a = cross-sectional area of of the transmission line conductor]

2. **Volume of wire** = length x cross-section of wire (a)
   for 2 conductors – Volume = l . 2 a
   for 3 conductors – Volume = l . 3 a
3. **Weight of material for wire** = Volume × density of material
4. **Three phase power** = $\sqrt{3} \cdot V_L \cdot I_L \cdot \cos\phi$
5. **Kelvin's Law** = It states that the best cost-effective cross-sectional area of line conductor is one for which the rate of power transmission line is the lowest annually.
   Annual charges of variable part = Cost of energy wasted annually
6. **Star connections:**

$$V_L = \sqrt{3}\, V_P$$
$$I_L = I_P$$
$$P = \sqrt{3} \cdot V_L \cdot I_L \cdot \cos\phi = 3 \cdot V_P \cdot I_P \cdot \cos\phi$$

   [V_P=Phase Voltage, I_P=Phase Current, V_L=Line Voltage, I_L=Line Current]
7. **In Delta connections:**

$$V_L = V_P$$
$$I_L = \sqrt{3}\, I_P$$
$$P = \sqrt{3} \cdot V_L \cdot I_L \cdot \cos\phi = 3 \cdot V_P \cdot I_P \cdot \cos\phi$$

   [V_P = Phase Voltage, I_P = Phase Current, V_L = Line Voltage, I_L = Line Current]
8. **Approximate economical voltage for transmission in kV**

$$5.5\sqrt{(km/1.6)+(load\ in\ kVA/150)}$$

SOLVED NUMERICAL

1. A two-core cable having length 10 km is used to deliver a fixed load of 200 amperes in a year. Transmission cable costs Rs (150a + 60) per-metre, here the conductor has the cross-sectional area of 'a' cm². 15 paisa per kilowatt hour is the energy cost and has 10% depreciation and interest charges. Specific resistivity of copper is 1.75 μΩ-cm. Find the line conductor cross-sectional area 'a'.

Ans. Resistance of every line conductor of area a cm² and 10 km in length

$$R = \rho \cdot \frac{l}{a}$$
$$= 1.75 \times 10^{-6} \times \frac{10 \times 1000 \times 100}{a}$$
$$= \frac{1.75}{a}\ \Omega$$

Energy loss per annum

$$= \frac{2I^2R \times 8760}{1000}$$

$$= \frac{2\times200^2\times1.75\times8760}{1000\times a} = \frac{1226400}{a}\ \text{kWh}$$

Annual cost of energy loss

$$\frac{K3}{a} = \text{Rs}\ \frac{15}{100}\times\frac{1226400}{a} = \text{Rs}\ \frac{183960}{a}$$

Capital cost of feeder cable (variable cost)

= Rs 150 × a × 10 × 1000 = Rs 1500000a

For interest and depreciation, the annual charges on variable cost of feeder cable are;

$$K_2\,a = \text{Rs } 1500000\,a \times \frac{10}{100} = \text{Rs } 150000a$$

For most economical cross-sectional area of conductor

$$\frac{183960}{a} = 150000a$$

$$a = \sqrt{(183960/150000)}$$

a = 1.23 cm² (Ans.)

Q.2 A power of 50 MW at power factor (p.f.) 0.9 is being transmitted over 220 kV, 3-ϕ transmission line with transmission line length of 300 kilometers and efficiency of 90%. For the similar line voltage and losses find separately the weight of copper used for 3-ϕ and 1-ϕ power transmission line. Assuming the resistance(R) of 5-kilometer-long power transmission line is 0.183 Ω, the specific density of copper is 8.8 and the resistivity of material is 1.73 × 10⁻⁸ Ωm.

Ans. Power to be transmitted = 50 MW = 50×10^6 watts

Voltage V = 220×10^3 volts

length = 300×10^3 m

efficiency η = 90%

power factor = cos ϕ = 0.9

(i) Three phase three wire: Line current = $\dfrac{P}{\sqrt{3}.\ V.\cos\phi}$

$$= \frac{50\times10^6}{\sqrt{3}.220.1000.0.9}$$

= 145.795 Amp.

$$\text{Line losses} = \frac{10}{100}\times 50\times10^6$$

$= 5 \times 10^6$ watts [η = 90%, loss = 10%]

Therefore, Area of cross section

$$a = 3\,I^2 \times \rho \times \frac{l}{W}\quad \text{(The system has 3 wires)}$$

$$= 3 \times 145.795 \times 145.795 \times 1.73 \times 10^{-8} \times \frac{300 \times 1000}{5 \times 1000000}$$

$$= 6.62 \times 10^{-5} \text{ m}^2$$

Therefore, volume of copper required = 3al

$$= 3 \times 6.62 \times 10^{-5} \times 300 \times 10^3$$

$$= 59.58 \text{ m}^3$$

Weight of copper = 59.58 × 8.8

= **524.304 Tonnes (Ans.)**

(ii) Single phase two wire: Line current $= \dfrac{P}{V.\cos\phi}$

$$= \frac{50 \times 10^6}{220.1000.0.9}$$

$$= 252.53 \text{ Amp.}$$

Therefore, Area of cross section

$$a = 2\, I^2 \times \rho \times \frac{l}{W}$$

(The system has 2 wires)

$$= 2 \times 252.53 \times 252.53 \times 1.73 \times 10^{-8} \times \frac{300 \times 1000}{5 \times 1000000}$$

$$= 13.24 \times 10^{-5} \text{ m}^2$$

Therefore, volume of copper required = 2al

$$= 2 \times 13.24 \times 10^{-5} \times 300 \times 10^3$$

$$= 79.44 \text{ m}^3$$

Weight of copper = 79.44 × 8.8

= **699.07 Tonnes (Ans.)**

3. Rate of a 3-ϕ, over-head power transmission line having cross-sectional area 'a' cm² is Rs (1000+4000a) per km. Calculate the effective current density of the required line conductor. 15% p.a (per-annum) is the rate of depreciation and interest is, cost of energy wasted is Rs 0.08/kWh and each conductor having resistance of $\frac{0.27}{a}$ ohm/km. Take load factor for losses = 15%.

Ans. For interest and depreciation, the annual charges on variable cost of transmission line is

$$K_2\, a = ₹4000\, a \times \frac{15}{100}$$

= ₹600 a per conductor per km length

Each conductor resistance,

$$R = \frac{0.27}{a} \text{ ohm per km of length}$$

Power loss in each conductor for a length of one km:

$$W = I^2 R = \frac{0.27}{a} I^2 \text{ watts}$$

Where I is the current in amperes in each conductor

Energy loss per annum per conductor for a length of one km

$$= \frac{0{,}27 \times I^2 \times 0.15 \times 8760}{a \times 1000} = \frac{0.35478 I^2}{a} \text{ kWh}$$

Annual cost of energy loss for a length of one km

$$\frac{K3}{a} = ₹\frac{0.05 \times 0.35478 I^2}{a} = ₹\frac{0.017739 I^2}{a}$$

For most economical cross section of conductor

$$K_2 a = \frac{K3}{a}$$

$$600 a = \frac{0.017739 I^2}{a}$$

Most economical current density

$$= \frac{I}{a} = \sqrt{(600 / 0.017739)}$$

$$= \mathbf{183.92 \ A / cm^2 \ (Ans.)}$$

4. A d.c. supply with a three-wire transmission system has to be changed into a 3-ϕ, four-wire transmission system by addition of 4th-wire equal in cross-sectional area to each line conductor of the dc transmission system. Assuming same supply voltage and load voltage to neutral and balanced conditions, calculate the extra transmission power at unity cos ϕ which can be delivered by the new a.c. transmission system.

Ans. Let the supply voltage V_S and load voltage V_L to neutral and conductor resistance be R ohms each.

In three-wire dc system,

Line Current, $I_1 = (V_S - V_L) / R$

Power supplied,

$$P_1 = 2 V_L I_1 = 2 V_L \times [(V_S - V_L) / R] \quad \text{... (a)}$$

In three phase four wire ac system,

Line current, $I_2 = (V_S - V_L) / R$

Power supplied,

$$P_2 = 3 V_L I_2 \cos\phi = 3 V_L \times [(V_S - V_L) / R] \times 1 \quad \text{... (b)}$$

Comparing equations, (a) and (b), we get

$$P_2 = \frac{3}{2} P_1$$

Therefore, for a three-phase four-wire system, 50 percent more power which can be delivered at unity cos ϕ. (Ans.)

5. Determine the reduction in conductor material usage when increasing the voltage of the two-wire DC transmission system from 300 to 700 volts while maintaining the same transmitted power.

Ans. Assume that in both the cases:

(i) Power is same (as given) = P

(ii) Length of line is same = l

(iii) Line losses are same = W

$$\text{Now, line current } I = \frac{P}{V}$$

As the resistivity will be the same in both the cases as the material is same, the losses in both the wires are

$$W = 2\,I^2\,R$$

$$= 2.\left(\frac{P}{V}\right).\left(\frac{P}{V}\right).\rho.\frac{l}{a}$$

$$= \frac{2.P^2.\rho.l}{V^2.a}$$

Cross-section area of the conductor:

$$a = \frac{2.P^2.\rho.l}{V^2.W}$$

Volume of the conductor = 2 a l

$$= \frac{2.2.P^2.\rho.l.l}{V^2.W}$$

$$= \frac{4.P^2.\rho.l^2}{V^2.W}$$

It is clear from this equation that the volume is inversely proportional to the voltages as P, ρ and W are constants

$$\text{So, Volume } \alpha = \frac{1}{V^2} = \frac{K}{V^2}, \text{ where K is a constant}$$

(i) At 300 V, $\quad V_1 = \dfrac{K}{300\times300} = 0.11 \times 10^{-4} \times K$

(ii) At 700 V, $\quad V_2 = \dfrac{K}{700\times700} = 0.02 \times 10^{-4} \times K$

The percentage saving of copper,

$[(V_1 - V_2) / V_1] \times 100$

$= [(0.11 \times 10^{-4} \times K - 0.02 \times 10^{-4} \times K) / 0.11 \times 10^{-4} \times K] \times 100$

= 0.82

Thus, saving in copper = 82% (Ans.)

6. The cost for a 3-phase overhead power transmission line is expressed as Rs[25,000k + 2,500] per kilometer, where 'k' represents the cross-sectional area of each conductor in square centimeters (cm^2). The load supplied by the line is 20 megawatt at 33 kilovolts & 0.8 power factor (lagging). Load is considered constant all around the year. The energy cost Rs 0.70 per kilowatt hour, depreciation & interest charges are 15% p.a. Calculate the effective size of the transmission line conductor. The resistivity (ρ) of the conducting material is 4 μΩ – cm.

Ans. Cost of line = ₹[25000 a +2500] per km

Power to be transmitted, P = 20 MW = 20×10^6 watts

Line Voltage, V = 33 kV = 33×10^3 volts

Power factor, cos = 0.8 lagging

cost of energy per kWh = ₹0.70 = 70 paisa

Interest and Depreciation = 15%

Resistivity of conductor, = 4 μΩ – cm = 4×10^{-6} Ω-cm

length of line, = 1 km = 10^5 cm

therefore, Resistance of conductor material,

$$R = \rho \cdot \frac{l}{a}$$

$$= \frac{4 \times 10^{-6} \times 10^5}{k}$$

$$= \frac{0.4}{k} \Omega$$

$$\text{Load current, } I = \frac{P}{\sqrt{3}.\ V\ .\cos\phi}$$

$$= \frac{20 \times 10^6}{\sqrt{3} \times 33 \times 10^3 \times 0.8} = 437.39 \text{ A}$$

$$\text{Energy lost per annum} = \frac{3.I^2.\ R\ .\ t}{1000} \text{kWh}$$

$$= \frac{3 \times 437.39 \times 437.39 \times 0.4 \times 8760}{1000 \times k} = \frac{2011050.85}{k} \text{ kWh}$$

$$\text{Annual cost due to energy lost} = ₹\ \frac{0.70 \times 2011050.85}{k} = ₹\ \frac{1407735.59}{k}$$

Capital cost of cable = 25000 k

Annual charges because of interest and depreciation = ₹ 0.15 × 25000k

= ₹3750 k

Most economical cross-sectional area

$$\frac{1407735.59}{k} = 3750\ k$$

therefore, k (area of cross section) $= \sqrt{1407735.59/3750}$

$= \mathbf{19.37\ cm^2}$ **(Ans.)**

UNSOLVED NUMERICAL

1. For a line voltage (V_L) with a two-wire dc transmission system, voltage is increased from 200 to 400 volts. Power is to be transferred to the samc distance keeping power loss the same. Find the percentage saving in feeder conductor material? **(Ans.: 75%)**
2. 1-ϕ 10 megawatt Overhead conductors with a cross-sectional area of ‹a› are used to transfer ac power of 10 MW. A 3rd conductor is having similar cross-sectional area which is added to convert this 1-ϕ system to 3-ϕ, 3-wire supply system. If voltage stays unchanged between the wires and %age loss, Find the 3-ϕ load power which can be delivered by this power transmission line. **(Ans.: 20 MW)**
3. A dual-core 11 kV cable is employed to supply a load of 1 MW at a lagging power factor of 0.8 (cos-ϕ) for a duration of 125 days in a year. The electrical cable has a capital cost of Rs. [400k + 20] /m (per-meter) here 'k' is the cross-sectional area of the core in square centimetre. The combined depreciation and interest on the capital investments amount to 10%. Find the effective cross-sectional area for the conductor. The energy cost per unit is 15 paisa and the cable length is 1 kilometre. Take specific resistance of copper as 1.75 μΩ-cm. **(Ans.: 0.2255 cm²)**
4. At a transmission voltage of 10 kV, determine the suitable cross-sectional size of a 3-phase power transmission line capable of supplying power to the load under the following conditions:

   (a) 100 kW at 0.8 power factor (lagging) for 10 hours.

   (b) 100 kW at unity power factor (lagging) for 6 hours.

   (c) 500 kW at 0.9 power factor (lagging) for 8 hours.

   Above are the daily load cycles. Cost per-kilometre of the fully established power transmission line is Rs. [8000k+1500], here k is each line conductor cross-sectional area. Per annum capital cost having depreciation & interest is 10 percent. 5 paisa per-kWh loss is the cost of energy. Conductor material having Resistivity (ρ) of 1.72 μΩ-cm. **(Ans.: 0.844 cm²)**
5. A 1-ϕ, a.c. system supplies a certain amount of power. By running a similar 3rd conductor, this transmission structure is changed to 1-ϕ, 3 wire a.c. power transmission system. Between the conductors and for the same %age loss, determine the extra load %age which is to be delivered for the same voltage. **(Ans.: 100%)**
6. For each copper conductor having x-section area "a" cm², the cost of 1 km of transmission line is Rs. [2000a + 1300], load factor is 80% of load current (I_L) & losses are 65% of the load. Depreciation & interest is 10 percent and energy cost is 5 paisa per kilowatt hour. Using Kelvin's law, for the power transmission line find the efficient current density. The resistivity (ρ) of the line conductor material is 1.78 μΩ-cm. **(Ans. : 74 A/cm²)**

Practical

Practical -1: Collect the information on components of the transmission line.

Objective: The objective is to collect data/information related to components of a transmission line as per Indian standards.

List of Components of a Transmission line:

Prepare a list of various components used in 220kV 3-ϕ 3-wire AC transmission lines.

- line conductors: give a list of standard conductors used in transmission lines.
- Line supports: give a detailed list of various types of line supports along with their photographs.
- Cross arms
- Ground wire: Give details of wires used a ground wire as per Indian standards
- Spacers: Paste photo of spacers
- Power line markers: Paste photo of spacers
- Vibration dampers: Mark vibration dampers on picture of a transmission line
- Danger plates: Specification of danger plates
- Anti climbing devices: why it is required. Give a picture of anti-climbing devices.

Practical -2: Prepare a report based on the transmission line network of your state.

Objective: The objective is to collect data/information related to the transmission line network of your state/country to know the transmission capacity of your state/ country.

Procedure: Annual/monthly/ daily reports of central / state electricity authorities may be referred for preparing the report.

KNOW MORE

Students are advised to visit following websites to understand the transmission and distribution system in India and the latest developments going on more deeply:

- Ministry of power, Govt of India - https://powermin.gov.in/
- Central Electricity Authority, Govt of India - https://cea.nic.in/?lang=en
- Ministry of new and renewable energy -https://mnre.gov.in/
- Any state electrical transmission utility.

REFERENCES AND SUGGESTED READINGS

1. https://nptel.ac.in/courses/108102047
2. https://nptel.ac.in/courses/108107112
3. https://nptel.ac.in/courses/108105104

2 Transmission Line Parameters and Performance

UNIT SPECIFICS

Through this unit we will discuss the following aspects:

- What are the transmission line parameters and why is it important to calculate transmission line parameters?
- How to compute these line parameters?
- How do transmission line parameters affect the performance of transmission lines?
- Methods of calculating performance, i.e., efficiency, voltage regulation and power factor of short and medium transmission lines.
- To understand the skin and proximity effects.

The importance of the transmission line parameters, methods of calculating for different types of transmission lines, and their usage for calculating the performance of a transmission line are discussed in detail in this unit. The information on power transmission line parameters is essential to compute the efficiency of the transmission line, power factor, and voltage regulation, like quantities of practical use for any engineer, are given in this unit. The voltage, current, and power factor quantities are known for either sending or receiving end of a power transmission line. We can find out the unknown quantities at any end of the power transmission line with the help of transmission line parameters if one-end quantities are known.

After the unit summary, students are given practice resources, including solved and unsolved problems, exercise questions, multiple choice questions, fill-in-the-blank questions, and true/false questions to further strengthen the learning of the students. The questions are prepared as per revised bloom's taxonomy targeting lower and higher orders questions for slow and fast learners. Web links are provided under the category of knowing more to create curiosity among the students related to the subject. Some reference links are also provided for further study related to the topics given in unit number 2.

Applications of the topics in daily life are supplemented through the lab practical given at the end of the unit. This unit will build the foundation for a detailed analysis of the power system i.e., the transmission and distribution supply systems under various conditions.

RATIONALE

This unit on the parameters of a transmission line and its performance will help the students to get a primary idea about the line parameters such as resistance capacitance and inductance of a transmission line. The unit explains the method of calculating transmission line parameters to evaluate the performance and to compute the voltage, current at sending or receiving end, regulation, and power factor etc. of the power transmission line. Voltage drop throughout the length of the transmission line is dependent on online parameters, and hence the efficiency can be calculated only if you know the parameters of the power transmission line. Further, to keep the voltages and other quantities of the power transmission line within the specified limits the knowledge of these parameters becomes even more important.

Comprehensive information on techniques for determining line parameters for short and medium transmission lines is one of the unit's primary features. The effect of line parameters on the performance of transmission lines, effects due to flow of AC current such as proximity effect, skin effect, and corona effect are studied. Power system engineers are guided to take necessary measures so as to improve the performance of power transmission lines.

Proper explanations with examples; photographs that enable students to imagine the various components of power transmission systems; solved examples at the end of every unit to add to the learning of students.

PRE-REQUISITES

No pre-requisites are required.

UNIT OUTCOMES

The students will be able to:

U2-O1: Calculate line parameters of a transmission line.

U2-O2: Use the calculated line parameters for performance evaluation of a transmission line.

U2-O3: Understand the proximity, skin effect and corona effect in AC transmission lines.

U2-O4: Infer methods to improve efficiency of transmission lines.

Unit-2 Outcome	EXPECTED MAPPING WITH COURSE OUTCOMES (1 - Weak Correlation; 2 - Medium Correlation; 3 - Strong Correlation)				
	CO-1	CO-2	CO-3	CO-4	CO-5
U2-O1	3	3	3	2	2
U2-O2	2	3	3	1	1
U2-O3	1	1	2	1	1
U2-O4	2	3	3	2	2

2.1 INTRODUCTION

Electric power, in bulk, is transmitted over long distances using 3-phase 3-wire transmission lines at high AC voltages. The performance of the transmission lines depends upon the electrical equivalent parameters viz; resistance (R), inductance (L), capacitance (C) and conductance (G). Resistance and inductance are called series parameters and capacitance and conductance are called shunt parameters.

All of these parameters are spread along the length of the transmission line. Hence, it is not possible to represent these parameters lumped at any single point on the power transmission line. The values of these parameters are given as per kilometre values. The values of series parameters depend upon the conductor material and conductors' size and the transmission line geometry. The conductance of the line arises from the leakage current that flows across the insulators, which is of very small value, hence, it is neglected in overhead transmission lines.

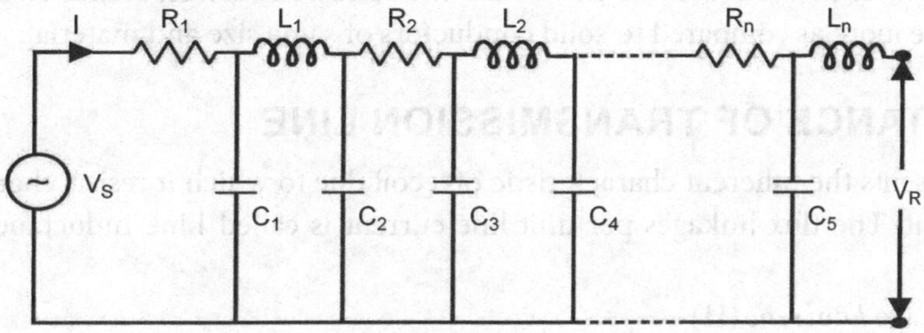

Fig. 2.1: Transmission Line representation

2.2 RESISTANCE OF A POWER TRANSMISSION LINE

Resistance is defined as the opposition offered to flow of current through a conductor. It is measured in ohms (Ω). The conductor material, size and temperature conditions affect the resistance values of any transmission line. The resistance offered to DC current is called DC resistance and that offered to AC current is called AC resistance. The dc and ac resistance values can be different for the same current and material due to the skin effect of ac current and are dependent on frequency of ac supply. The power loss i.e. I^2R loss in the transmission line occurs because of resistance.

$$\text{Power loss} = I^2 R \qquad \dots (2.1)$$

$$R = \frac{\text{Power loss}}{I^2} \text{ ohm } (\Omega) \qquad \dots (2.2)$$

also, DC resistance is given by $R_{dc} = \dfrac{\rho\, l}{a}\ \Omega$ ... (2.3)

Where, resistivity of conductor material is denoted by ρ and its units are in Ωs; length of the conductor is measured in meters (m) and is denoted by l, and 'a' is the area of cross- section of conductor (m^2).

Another factor on which the resistance of a conductor depends is the temperature. The resistance of the conductor generally varies linearly with temperature. In India, ambient temperature variations are large (–30°C to + 47°C) depending upon the regions and seasons.

2.2.1 Variation of Resistance with Temperature

The value of resistance of the conductor material is temperature dependent. If we know the resistance at one temperature, the value of the resistance can be calculated for another temperature also. Let R_1 and R_2 are the resistance values at temperature t_1°C and t_2 °C, the temperature $t_1°C < t_2$ °C; α_1 is the temperature coefficient of resistance of the material used for conductors at temperature t_1°C then,

$$R_2 = R_1[1+ \propto_1(t_2 - t_1)] \qquad \dots (2.4)$$

where $$\propto_1 = \frac{\propto o}{1+ \propto ot1} \qquad \dots (2.5)$$

$\propto_o$ = temperature coefficient of resistance at 0 °C

Generally, stranded (spiralled) line conductors are used in overhead power transmission lines. Due to strand the length of the conductor is more than the solid conductors. Hence resistance of stranded conductors is little more as compared to solid conductors of same size and material.

2.3 INDUCTANCE OF TRANSMISSION LINE

Inductance represents the inherent characteristic of a coil due to which it resists changes in the current flowing through it. The flux linkages per unit line current is called Line Inductance and is generally denoted by L.

L = Flux linkage / current (H)

$L = \psi / I$ (H)

where; $\psi = N\,\Phi$ = flux linkages (Wb-T)

I = current (A)

2.3.1 Flux-linkages in Relation to Internal Flux

In over-head transmission lines, it is supposed that the current is distributed uniformly inside the line conductor. Cross-sectional area of the line conductor shows in figure 2.2.

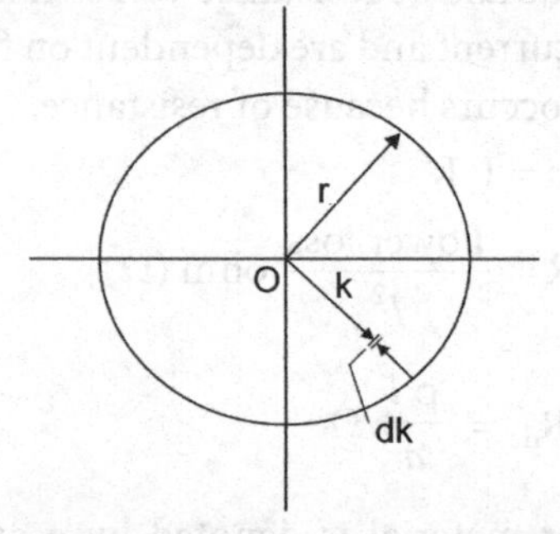

Fig. 2.2: Cross-sectional area of the line conductor (flux-linkage in relation to internal flux)

Let from the centre, the conductor is at a distance of 'k' meters. Thus the field strength inside the conductor is given by:

$$H_k = \frac{\text{current}}{\text{distance} \times 2\pi}$$

$$= I_k / (2 \, . \, k)$$

let there be a uniform current density,

$$I_k = \frac{k^2 \, . \, \pi}{r^2 \, . \, \pi} \, . \, I$$

$$= \frac{k^2}{r^2} . \mathrm{I}$$

Therefore, $$\mathrm{H_k} = \frac{k^2}{r^2} .\mathrm{I}. \frac{1}{k \times 2\pi}$$

$$= \frac{k}{2\pi . r^2} . \mathrm{I} \quad \text{ampere turns / meter}$$

Since, $\mathrm{B_k / H_k = \mu_o . \mu_r}$

Therefore,

Flux density, $$\mathrm{B_k = \mu_o . \mu_r . H_k}$$

$$\mathrm{B_k} = \mu_o . \mu_r . \frac{k}{2\pi . r^2} .\mathrm{I}$$

$$= \frac{k}{2\pi . r^2} . \mathrm{I} . \mu_o$$

[Because, for non-magnetic material $\mu_r = 1$]

Thus, the flux of radial thickness 'dk' through a cylindrical shell and one meter axial length is given by,

$$d\phi = \mathrm{B_k . dk . 1}$$

$$= \frac{k}{2\pi . r^2} . \mathrm{I} . \mu_o . \mathrm{dk} \quad \text{weber}$$

Therefore, when magnetic flux links with the line current inside the circular boundary of a given radius 'k' only i.e. $\mathrm{I_k}$.

Therefore,

$$\text{Flux Linkages} = \frac{k}{2\pi . r^2} . \mathrm{I_k} . \mu_o . \mathrm{dk}$$

$$= \frac{k}{2\pi . r^2} . \frac{k^2}{r^2} . \mathrm{I} . \mu_o . \mathrm{dk} \qquad \text{(because } \mathrm{I_k}\text{=.I)}$$

$$= \frac{k}{2\pi . r^2} .\mathrm{I}.\mu_o.\mathrm{dk}$$

From centre to the conductor surface, the total flux linkages are:

$$= \int_0^r \frac{k^3}{2\pi . r^4} . \mathrm{I} . \mu_o . \mathrm{dk}$$

$$= \mu_o . \frac{I}{8. \pi} \quad \text{Weber turns per meter length} \qquad \text{... (2.6)}$$

2.3.2 Flux-linkages in Relation to External Flux

Now considering the magnetic lines of force set up outside the conductor only.

From the centre, the conductor is at a distance of 'k' meters. Thus, the field strength outside the conductor is given by:

$$H_k = \frac{\text{current}}{\text{distance} \times 2\pi}$$

$$= \frac{I}{2.\pi.k} \text{ AT/m}$$

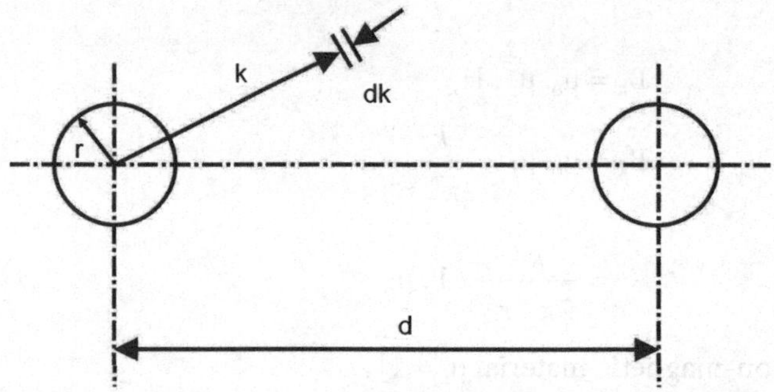

Fig. 2.3: Cross-sectional area of the line conductor (flux-linkage in relation to external flux)

Therefore,

Flux density, $B_k = \mu_o . H_k$ [Because, for non-magnetic material $\mu_r = 1$]

$$B_k = \mu_o . \frac{I}{2.\pi.k} \text{ Wb/m}^2$$

Thus, the flux of radial thickness 'dk' through a cylindrical shell and one meter axial length is given by,

$$d\phi = B_k . dk . 1$$

$$= \mu_o . \frac{I}{2.\pi.k} . dk \text{ webers}$$

The flux dϕ links with the conductor itself.

Therefore,

Flux linkages, $d\phi = \mu_o . . dk$ weber-turns

Total flux linkages outside the conductor:

$$\text{Flux linkages, } d\phi = \int_r^d \mu_o . \frac{I}{2.\pi.k} . dk$$

$$= \mu_o . \frac{I}{2.\pi} \log e^{(d/r)}$$

Overall flux linkages = Flux linkages in relation to internal flux + external flux

$$= \frac{I}{8.\pi} \mu_o . \frac{I}{2.\pi} + \mu_o . \log e^{(d/r)}$$

$$= \mu_o . \frac{I}{4.\pi} [0.5 + 2 . \log e^{(d/r)}]$$

Total flux linkages for both the conductors

$$= 2 \times \mu_o . \frac{I}{4.\pi} [0.5 + 2 . \log e^{(d/r)}]$$

$$= \mu_o . \frac{I}{4.\pi} [1 + 4 . \log e^{(d/r)}]$$

Flux linkages/ ampere = loop inductance of line

Therefore, $L = \mu_o . \frac{I}{4.\pi} [1 + 4 . \log e^{(d/r)}]$

or $L = 4 \times 10^{-7} . [1 + 4 . \log e^{(d/r)}]$

or $L = [1 + 4 . \log e^{(d/r)}] \times 10^{(-7)}$ H/m ... (2.7)

For a single phase line the loop inductance is considered.

2.3.3 Inductance of Three Phase Overhead Power Transmission Line

In a 3-, overhead power transmission line, instead of loop inductance, the inductance of each line conductor is considered. Figure (2.4.a) shows the three conductors placed symmetrically on the tower of the power transmission line, whereas figure-2.4 (b & c) shows the different positions of the conductors placed unsymmetrically.

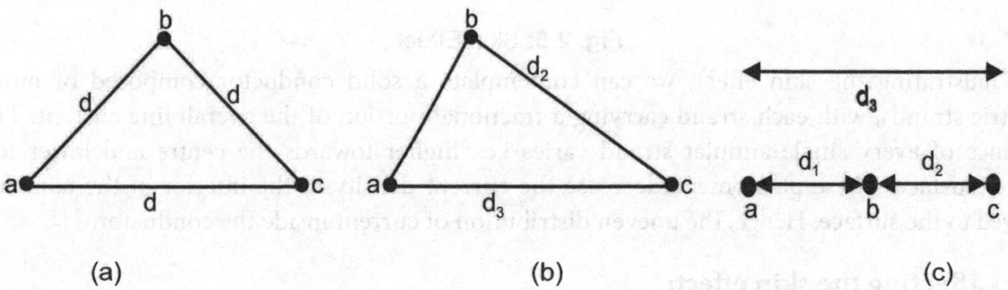

Fig. 2.4: (a) Three conductors placed symmetrically on the tower of the power transmission (b, c) Different positions of the conductors placed unsymmetrically

In the case of a 3-ϕ configuration for an overhead power transmission line, where the distance between two conductors remains constant i.e., if at the corners of an equilateral, the conductors are placed as shown in figure 2.4.a, the line is called a symmetrical line.

In this case, the inductance of each conductor can be determined by the expression:

$$L = [0.5 + 2 . \log e^{(d/r)}] \times 10^{(-7)} \text{ Henry/ meter}$$

A overhead transmission line in which the spacing between the conductor is different as per figure 2.4 (b & c), it is called unsymmetrical line, and the inductance per conductor (per phase) is determined by the relation:

$$L = [\,0.5 + 2\,.\,\log e^{(d/r)}\,] \times 10^{(-7)} \text{ Henry/ meter} \quad \ldots (2.8)$$

$$[\text{where } d = (d_1\,.\,d_2\,.\,d_3)^{1/3}]$$

From the above expression, it is concluded:

(a) If spacing between the conductors is more, larger will be the inductance.

(b) If the radius of the conductor is more, smaller will be the inductance.

(c) If the length of the line is increased, more will be the inductance.

2.4 SKIN EFFECT

In the AC supply systems, because of inductance, the current flowing through the conductor tends to concentrate near the surface rather than getting distributed uniformly in the conductor. This results in an increase in its resistance with a decrease in the effective cross-sectional area of the line conductor. This concentration of current near/ across the surface of the line conductor is called the skin effect.

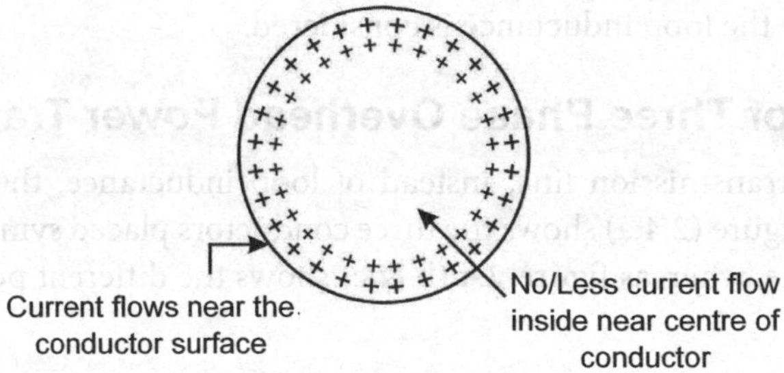

Fig. 2.5: Skin Effect

In illustrating the skin effect, we can contemplate a solid conductor composed of numerous concentric strands, with each strand carrying a fractional portion of the overall line current. The line inductance of every single annular strand varies i.e., higher towards the centre and lower towards the outer surface. These phenomena decrease the current density in the interior of the conductor as compared to the surface. Hence, the uneven distribution of current inside the conductor.

Factors affecting the skin effect:

(a) Shape of conducting wire

(b) Material type

(c) Frequency

(d) Diameter of conducting wire

2.5 PROXIMITY EFFECT

Proximity effect is the phenomenon by which the distribution of the current inside the conductor becomes non-uniform and resistance of a line conductor is increased due to the presence of another current-carrying conductor in the vicinity. When there is a current carrying conductor in the proximity of other conductors their electromagnetic fields interact with each other resulting in redistribution of current in conductors as shown in figure (2.6). The current in two conductors is flowing in opposite direction.

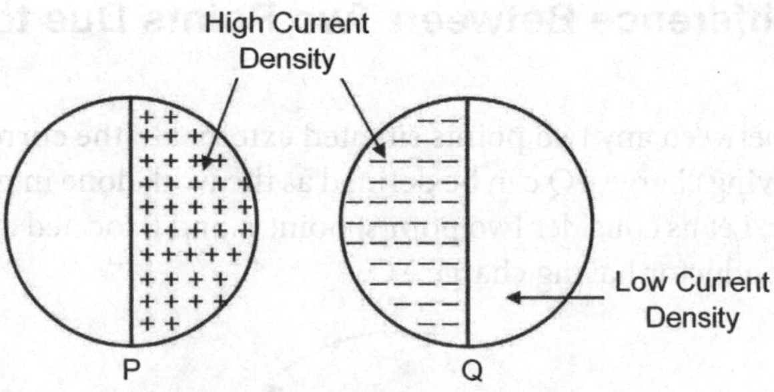

Fig. 2.6: Proximity Effect

As shown in figure 2.6, the side of the conductor Q that is nearer to the other conductor P has more flux linkages than the far side of the conductor Q. Hence the inductance of the conductor Q on the farther side is more as compared to the side nearer to the other conductor P. The current density in the farther part will be less than the side situated near the other conductor P. This results in an increase in the effective resistance due to non-uniform distribution of the current in the conductor. The various factors that affect the proximity effect in conductors are the distance between the two conductors, frequency of power supply, conductor size and resistivity of the material conductor material. Since in underground cables the conductors are very near to each other the proximity effect is more predominant whereas, in overhead transmission lines where the conductors are at a distance from each other the proximity effect can be neglected.

2.6 CAPACITANCE OF TRANSMISSION LINE

Before understanding the capacitance of the power transmission line, we need to briefly review the capacitance and the concept of potential difference (p.d.) between any two points due to the presence of a charge. Two conducting plates having positive and negative charge separated by a dielectric medium or insulator is called a capacitor. The current carrying conductors of the transmission line separated by a dielectric (air in case of overhead lines) forms a capacitor. Capacitance (C) is the measure of charge per unit potential difference and its units are farad (F).

$$C = \frac{Q}{V}\ \text{F} \qquad \ldots(2.9)$$

where; Q is the value of charge and its units are coulombs

C is the value of the capacitance, its units are farads (F)

and V is the value of potential difference in volts (V)

The capacitance of the power transmission line is evenly distributed along the entire length of the transmission line. Value of the capacitance for short transmission lines is very small and generally neglected, however in medium and long transmission lines the effect of capacitance is considered as it affects the performance of the transmission line.

When the transmission line is switched on the current starts flowing in the power transmission line even though there is no load connected at the receiving end of the transmission line. This current is called the charging current and its value depends upon the frequency, voltage and line capacitance.

2.6.1 Potential Difference Between Two Points Due to Electric Field of a Conductor

The potential difference between any two points situated external to the current-carrying conductor (as depicted in figure 2.7), having charge +Q can be defined as the work done in moving unit positive charge from one point to another. Let us consider two points, point A and B located at a distance D_1 and D_2 from a long current carrying conductor having charge +Q.

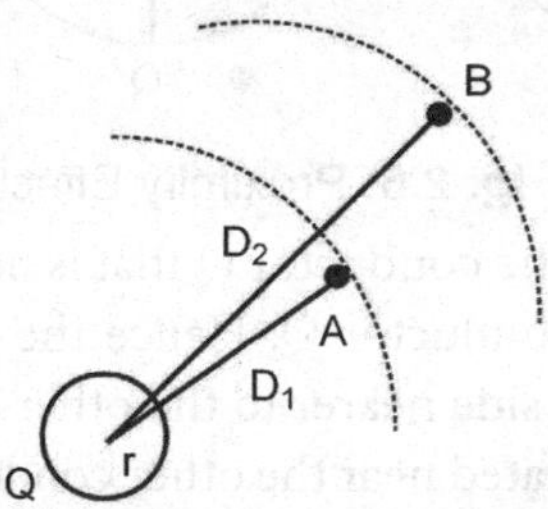

Fig. 2.7: Potential difference between any two points located outside the current carrying conductors

The electric field intensity as per Gauss's law at any distance x from the centre of the conductor is given by following equation:

$$E = \frac{Q}{2\pi\varepsilon x} V/m \qquad \ldots(2.10)$$

The potential difference at any point is dependent upon the radial distance from the charge. Points A and B are situated at distances D_1 and D_2 away from the center of the conductor The p.d. between the point A and B can be calculated by integrating the field intensity between the two equipotential surfaces. Thus, the p.d. between the two points A and B can be given by the following equation;

$$V_{AB} = \int_{D1}^{D2} E * dx = \int_{D1}^{D2} \frac{Q}{2\pi\varepsilon x} * dx$$

$$V_{AB} = \left(\frac{Q}{2\pi\varepsilon}\right) \ln\left(\frac{D2}{D1}\right) \text{ V} \qquad \ldots(2.11)$$

In a 3-phase single circuit transmission line there are three conductors and in a 3-phase double circuit line there are six conductors. The equation (2.11) mentioned above can be applied to determine the potential difference between the two conductors when arranged within a configuration of multiple conductors.

2.6.2 Potential at Conductor in an Array of Charged Conductors

Let us consider an array of n conductors having conductors A, B,C, D ....N. Let the charges on these conductors are q1, q2, q3, q4........ ....qn and are uniformly distributed over the complete length of the conductor as the spacing between the conductors is considerably greater than the diameter of the conductors. The potential difference between any two conductors can be calculated using the principle of superposition. To find potential difference between A and B due to all the conductors of the arrey is the sum of potential difference due to each charged conductor acting alone. The following equation gives the potential difference between two conductors A and B due of other charged conductors of the array:

$$V_{AB} = \frac{1}{2\pi\varepsilon}\left[q1\ln\frac{D12}{r1} + q2\ln\frac{r2}{D21} + q3\ln\frac{D32}{D31} + \ldots\ldots\ldots\ldots + qn\ ln\frac{Dn2}{Dn1}\right] \quad \ldots (2.12)$$

Likewise potential difference between any two conductors can be calculated.

2.6.3 Capacitance of a Single Phase Two Wire AC Transmission Line

For calculating the capacitance of a power transmission line first we need to calculate the potential difference between the two conductors as the capacitance per unit length is the ratio of charge to potential difference. Figure 2.8 shows a single phase two wire ac line. The charge per unit on conductor 1 is +q and on conductor 2 is -q. The distance between the two conductors is d meters.

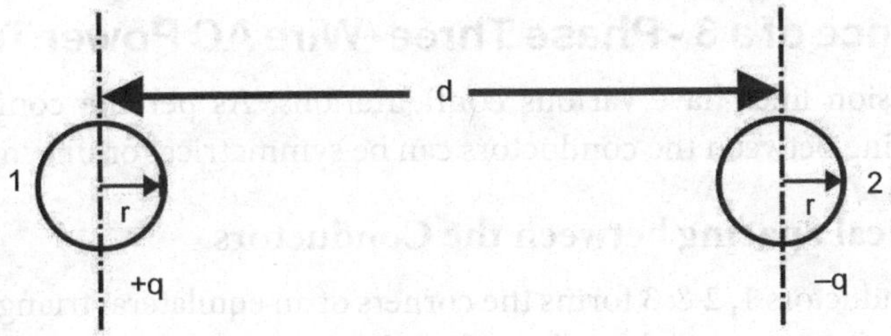

Fig. 2.8: Single phase two wire ac line

The potential difference between the two conductors is given by the equation:

$$V_{12} = \frac{1}{2\pi\varepsilon}\left[q\ ln\frac{d}{r} + (-q)\ln\frac{r}{d}\right]$$

$$V_{12} = \frac{1}{2\pi\varepsilon}\ln\frac{d2}{r2} \quad \ldots (2.13)$$

$$C_{12} = \frac{q}{V12}$$

$$= \frac{2\pi\varepsilon}{\ln\frac{d2}{r1r2}} = \frac{\pi\varepsilon}{\ln\left(\frac{d}{r}\right)} \text{ farads/ meter} \quad \ldots (2.14)$$

where, $\varepsilon = \varepsilon_0\,\varepsilon_r$ is the permittivity of the medium. ε_0 is the permittivity of the free space having value 0.0088464×10^{-9}; ε_r is the relative permittivity and relative permittivity of air is 1.

Substituting the values in eq 2.14 we get:

$$C_{12} = \frac{0.0121}{\log\left(\frac{d}{r}\right)} \ \mu F/km \qquad \ldots(2.15)$$

The line to line and line to neutral capacitance is are shown in figure 2.9 below:

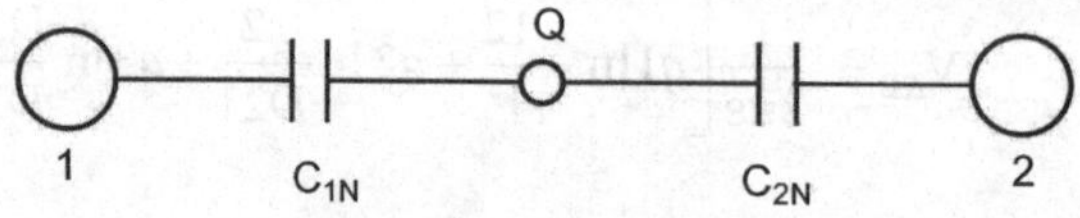

$C_{IN} = 2C_{12}$; $C_{2N} = 2C_{12}$

Fig. 2.9: Line to line and line to neutral capacitance

The charging current value due to capacitance for a 1-ϕ two wire line is given by the following equation:

$$I_c = j\omega\, C_{12} V \ \text{Amps}$$

where ; V is the voltage between two conductors 1 and 2.

2.6.4 Capacitance of a 3 - Phase Three- Wire AC Power Transmission Line

Three phase transmission lines have various configurations. As per the configuration of the power transmission line spacing between the conductors can be symmetrical or unsymmetrical.

2.6.4.1 Symmetrical Spacing between the Conductors

Let the three phase conductors 1, 2 & 3 forms the corners of an equilateral triangle. The spacing between conductors is equal i.e. D meters and the radius of conductors is r meters. The charge on each conductor is q1, q2 and q3 and some of these charges at any instance are equal to zero. The P.D. between conductor 1 and point P at infinite neutral point is given by following equation:

$$V_1 = \frac{1}{2\pi\varepsilon}\left[q1\ln\frac{1}{r} + q2\ln\frac{1}{d} + q3\ln\frac{1}{d}\right]$$

$$= \frac{1}{2\pi\varepsilon}\left[q1\ln\frac{1}{r} + (q2+q3)\ln\frac{1}{d}\right] \qquad \ldots(2.16)$$

Since $\quad q1 + q2 + q3 = 0$

$$(q2 + q3) = -q1$$

Substituting in eq 2.16

$$V_1 = \frac{1}{2\pi\varepsilon}\left[q1\ln\frac{1}{r} - q1\ln\frac{1}{d}\right] = \frac{q1}{2\pi\varepsilon}\ln\frac{d}{r} \qquad \ldots(2.17)$$

From this we can calculate capacitance of Conductor 1 w.r.t neutral

$$C_1 = \frac{q1}{V1} = \frac{q1}{\frac{q1}{2\pi\varepsilon}\ln\frac{d}{r}} = \frac{2\pi\varepsilon}{\ln\frac{d}{r}} \qquad \ldots(2.18)$$

2.6.4.2 Unsymmetrical Spacing between the Conductors

Let the three phase conductors 1, 2 & 3 are in the same plane. The distance between conductors 1 & 2 and 2 & 3 is d meters and between conductors 1 & 3 is 2d meters as shown in figure 2.10. Let us consider conductor 1 in the transposed line at three different positions i.e. a,b & c.

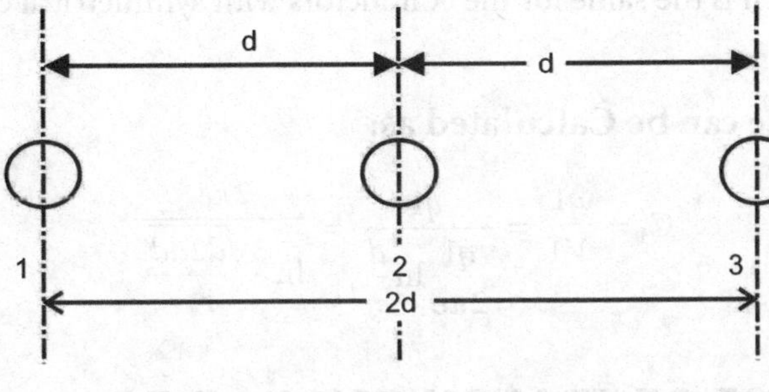

Fig. 2.10: Unsymmetrical spacing between conductors

Potential difference at position a

$$V_a = \frac{1}{2\pi\varepsilon}\left[q1\ln\frac{1}{r} + q2\ln\frac{1}{d} + q3\ln\frac{1}{2d}\right]$$

Potential difference at position b

$$V_b = \frac{1}{2\pi\varepsilon}\left[q1\ln\frac{1}{r} + q3\ln\frac{1}{d} + q2\ln\frac{1}{2d}\right]$$

Potential difference at position c

$$V_c = \frac{1}{2\pi\varepsilon}\left[q1\ln\frac{1}{r} + q2\ln\frac{1}{d} + q3\ln\frac{1}{d}\right]$$

Average potential difference of conductor 1

$$V_1 = (V_a + V_b + V_c)$$

In balance system

Since $q_1 + q_2 + q_3 = 0$

$$(q_2 + q_3) = -q_1$$

$$V_1 = \frac{1}{3*2\pi\varepsilon}\left[q1\ln\frac{1}{r3} + (q2+q3)\frac{1}{d2dd}\right]$$

$$V_1 = \frac{1}{3*2\pi\varepsilon}\left[q1\ln\frac{1}{r3} - q1\frac{1}{d2dd}\right]$$

$$V_1 = \frac{q1}{6\pi\varepsilon}\ln\frac{d2dd}{r3}$$

$$V_1 = \frac{q1}{2\pi\varepsilon}\ln\left(\frac{3\sqrt{d2dd}}{r}\right) \quad \ldots(2.19)$$

With this we can find out the capacitance for any type of configuration by changing the distance values between the conductors.

in case d=2d the equation 2.13 becomes

$V_1 = \frac{ql}{2\pi\varepsilon}\ln\left(\frac{d}{r}\right)$ which is the same for the conductors with symmetrical distance.

Further the Capacitance can be Calculated as:

$$C_1 = \frac{ql}{V1} = \frac{ql}{\frac{ql}{2\pi\varepsilon}\ln\frac{d}{r}} = \frac{2\pi\varepsilon}{\ln\frac{3\sqrt{d2dd}}{r}} \qquad \text{...(2.20)}$$

2.7 PERFORMANCE OF TRANSMISSION LINES

Generally, the values of power, voltage, current, and power factor are known for either receiving or sending end of a power transmission line. Also we are interested to find out the efficiency of a power transmission line for comparison and other purposes. The performance of a power transmission line means calculating the unknown parameters from the given parameters such as if sending and parameters are known we should be able to calculate the receiving and parameters. For evaluating the performance of a power transmission line the parameter of the line must be known beforehand. In case of short transmission lines the line parameters are assumed lump whereas in case of medium transmission line parameters are distributed along the line.

2.7.1 Performance of Short Transmission Line

Transmission lines with a length shorter than 100 km are classified as short transmission lines. The standard operational voltage for these transmission lines ranges up to 22 kV. The value of a capacitance for short transmission lines is generally small. Due to short length of transmission line and low operating voltages the capacitance and charging current is of very small value and its effect can be neglected on the performance of transmission lines. The equivalent model of a short transmission line showing resistance and inductive reactance are shown in the figure 2.11.

$$Vr = Vs - IZ = Vs - I\,(R+jX)$$

where; Vr is the voltage in kV at sending end of transmission line

Vs is the voltage in kV receiving end

I =Ir =Is is the current through transmission line in kA

Z is the impedance of short transmission line

from the phasor diagram as shown in figure 2.11(b)

Vs is approximately equal to Vr + I.R $\cos\phi_r$ + I.X $\sin\phi_r$

$Vs \cong Vr + I.R\ Cos\phi_r + I.X\ Sin\phi_r$

Voltage regulation is given as

$$\%\ \text{voltage regulation} = \frac{Vs - Vr}{Vr} \times 100$$

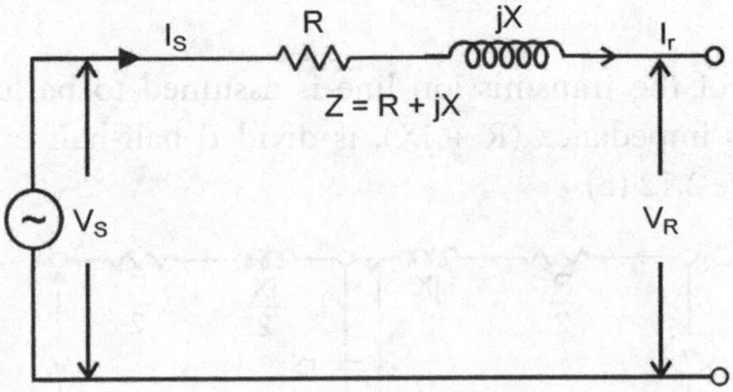

(a)

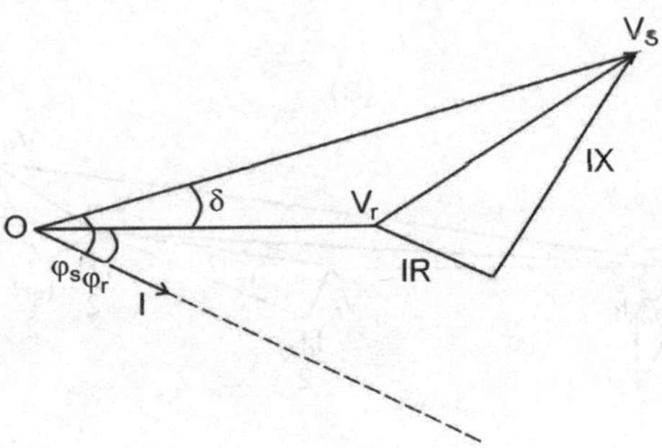

(b)

Fig. 2.11: Equivalent model of a short transmission line

$$= \frac{Vr + I.R\ \cos\phi r + I.\times\ \sin\phi r - Vr}{Vr} \times 100$$

$$= \frac{I.R\ \cos\phi r + I.\times\ \sin\phi r}{Vr} \times 100$$

The regulation of transmission lines should be within specified limits.

Efficiency: The efficiency of a power transmission line is the ratio of receiving and power to sending and power. The efficiency is generally expressed in percentage.

Sending and power in short transmission line $Pr = VrI\ \cos\phi_r$

Receiving and power $Ps = VrI\ \cos\phi_r$

Line loss per phase $= I^2R$

$$\text{Efficiency} = \frac{Pr}{Ps} \times 100$$

The efficiency of the transmission line should be high.

2.7.2 Performance of Medium Transmission Line

Power transmission lines with lengths ranging from 100 kilometers to 250 kilometers and operating voltages spanning 20 kV to 100 kV are referred to as medium transmission lines. The transmission line parameters (R, L & C) in medium transmission lines are considered as lump at particular locations. The medium transmission lines are modelled as nominal T-method and nominal π-method.

Nominal T-method:

In this method capacitance of the transmission line is assumed to be lumped at the centre of the transmission line. The series impedance (R + jX), is divided half-half on the other side of the line capacitance as shown in figure 2.12 (a)

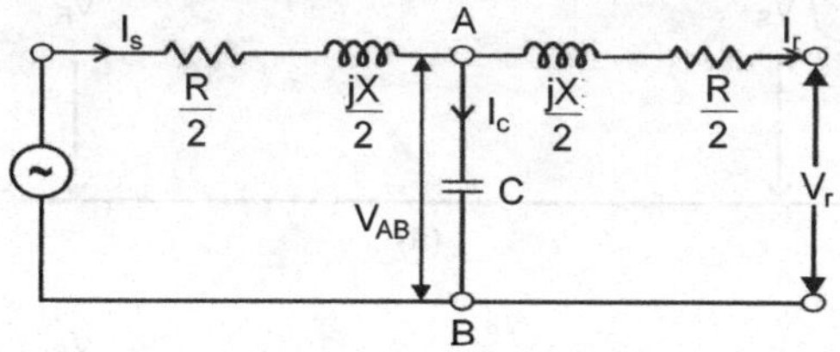

(a)

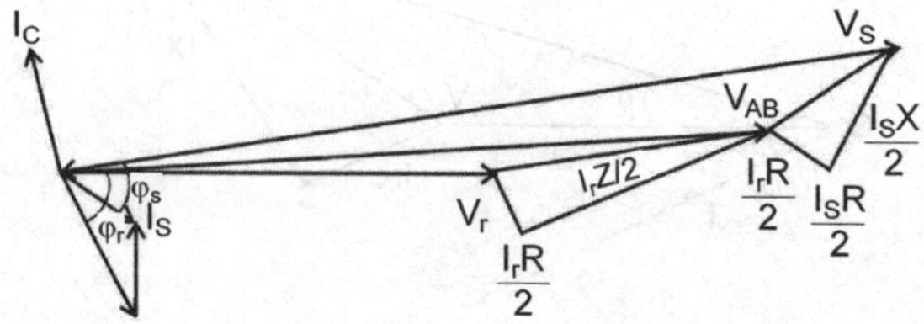

(b)

Fig. 2.12: (a) Nominal T method (b) Phasor diagram of nominal T method

Phasor diagram of nominal T method is shown in figure 2.12 (b). Apply kirchhoff's current law to node A.

$$I_s = I_r + I_c$$

Voltage across capacitance can be found using kirchhoff's voltage law:

$$V_{AB} = V_r + \frac{(R + jX)}{2} Ir$$

Current the shunt capacitance = $I_c = I_{AB} = V_{AB}\, Y$

Hence we can calculator the send end voltage and sending end current

$$I_s = I_r + I_{AB} = Ir + V_{AB}\, Y$$

$$I_s = Ir + (V_r + \frac{(R + jX)}{2} Ir\ )\ Y = Ir + (V_rY + \frac{ZY}{2} Ir\ )$$

Similarly, the sending end voltage can be calculated:

$$V_s = V_r + \frac{(R + jX)}{2} Ir\ + \frac{(R + jX)}{2} Is$$

$$V_s = V_r + \frac{Z}{2} Ir + \frac{Z}{2}(Is)$$

$$V_s = V_r + \frac{Z}{2} Ir + \frac{Z}{2}[Ir + VrY + \frac{ZY}{2} Ir]$$

$$V_s = V_r(1+\frac{ZY}{2}) + IrZ(1+\frac{ZY}{4})$$

Nominal π-Method

In this method impedance is assumed to be lumped at the centre of the transmission line and half of the total line capacitance is lumped at the receiving end and half of line capacitance is lumped at the sending end as shown in figure 2.13 (a).

Phasor diagram of nominal π-method is shown in figure 2.13 (b). Apply Kirchhoff›s current law to node B.

$$I_l = I_r + I_{c2} = I_r + V_r \frac{Y}{2}$$

$$V_s = V_r + I_l (R+jX) = V_r + I_l Z$$

$$V_s = V_r + (I_r + V_r \frac{Y}{2}) Z$$

$$V_s = V_r \left(1+\frac{ZY}{2}\right) + I_r Z$$

Apply kirchhoff's current law to node A.

$$I_s = I_l + I_{c1} = I_l + V_s \frac{Y}{2}$$

$$= I_r + V_r \frac{Y}{2} + V_s \frac{Y}{2}$$

$$= I_r + V_r \frac{Y}{2} + [V_r \left(1+\frac{ZY}{2}\right) + I_r Z] \frac{Y}{2}$$

$$= V_r Y \left(1+\frac{ZY}{4}\right) + I_r \left(1+\frac{ZY}{2}\right)$$

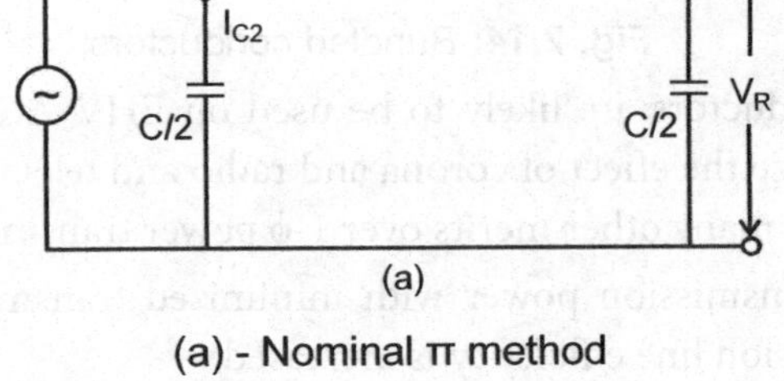

(a)

(a) - Nominal π method

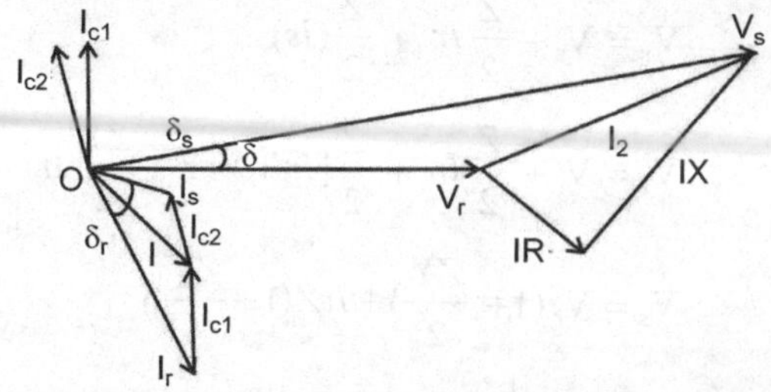

(b) - Phasor diagram of nominal π method

Fig. 2.13:

Nominal T- method and nominal π-method for evaluating the performance of medium transmission lines are not equivalent representations of transmission lines. However, these are the closest approximations to equivalent representations.

2.8 BUNDLED CONDUCTORS

When we increase the voltage level of transmission; there is an increase in transmission efficiency (η_T), reduction in transmission line losses, improvement in voltage regulation profile and reduction in cross-sectional area of conductor material required. At 300 kV and above voltages, for a round single conductor per phase, skin effect and corona cause power losses and interference with radio and communication circuits. As current flows near the surface of the conductor therefore, at the centre conductor does not carry much current. Thus, in place of hollow conductor, bundling of conductors is beneficial i.e., more than one conductor per phase.

Two or more sub-conductors forming a power transmission line conductor are called the bundled conductors, per phase compared between the spacing between phases in close proximity as shown in figure 2.14. The distinction between a composite conductor and a bundled conductor lies in the fact that the sub-conductors within a bundled conductor are spaced apart at a consistent distance, which can vary from 0.2 meters to 0.6 meters based on factors such as environmental conditions and the designated voltage level.

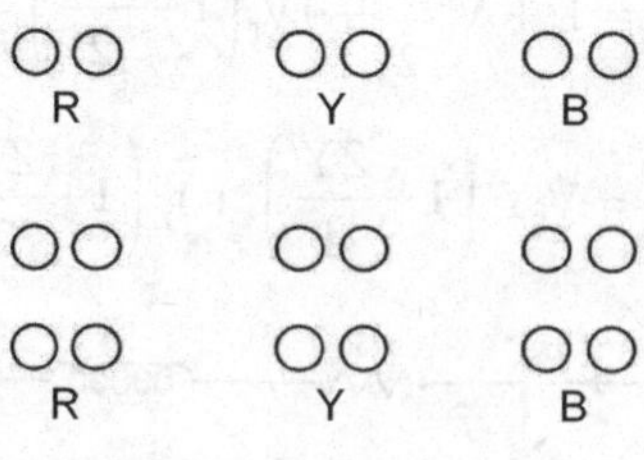

Fig. 2.14: Bundled conductors

Therefore, bundled conductors are likely to be used on EHV AC (extra high voltage ac) power transmission lines to minimize the effect of corona and radio and television interference/ disturbances, but bundled conductors have many other merits over 1-ϕ power transmission line conductor i.e.:

(a) They transmit bulk transmission power with minimized transmission line losses and thus the overall power transmission line efficiency is increased.

(b) Bundled conductors have higher capacitance or charging current which helps in improving the cos-ϕ (because bundled conductors have more capacitance to neutral as compared to single conductor lines).

(c) They have lesser inductance per-phase as compared to single conductor lines, thus giving lower reactance per-phase (because by bundling, the geometrical mean distance and radius is increased).

(d) The transmission line has surge impedance given by $Z_o = \sqrt{\frac{L}{C}}$ and bundled conductors have more capacitance and less inductance. Therefore, they have lower surge impedance with a capability of maximum power transfer. The following table represents the relative power transfer with the number of sub conductors forming a bundled conductor.

No of Sub conductors	1	2	4	8
Relative transfer power	1.0	1.3	1.6	1.7

The Geometric Mean Radius (GMR) of a bundled conductor arrangement is shown in figure 2.15 and can be determined by:

(a) For Duplex arrangement: $D_S = \sqrt{r's}$

(b) For Triplex arrangement: $D_S = \sqrt[3]{r's^2}$

(c) For Quadruplex arrangement: $D_S = 1.09\sqrt[4]{r's^3}$

where,

r' = the GMR of all sub conductor of bundled conductor

s = spacing between sub conductor of bundled conductor

(a) Two-conductor (Duplex)

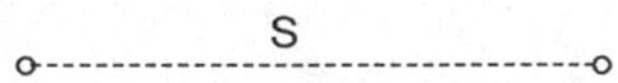

(b) Three-conductor (Triplex)

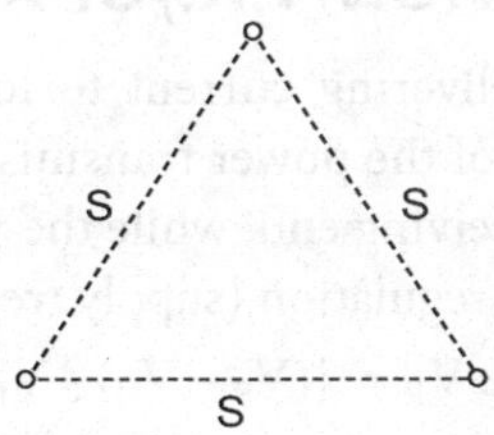

(c) Four-conductor (Quadruplex)

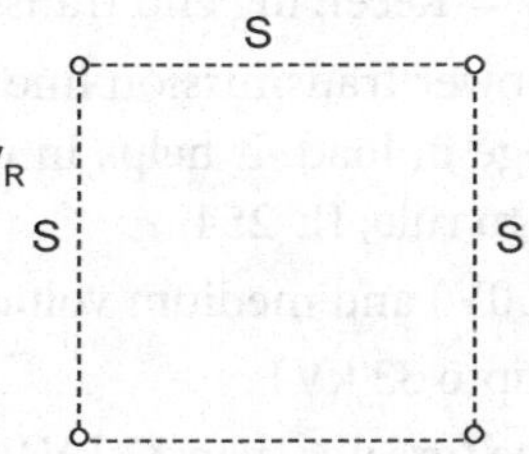

Fig. 2.15: Geometric mean radius (GMR) of a bundled conductor's arrangement

2.9 TRANSPOSITION OF CONDUCTORS

As previously mentioned, in 3-ϕ power transmission lines, the non-uniform spacing of line conductors results in distinct inductance (L) and capacitance (C) values for each phase. The apparent resistance of a transmission line conductor is additionally influenced due to the proximity effect. Therefore, the irregular spacing of the conductors affects the line parameters/ constants for a 3-ϕ power transmission line.

Due to irregular spacing of the conductors, since voltage drops in three are different, lead to different line voltages $V_{R(L)}$ at the receiving end. This discrepancy can result in disruptions to nearby telephone lines, as electromagnetic currents are induced within them. Thus, by transposition of conductors, unbalancing effect can be avoided as per figure 2.16.

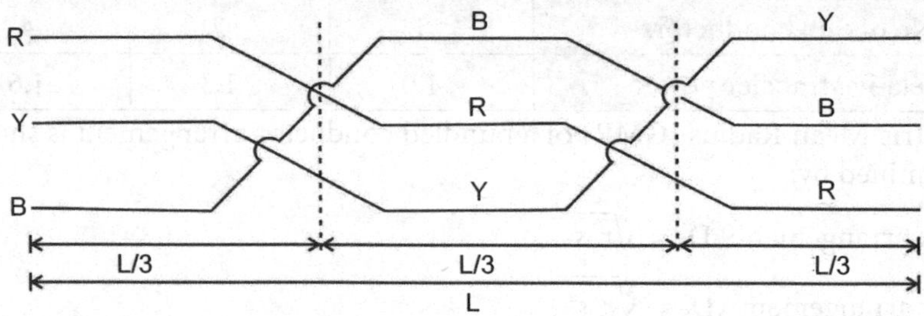

Fig. 2.16: Transposition of conductors

In practice, the transmission line conductors should be so transposed that they exist for one third of the overall length of the power transmission line for each of the three possible arrangements of the conductors. The conductors are transposed regularly at intervals to neutralize the effect of unbalanced currents. Therefore, the disturbances to the nearby communication circuits are also reduced by transposition of conductors.

2.10 VOLTAGE REGULATION (V.R.) OF A POWER TRANSMISSION LINE

When the transmission lines are delivering current to load, there is a drop in voltage due to line inductance(L) and line resistance(R) of the power transmission line. Upon disconnection of the load, a voltage increase is observed at the receiving end, while the voltage at the sending end remains constant. This phenomenon is termed "voltage regulation (supply frequency (Hz) remains unchanged).

%age Voltage Regulation or %age $V_R = [(V_S - V_R) / V_R] \times 100$

where, V_S = Sending end transmission line voltage and

V_R = Receiving end transmission line voltage

The voltage regulation of the power transmission line should be low as the variations in receiving end voltage will be small with change in load. It helps in maintaining the voltage at the load terminal within prescribed limits. According to rule, IE-254:

(a) (±6%) for low voltage (upto 250V) and medium voltage (upto 650V)

(b) (± 6 to 9 %) for high voltage (upto 33 kV)

(c) (± 12.5%) for extra high voltage (greater than 33 kV)

2.11 EFFICIENCY OF A TRANSMISSION LINE

Due to line resistance and line inductance of a 3-ϕ transmission line, I^2R (ohmic loss) losses occurs when delivering power i.e. (V_R . I . cos ϕ_R) at the load end of a power transmission line. The power received at the the receiving end is less than the supplied power i.e. (V_S . I . cos ϕ_S) at the sending end.

Hence, efficiency can be defined as the ratio of power received at the receiving end to the power sent at the sending end of a power transmission line.

$$\text{Efficiency of power transmission line} = \frac{\text{power received}}{\text{power sent}} \times 100$$

$$\eta_T = [\,(V_R \,.\, I \,.\, \cos \phi_R) \,/\, (V_S \,.\, I \,.\, \cos \phi_S)\,] \times 100$$

Where,

V_R Refers to the phase voltage of the power transmission line at the receiving end.

V_S Represents the phase voltage of the power transmission line at the sending end.

I Denotes the load current flowing through the transmission line conductor.

cos ϕ_R is the receiving end power transmission line p.f.

cos ϕ_S is the sending end power transmission line p.f.

$$\text{Also, Transmission efficiency, } \eta_T = \frac{\text{output power}}{\text{output power+transmission line losses}}$$

$$\eta_T = [(V_R \,.I \,.\, \cos\phi_R) \,/\, \{(V_R \,.I \,.\, \cos\phi_R) + \text{Line losses}\}] \times 100$$

$$\eta_T = [(V_R \,.I \,.\, \cos\phi_R) \,/\, \{(V_R \,.I \,.\, \cos\phi_R) + I^2.R\}] \times 100$$

2.12 EFFECT OF LOAD POWER FACTOR ON VOLTAGE REGULATION (V.R.) AND TRANSMISSION EFFICIENCY(H_T)

The voltage regulation (V.R.) and transmission efficiency (η_T) of a power transmission line depends upon the values of cos ϕ (power factor) as given below:

(a) Effect on Voltage regulation for 3-phase short transmission line:

(i) **For Inductive load (unity and lagging (cos ϕ) power factor):**

[(IR. cos ϕ_R + IX_L . sin ϕ_R) / V_R]

(ii) For Capacitive load (leading (cos ϕ) power factor)

[(IR. cos ϕ_R - IX_L . sin ϕ_R) / V_R]

The following observations are drawn from above two expressions:

(a) For unity and lagging cos ϕ, i.e. (IR. cos ϕ_R) is more than (IX_L . sin ϕ_R). Therefore, the voltage regulation is positive and thus, V_R is less than V_S.

(b) With the decrease in cos ϕ, for given load current and V_R, the load current increases, thus there is an increase in voltage regulation.

(c) For leading cos ϕ (power factor), i.e. (IR. cos ϕ_R) is less than (IX_L . sin ϕ_R). Therefore, the voltage regulation is negative and thus, V_R is more than V_S.

(d) With the increase in cos ϕ, for given load current and V_R, the load current decreases, thus there is an decrease in voltage regulation.

(b) Effect on transmission efficiency: For 3-ϕ, transmission line, the transmission efficiency is given by:

$$\% \eta_T = \frac{\text{receiving end power}}{\text{sending end power}} \times 100$$

$$\%\eta_T = [(\sqrt{3} . V_{R(L)} . I . \cos \phi_R) / (\sqrt{3} .V_{S(L)} . I . \cos \phi_S)] \times 100$$

Also,

$$\%\eta_T = \frac{\text{receiving end power}}{\text{receiving end power + line losses}} \times 100$$

$$\%\eta_T = [(\sqrt{3} . V_{R(L)} . I . \cos \phi_R) / \{(\sqrt{3} .V_{R(L)} . I . \cos \phi_R) + 3. I^2. R\}] \times 100$$

or

$$\%\eta_T = [(3 . V_{R(ph)} . I . \cos \phi_R) / \{(3 .V_{R(ph)} . I . \cos \phi_R) + 3. I^2. R \}] \times 100$$

Where,

$V_{R(ph)}$ represents the phase voltage at the receiving end of the power transmission line.

$V_{S(ph)}$ signifies the phase voltage at the sending end of the power transmission line.

$V_{R(L)}$ indicates the line voltage at the receiving end of the power transmission line.

$V_{S(L)}$ denotes the line voltage at the sending end of the power transmission line

I is the line load current flowing through transmission line conductor

$\cos \phi_R$ corresponds to the power factor (cosine of the phase angle) at the receiving end.

$\cos \phi_S$ refers to the power factor (cosine of the phase angle) at the sending end.

From the above expression, it is observed that the delivered power is $3.V_R. I. \cos \phi_R$

Therefore,

$$\text{Power (P)} = V_R.I.\cos \phi_R$$

$$I = P \;/\; V_R \cos \phi_R$$

Therefore, for given voltage and power, cos ϕ is inversely proportional to load current. Thus, with decrease in cos ϕ, line losses will increase and transmission efficiency decreases.

Therefore, it is summarized that with the decrease in transmission efficiency there is decrease in the ($\cos \phi_R$) load power factor.

UNIT SUMMARY

This unit describes the importance of the line parameters/ constants of a power transmission line (R,L &C) and methods to evaluate the performance of the transmission line. The various transmission line parameters which affect the performance of a transmission line are discussed and methods to calculate these parameters are discussed in detail. Further, the use of these parameters for calculating performances of transmission lines is given in this unit. Comprehensive discussions are presented regarding the performance evaluation of transmission lines, categorized into short and medium transmission lines. The methodologies for evaluating these short and medium lines are explored in depth. Moreover, the effect of load power factor on transmission line performance, particularly with respect to efficiency and voltage regulation, is extensively elucidated. The effects of AC currents when flowing through the conductors such as Skin effect and proximity effect are also given in detail.

UNIT Highlights

1. **Transmission line parameters (line constants):** The line resistance (R), line inductance (L) & line capacitance (C) of a power transmission line are called line parameters or constants of a line.
2. **Skin effect:** the current flowing across the conductor tends to concentrate near the surface rather than getting distributed uniformly. This leads to an increase in its resistance with a decrease in the effective area of the conductor. This is known as skin effect as there is increased current concentration at the very skin of the conductor.

   Factors affecting the skin effect:

   (a) Shape of conducting wire

   (b) Material type

   (c) **Frequency:** The effect is minimal at lower frequencies but increases with increase in frequency.

   (d) Diameter of conducting wire: more the diameter, more is the skin effect.
3. **Resistance:** It's an obstruction/ opposition of flow of electrons/ current.

   The value of resistance is: $\mathbf{R} = \rho \dfrac{l}{a}$ ohms (Ω)
4. **Inductance:** Property of opposing any change in direction and magnitude of alternating current passing through the conductor. or An alternating flux is set up, when alternating current (electrons) flows through a conductor, which links the conductor.

   Thus, the conductor possesses inductance due to these flux linkages.

   $$L = \frac{N \cdot \phi}{I} \text{ Henry}$$

   The value of inductance in a 1- overhead power transmission line is:

   $$L = [\,1 + 4\,.\,(\log e^{(d/r)})] \times 10^{(-7)} \text{ Henry/ meter}$$

   The value of inductance per phase in a 3- overhead power transmission line is:

   $$L = [\,0.5 + 2\,.\,(\log e^{(d/r)})] \times 10^{(-7)} \text{ Henry/ meter}$$
5. **Factors affecting the Inductance of transmission line:**

   (a) **Line length of power transmission line conductor:** More the line length of conductor, more the inductance of transmission line.

   (b) **Radius of power transmission line conductor:** With increase in the radius of conductor, there is decrease in inductance of transmission line conductor.

   (c) **Spacing between power transmission line conductor:** Larger the spacing between the conductor, more will be the inductance of the conductor.
6. **Capacitance:** "Capacitance" refers to the inherent property of an electrical component or system that determines its ability to store electric charge when a voltage difference exists across its terminals.

The value of capacitance, $C = \frac{Q}{V}$

Where, Q = charge (coulombs) & V = potential difference (volts)
The value of Capacitance in a 1-ϕ over-head transmission line is:
$C = [.\, \varepsilon_0 / \log e^{(d/r)}]$ Farad/meter (F/m)
The value of Capacitance per phase in a 3-ϕ over-head transmission line is:
$C = [2..\, \varepsilon_0 / \log e^{(d/r)}]$ Farad/meter (F/m)

7. **Equilateral spacing: $d = [d_1 . d_2 . d_3]^{1/3}$,** for unsymmetrical conductor positioning.
8. **Transposition of 3- transmission line:** Due to unsymmetrical spacing, the process of changing the position of conductors of a 3-ϕ, over-head transmission line at regular distance in order to make the line constants of 3-ϕ symmetrical is called transposition of 3-ϕ transmission line. It also serves to minimize disturbances in communication circuits located in close proximity."
9. **Bundled Conductors:** Two or more sub-conductors forming a line conductor are called the bundled conductors. Therefore, these bundled conductors are used on EHV-AC (extra high voltage ac) power transmission lines in order to minimize the effect of corona and radio and television interference.

   Table represents the relative power transfer with the number of sub conductors forming a bundled conductor.

Number of Sub conductors	1	2	4	8
Relative transfer power	1.0	1.3	1.6	1.7

10. **Classification of overhead transmission line:** These are classified as under;
    (a) Short transmission lines: Lines with working voltage of lower than 20 kV and their line length is less than 60 km.
    (b) Medium transmission lines: Lines with working voltage of upto 132 kV and their line length is around 60 km to 150 km.
    (c) Long Transmission lines: Lines with working voltage of 120 kV or more than 120 kV and their line length is more than 150 km.
11. **Voltage regulation (V.R.) of a transmission line:** There is a drop in voltage, when the transmission lines are delivering current to load, due to inductance and resistance of the line. When the load is thrown off, there is a rise in voltage at the receiving end and the sending end voltage remains the same, called voltage regulation (supply frequency (Hz) remains unchanged).
    %age (V.R.) Voltage Regulation $= [(V_S - V_R)/V_R] \times 100$
    where, V_S = Sending end voltage
    V_R = Receiving end voltage
12. **Transmission efficiency:** Transmission Efficiency (η_T) is the ratio of transmission power received to the power sent through a power transmission line.

    Therefore, (η_T) Transmission Efficiency $= \frac{\text{power received}}{\text{power sent}} \times 100$

$\eta_T = [(V_R . I . \cos \phi_R) / (V_S . I . \cos \phi_S)] \times 100$

How the load p.f. effect the voltage regulation and transmission line efficiency:

For unity and lagging cos ϕ (power factor), the regulation is positive and for leading cos ϕ (power factor), the regulation is negative.

For constant power (P) and voltage (V), if the cos ϕ (power factor) is decreased, there is a rise in load current and line losses. Therefore, the efficiency of the line will also decrease.

EXERCISES

1. Examine the distinctions between the Proximity Effect and Skin Effect.
2. "The effective a.c. resistance (R_{ac}) is greater than d.c. resistance (R_{dc}) of an overhead transmission line" Why?
3. Mention the merits of using bundled conductors in EHV AC overhead transmission lines?
4. Deduce an expression of inductance (L) per-phase per-kilometer for a 3-ϕ, over-head transmission line when:
   (a) symmetrical spacing
   (b) unsymmetrical spacing (when conductors are transposed regularly).
5. For a 3-ϕ, *over-head transmission line, explain* the transposition of conductors along with its advantage. How and why is it carried out?
6. Deduce an expression of line capacitance (C) per phase for a 3-ϕ overhead power transmission line when:
   (a) symmetrical spacing
   (b) unsymmetrical spacing (when conductors are transposed regularly).
7. Write short notes on the following:
   (a) Bundled Conductors
   (b) Proximity effect
   (c) Transposition of Conductors
   (d) Skin effect
   (e) Voltage regulation of overhead transmission line
8. How does Proximity-effect affect the resistance of the transmission line conductor?
9. What factors govern the capacitance of a transmission line?
10. Give comparison of Short, Medium, and Long Transmission Lines
11. Explain the transmission efficiency (η_T) and voltage regulation (V.R.) of a power transmission line on the basis of load power factor cos-ϕ.
12. Explain the term Voltage regulation (V.R.) of transmission lines?

Multiple Choice Questions

1. Transmission line parameters (line constants) are:
   (a) Inductance (L) (b) Resistance (R)
   (c) Capacitance (C) (d) All of the above

2. The inductance (L) per kilometer gets doubled for a 1-ϕ, 2-wire power transmission line when the distance between
   (a) wires is half
   (b) wires is increased as square of the original distance
   (c) wires is triple
   (d) wires is increased four-fold
3. The Inductance (L) of power transmission line increases with:
   (a) Increase in load current carried by the conductor
   (b) Increase in conductor diameter
   (c) Decrease in line length
   (d) Increase in spacing between the phase conductors
4. Bundled conductors reduce
   (a) line inductance and corona loss
   (b) corona loss
   (c) line inductance
   (d) both line inductance and capacitance
5. Transmission line transposition is performed in order to decrease
   (a) Capacitive effect
   (b) Line losses
   (c) Effect of surge voltages induced on the line
   (d) Disturbances to nearby communication circuits
6. The current in a transmission line under no-load conditions is because of
   (a) Ferranti effect (b) Proximity effect
   (c) Capacitive effect (d) Corona effect
7. With increase in line voltage at the receiving end of the lightly load and the open circuited line is known as
   (a) Ferranti effect (b) Proximity effect
   (c) Corona effect (d) Skin effect
8. To increase the capacity of a (HV) high voltage, long power transmission line
   (a) Resistance can be decreased (b) Resistance can be increased
   (c) Shunt admittance can be reduced (d) Series reactance can be added
9. For a short power transmission line, R & X_L are equal and voltage regulation is zero, then the load in a short power transmission line will
   (a) Have zero cos ϕ (b) Have unity cos ϕ
   (c) Be 0.707 lagging (d) Be 0.707 leading
10. Transmission efficiency (η_T) of a power transmission lines increase with the
    (a) Increase in line voltage but decrease in load power factor
    (b) Decrease in line voltage but increase in load power factor
    (c) Increase in line voltage and load power factor
    (d) Decrease in line voltage and load power factor

11. While finding the relation between receiving end voltage and sending end voltage, the capacitance of the line is neglected in
    (a) Short power transmission line (b) Medium power transmission line
    (c) Long power transmission line (d) None of the above
12. For analysing the performance of transmission line of equivalent π-model is quite suitable for line length of
    (a) 50 km (b) 150 km
    (c) 250 km (d) All of the above

ANSWERS															
1.	(d)	2.	(b)	3.	(d)	4.	(a)	5.	(d)	6.	(c)	7.	(a)	8.	(d)
9.	(d)	10.	(c)	11.	(a)	12.	(c)								

Fill in the Blanks

1. The effect of .... is neglected in short transmission lines.
2. The voltage regulation of transmission lines .... , with the increase in voltage.
3. For a transmission line, during on load the voltage at the sending end may be equal to the voltage at the receiving end, only when the cos ϕ of the line load is ....
4. An electric power transmission line has four constants/ parameters viz line resistance, line inductance, line capacitance and line ....
5. With the decrease in conductor diameter,, the inductance of the line ....
6. With the increase in supply frequency, the skin effect ....
7. Normally, the voltage regulation (V.R.) has to be kept .... for a power transmission line.
8. Only ....is considered, for the analysis of 3-ϕ transmission line.
9. Effects of .... are to be considered in medium power transmission lines.
10. The over-head transmission lines are basically electrical circuits having .... constants.

ANSWERS							
1.	Capacitance	2.	improves	3.	leading	4.	Shunt conductance
5.	Increases	6.	increases	7.	low	8.	Single phase (1- ϕ)
9.	Capacitance	10.	distributed				

True or False

1. At high frequency, the skin effect is very large.
2. In ac systems, skin effect is absent and line losses are less than that in dc systems.
3. The proximity effect alters the value of line resistance.
4. The inductance of the transmission line is dependent on the height of the supports.
5. For power transmission lines, the skin effect is comparatively less for stranded conductors rather than the solid conductors.
6. With the improvement in cos-ϕ of the line load, the power transmission line losses are reduced.
7. The length (km) for a short power transmission line is up to about 150 kilometers.

8. In case of positive voltage regulation, the voltage at the receiving end is less than the voltage at the sending end.
9. The performance of a 3-phase line is evaluated considering all three phases
10. The line parameters/ constants of an overhead power transmission line are distributed instead of lumped.

ANSWERS									
1.	True	2.	False	3.	True	4.	False	5.	True
6.	True	7.	False	8.	True	9.	False	10.	True

Short and Long Answer Type Questions

1. Elaborate on the difference between alternating current (a.c.) and direct current (d.c.) resistance of a power transmission line conductor.

Ans. "When an overhead conductor offers resistance (R) to a direct current (d.c.) supply, it is referred to as d.c. resistance. On the other hand, the resistance offered to an alternating current (a.c.) supply is termed a.c. resistance. The a.c. resistance exceeds its d.c. counterpart for a given conductor due to the non-uniform distribution of alternating current inside the conductor. This phenomenon causes the current to concentrate near the surface of the line conductor. Consequently, the increase in a.c. resistance leads to a reduction in the effective cross-sectional area of the conductor."

2. Define the term Skin effect.

Ans. The a.c. supply systems, because of inductance, the current flowing through the conductor tends to concentrate near the surface rather than getting distributed uniformly in the conductor. This leads to an increase in its line resistance with a decrease in the effective area of the line conductor. This is called the skin effect as there is increased current concentration at the very skin of the conductor.

3. Mention the factors which affect the skin effect.

Ans. Factors which affect the skin effect are as follows:

(a) Shape of conducting wire.

(b) Material type.

(c) Frequency: The effect is minimal at lower frequencies but increases with increase in frequency.

(d) Diameter of conducting wire: more the diameter, more is the skin effect.

4. Why flux linkages are essential for determining the inductance of the circuit?

Ans. It is a well known fact that the concentric circles of magnetic lines are surrounded by current carrying conductors. In an a.c. system, the above field is not constant but varies around the conductor and also links with the other line conductor. Therefore, with these flux linkages, the power transmission line maintain transmission line inductance (L) known as the flux linkage per unit current. Thus, for determination of inductance, flux linkages are essential.

5. What is a Geometrical mean radius (GMR) of a Conductor?

Ans. The product of $(r \, . \, e^{(-1/4)})$ is known as GMR of a conductor and is 0.7788 times the conductor radius.

6. Define bundle conductors and why it is used?

Ans. Two or more sub-conductors forming a transmission line conductor are called the bundled conductors. Therefore, these bundled conductors are used on EHV-AC (extra high voltage ac) power transmission lines in order to minimize the effect of corona and radio and television interference, but bundled conductors have many other advantages over single phase transmission line conductor such as:

(a) They transmit bulk power with reduced losses, thus transmission efficiency of the transmission line increased.

(b) Bundled conductors have higher capacitance or charging current which helps in improving the Cos- (because bundled conductors have more capacitance to neutral as compared to single conductor lines).

(c) They have lesser inductance per-phase as compared to single conductor lines, thus giving lower reactance per-phase (because by bundling, the geometrical mean distance and radius is increased).

(d) *The transmission line has surge impedance given by* $Z_o = \sqrt{\frac{L}{C}}$ *and bundled conductors* have more capacitance and less inductance. Therefore, they have lower surge impedance with a capability of maximum power transfer. The following table represents the relative power transfer with the number of sub-conductors forming a bundled conductor.

Number of Sub-conductors	1	2	4	8
Relative transfer power	1.0	1.3	1.6	1.7

7. What do you mean by bundling of conductors?

Ans. The use of more than one conductor per phase is called bundling of conductors.

8. For a given transmission line, what will be the effect of ground on the capacitance?

Ans. There is an increase in the small amount of capacitance for the presence of ground for a given transmission line.

9. What do you mean by transposition of line conductors?

Ans. Due to irregular spacing of the conductors, there will be different voltage drops in 3-phases which results in different line voltages $V_{R(L)}$ at the receiving end and also causes disturbances in the nearby telephone lines due to electromagnetic currents being induced in them. Thus, by transposition of conductors the unbalancing effect can be avoided i.e. by changing the position of a 3-ϕ conductors on the line supports twice over the length of the line. In practice, the transmission line conductors should be so transposed that conductors exist for one third of the total length of the line for each of the three possible arrangements.

10. Enumerate the factors which affect the performance of power transmission lines.

Ans. The performance of a power transmission line is influenced by several factors, including series line resistance (R), line inductance (L), shunt line capacitance (C), and line conductance (G).

11. Define the term voltage regulation.

Ans. As current is being supplied to the load through transmission lines, a voltage drop occurs as a result of the line inductance (L) and line resistance (R) inherent in the power transmission system. When the load is thrown off, there is a rise in voltage at the receiving end and the sending end voltage remains the same, called voltage regulation (supply frequency (Hz) remains unchanged).

%age (V.R.) Voltage Regulation = $[(V_S - V_R) / V_R] \times 100$

where, V_S = Sending end voltage and V_R = Receiving end voltage

Lower the transmission line voltage regulation (V.R.), better it is because there is little change in voltage at the receiving end (V_R) due to change in load current.

It helps in maintaining the voltage at the load terminal within prescribed limits. According to rule, IE-254:

(a) (±6%) for low voltage (upto 250V) and medium voltage (upto 650V)
(b) (± 6 to 9 %) for high voltage (upto 33 kV)
(c) (± 12.5%) for extra high voltage (greater than 33 kV)

12. Explain transmission efficiency based on load power factor?

Ans. It is observed that the delivered power over power transmission line is

$= \sqrt{3}.\ V_R.\ I.\ \cos\phi_R$

Therefore,

$P = \sqrt{3}.\ V_R.\ I.\ \cos\phi_R$

$I = P\ /\ \sqrt{3}.V_R\ \cos\phi_R$

Therefore, for given voltage and power, current across load is inversely proportional to cos ϕ. Thus, with decrease in cos ϕ, line losses will increase and transmission efficiency decreases.

Therefore, it is summarized that the transmission efficiency (η_T) decreases with the decrease in the ($\cos\phi_R$) load power factor of power transmission line.

13. Why is line regulation more significant in long and medium transmission lines compared to voltage drop?

Ans. Because of the rise in voltage caused by the Ferranti effect, the line regulation is more important than voltage drop.

Numerical Problems

SOLVED NUMERICAL

1. For a 1-Φ transmission line operating at 220 volts, featuring parallel line conductors spaced 3 meters apart and each line conductor having a diameter of 1.4 cm, determine the loop inductance per kilometer of the power transmission line.

Ans. Voltage, V = 220 volts

Spacing between the line conductors, d = 3 m = 300 cm

Each conductor having diameter of, = 1.4 cm

Therefore,

conductor having radius, $r = \frac{1.4}{2} = 0.7$ cm

conductor line length, l = 1 km = 1000 m

Therefore,

Loop Inductance of 1-ϕ, transmission line:

$$L = [\,1 + 4\,.\,(\log_e{(d/r)})] \times 10^{(-7)}\ \text{Henry/ meter}$$

Therefore,

Total inductance of loop per km:

$$L = [\,1 + 4 \log e^{(300/0.7)}\,] \times 10^{-7} \times 1000$$

$$\mathbf{L = 2.524\ mH\ (Ans.)}$$

2. Calculate the inductance of a 3-Φ symmetrical power transmission line configuration. The line consists of conductors with a diameter of 2.5 cm, positioned at the corners of an equilateral triangle with a separation distance of 1.5 meters.

Ans. Spacing between any two-line conductors, d = 1.5 m = 150 cm

Each conductor having diameter of, = 2.4 cm

Therefore,

each conductor having radius, $r = \frac{2.4}{2} = 1.2$ cm

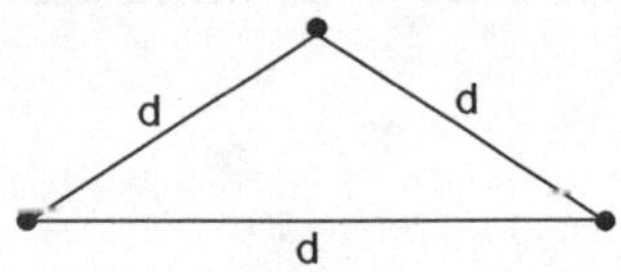

Fig. 2.17: Conductors of the equilateral triangle are equally placed at corners

As per symmetrical transmission, the conductors of the equilateral triangle are equally placed at corners of the as per figure 2.17. Therefore, Inductance per phase of the transmission line:

$$L = [\,0.5 + 2\,.\,(\log e^{(d/r)})] \times 10^{(-7)}\ \text{Henry/ meter}$$

$$L = [\,0.5 + 2 \log e^{(150/1.2)}\,] \times 10^{-7}$$

$$\mathbf{L = 10.16 \times 10^{-7}\ H/m\ (Ans.)}$$

3. In the case of a 3-Φ overhead power transmission line has three conductors of sides 2.5 m, 3 m and 5 m which are placed at the corner of a triangle and having each conductor diameter of 1.54 cm. Calculate the line inductance/ km (per-kilometer) of a power transmission line, when conductors are transposed regularly.

Ans. Figure (2.18) shows 3-ϕ, overhead power transmission line with three conductors of a triangle placed at the corner having their sides:

$d_1 = 2.5$ meters

$d_2 = 3.0$ meters

$d_3 = 5.0$ meters

where, diameter = 1.54 cm

Therefore,

Conductor having radius, $r = \frac{1.54}{2} = 0.77$ cm

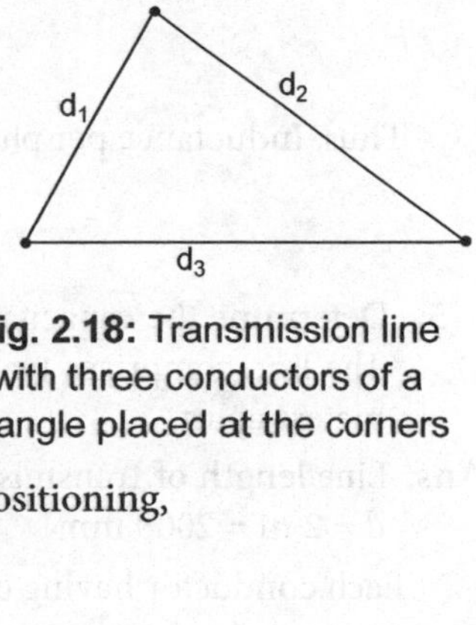

Fig. 2.18: Transmission line with three conductors of a triangle placed at the corners

Since, the overhead transmission line has unsymmetrical conductor positioning,

Therefore, the equivalent value of equilateral spacing:

$$\mathbf{d = (d_1 \times d_2 \times d_3)^{(1/3)}}$$

$$d = (\,2.5 \times 3 \times 5)^{1/3} = 3.35\ m\ =\ 335\ cm$$

Therefore,

Inductance per phase of the transmission line:

$$L = [0.5 + 2 . (\log e^{(d/r)})] \times 10^{(-7)} \text{ Henry/ meter}$$

$$L = [0.5 + 2 \log e^{(335/0.77)}] \times 10^{-7}$$

$$L = 12.65 \times 10^{-7} \text{ H/m}$$

Thus, Inductance per phase per kilometer of the transmission line:

$$L = 12.65 \times 10^{-7} \times 1000$$

$$\mathbf{L = 1.265 \text{ mH} \quad (Ans.)}$$

4. **A 3-ϕ, 3-wire overhead power transmission line has three conductors with spacing $d_1 = 3$ m, $d_2 = 3$ m and $d_3 = 6$ m placed in a horizontal plane. The conductors are transposed having each conductor diameter of 3.2 cm. Calculate the power transmission line inductance/ km (per kilometer).**

Ans. Figure (2.19) shows that the three conductors which are situated in a horizontal plane having spacing:

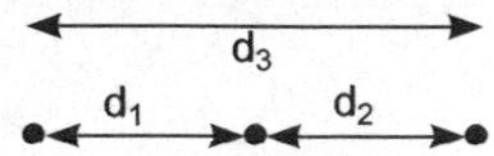

Fig. 2.19: Three conductors which are situated in a horizontal plane

$d_1 = 3$ m

$d_2 = 3$ m

$d_3 = 6$ m

where, diameter = 3.2 cm

Therefore,

conductor having radius, $r = \frac{3.2}{2} = 1.6$ cm

Therefore, the equivalent value of equilateral spacing:

$$d = (d_1 \times d_2 \times d_3)^{(1/3)}$$

$$d = (3 \times 3 \times 6)^{1/3} = 3.78 \text{ m} = 378 \text{ cm}$$

Therefore,

Inductance per phase of the transmission line:

$$L = [0.5 + 2 . (\log e^{(d/r)})] \times 10^{(-7)} \text{ Henry/ meter}$$

$$L = [0.5 + 2 \log e^{(378/1.6)}] \times 10^{-7}$$

$$L = 11.43 \times 10^{-7} \text{ H/m}$$

Thus, Inductance per phase per kilometer of the transmission line:

$$L = 11.43 \times 10^{-7} \times 1000$$

$$\mathbf{L = 1.143 \text{ mH} \quad (Ans.)}$$

5. **Determine the capacitance of a 1-Φ power transmission line spanning a length of 50 kilometers. The line comprises two parallel line conductors, each with a diameter of 24 mm and spaced 2 meters apart.**

Ans. Line length of transmission line, = 50 km = 50000 meters Spacing between any two conductors, d = 2 m = 2000 mm

Each conductor having diameter of, = 24 mm

Therefore,

radius of each conductor, $r = \frac{24}{2} = 12$ mm

Capacitance of transmission line, $C = [.\ \varepsilon_o / \log e^{(d/r)}\ ] \times$ line length

$$= (\ .8.854\ .\ 10^{-12}\ .\ 50000\ )\ /\ \log e^{(\ 2000\ /\ 12\ )}$$

C = 0.2715 F (Ans.)

6. Calculate the line capacitance per kilometer for each transmission line conductor in a 3-Φ overhead transmission line. The conductors are positioned at the corners of an equilateral triangle, with a separation distance of 2.5 meters between them. The diameter of each conductor measures 1.6 cm.

Ans. Line length of transmission line, = 1 km = 1000 meters

Spacing between any two line conductors: d = 2.5 m = 250 cm

Each conductor having diameter of, = 1.6 cm

Therefore,

Conductor having radius, $r = \frac{1.6}{2} = 0.8$ cm

Capacitance of each power transmission line conductor,

$$C = [2.\ \pi\ .\ \varepsilon_o / \log e^{(d/r)}\ ] \times \text{line length}$$

$$= (\ 2\ .\ \pi\ .\ 8.854\ .\ 10^{-12}\ .\ 1000\ )\ /\ \log e^{(\ 250\ /\ 0.8\ )}$$

C = 0.0096 F/km (Ans.)

7. A 3-ϕ, over-head transmission line has three conductors placed at the corner of sides 2.5 m, 3 m and 5 m of a triangle having each conductor diameter of 1.54 cm. Find the capacitance/ phase of a power transmission line, which are transposed regularly. The specified length of the power transmission line is 30 kilometers.

Ans. Figure (2.20) shows 3-, overhead transmission line with three conductors of a triangle situated at the corner with sides:

d_1 = 2.5 meters

d_2 = 3.0 meters

d_3 = 5.0 meters

where, diameter = 1.54 cm

Therefore,

conductor having radius, $r = \frac{1.54}{2} = 0.77$ cm

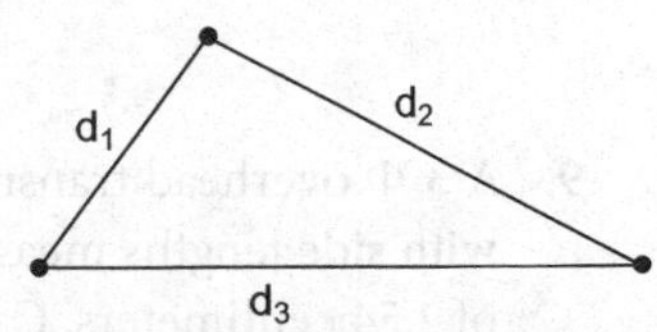

Fig. 2.20: Three conductors of a triangle situated at the corner

Line length of transmission line = l = 30 km = 30000 meters

Since, the overhead transmission line has unsymmetrical conductor positioning,

Therefore, the equivalent value of equilateral spacing:

$$d = (d_1 \times d_2 \times d_3)^{(1/3)}$$

$$d = (\ 2.5 \times 3 \times 5)^{1/3} = 3.35 \text{ m} = 335 \text{ cm}$$

Therefore,

Capacitance of each transmission line conductor,

$$C = [2.\pi.\varepsilon_o / \log e^{(d/r)}] \times \text{line length}$$
$$= (2.\pi.8.854.10^{-12}.30000)\ /\log e^{(335/0.77)}$$
$$\mathbf{C = 0.2744\ F\ (Ans.)}$$

8. A 3-ϕ, 3-wire over-head transmission line has three conductors with spacing $d_1 = 3.5$ m, $d_2 = 3.5$ m and $d_3 = 7$ m placed in a horizontal plane. The conductors are transposed having a diameter of 2.6 cm of each line conductor. If the power transmission line length is 120 km, find the line capacitance per-phase of a power transmission line.

Ans. Figure (2.21) shows horizontal plane having three conductors with spacing:

$d_1 = 3.5$ m

$d_2 = 3.5$ m

$d_3 = 7$ m

where, diameter = 2.6 cm

Therefore,

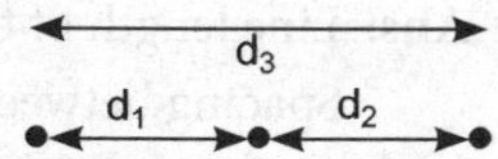

Fig. 2.21: Horizontal plane having three conductors

conductor having radius, $r = \dfrac{2.6}{2} = 1.3$ cm

Therefore, the equivalent value of equilateral spacing:

$$d = (d_1 \times d_2 \times d_3)^{(1/3}$$
$$d = (3.5 \times 3.5 \times 7)^{1/3} = 4.41 \text{ m} = 441 \text{ cm}$$

Line length of transmission line = l = 120 km = 120000 meters

Therefore,

Capacitance of each transmission line conductor,

$$C = [2.\pi.\varepsilon_o / \log e^{(d/r)}] \times \text{line length}$$
$$= (2.\pi.8.854.10^{-12} \times 120000)\ /\log e^{(441/1.3)}$$
$$\mathbf{C = 1.144\ F\ (Ans.)}$$

9. A 3-Φ overhead transmission line consists of three conductors placed at the vertices of a triangle, with side lengths measuring 2.5 m, 3.5 m, and 5.5 m, respectively. Each conductor has a diameter of 2.54 centimeters. Calculate

(a) Line-Inductance/ km (per-kilometer) of a power transmission line,

(b) capacitance/ phase (per-phase), when the power transmission line length is 120 km.

Assume conductors are transposed regularly.

Ans. Figure (2.22) shows 3-ϕ, overhead transmission line with three conductors of a triangle situated at the corner with sides:

$d_1 = 2.5$ meters

$d_2 = 3.5$ meters

$d_3 = 5.5$ meters

where, diameter = 2.54 cm

Therefore,

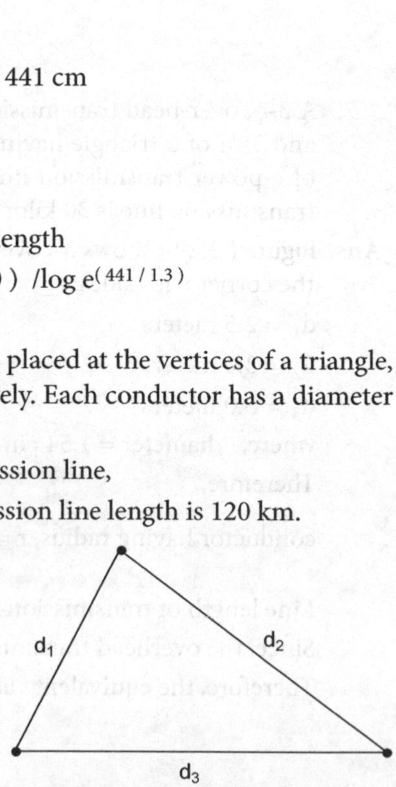

Fig. 2.22: Transmission line with three conductors of a triangle situated at the corner

conductor having radius, $r = \frac{2.54}{2} = 1.27$ centimeters Since, the overhead transmission line has unsymmetrical conductor positioning,

Therefore, the equivalent value of equilateral spacing:

$$d = (d_1 \times d_2 \times d_3)^{(1/3)}$$

$$d = (2.5 \times 3.5 \times 5.5)^{1/3} = 3.64 \text{ m} = 364 \text{ cm}$$

Therefore,

Inductance per phase of thc transmission line:

$$L = [\, 0.5 + 2\,.\,(\log e^{(d/r)})] \times 10^{(-7)} \text{ Henry/ meter}$$

$$L = [\, 0.5 + 2 \log e^{(364/1.27)}\,] \times 10^{-7}$$

$$L = 11.82 \times 10^{-7} \text{ H/m}$$

Thus, Inductance per phase per kilometer of the transmission line:

$$L = 11.82 \times 10^{-7} \times 1000$$

$$\mathbf{L = 1.182 \text{ mH (Ans.)}}$$

Line length of transmission line = l = 120 km = 120000 meters

Therefore,

Capacitance of each transmission line conductor per-phase,

$$C = [2.\,\pi.\,\varepsilon_o / \log e^{(d/r)}\,] \times \text{line length}$$

$$= (2\,.\,\pi\,.\,8.854\,.\,10^{-12}\,.\,120000\,)\ /\log e^{(364/1.27)}$$

$$\mathbf{C = 1.179 \text{ F (Ans.)}}$$

10. A 11, kV 1-ϕ, over-head transmission line delivers 900 kW at cos ϕ (power factor) 0.85 lagging. The total transmission line resistance (R) is 9 ohms and total inductive reactance (X_L) is 7 ohms. Find:
    (a) V_S, Sending end voltage
    (b) %age Voltage regulation
    (c) Sending end cos (power factor)
    (d) Transmission efficiency

Ans. Receiving end voltage, $V_R = 11$ kV

Delivered Power, $P = 900$ kW

Load cos $_R$ (power factor) = 0.85 lagging

Therefore, sin $_R$ = 0.53

Line resistance, R = 9 ohms

Inductive reactance, $X_L = 7$ ohms

Line current, $I = P / (V_R\,.\,\cos\phi_R)$

$$= \frac{900 \times 1000}{11 \times 1000 \times 0.85}$$

$$= 96.26 \text{ Amperes}$$

(a) Sending end-line voltage,

$$V_{S(L)} = [(V_R.\cos\phi_R + I.R)^2 + (V_R.\sin\phi_R + I.X_L)^2]^{(1/2)}$$

$$= [(11000 \times 0.85 + 96.26 \times 9)^2 + (11000 \times 0.53 + 96.26 \times 7)^2]^{(1/2)}$$

$$= [(9350 + 866.34)^2 + (5830 + 673.82)^2]^{(1/2)}$$

$$= [(104373603 + 42299674.59]^{(1/2)}$$

$$\mathbf{V_S = 12111 \text{ volts (Ans.)}}$$

(b) %age voltage regulation $= [(V_S - V_R) / V_R] \times 100$

$$= [(12111 - 11000) / 11000] \times 100$$

$$= \frac{1111 \times 100}{11000}$$

$$\mathbf{\% \text{ V.R.} = 10.1 \% \text{ (Ans.)}}$$

(c) Sending end cos (power factor), $\cos\phi_S = [(V_R \cos\phi_R + IR) / (V_S)]$

$$= \frac{11000 \times 0.85 + 96.26 \times 9}{12111}$$

$$= \frac{10216.34}{12111}$$

$$\mathbf{\cos\phi_S = 0.844 \text{ (Ans.)}}$$

Transmission line losses $= I^2R = (96.26)^2 \times 9 = 83394$ watts

(d) Transmission efficiency, $= \frac{900000}{900000 + 83394} \times 100$

$$= \frac{900000}{983394} \times 100$$

$$\mathbf{= 91.52\% \text{ (Ans.)}}$$

11. **A 3-Φ overhead transmission line transmits 4000 kW with a power factor (cos Φ) of 0.82 lagging. The total transmission line resistance (R) is 0.6 ohms and total inductive reactance (X_L) is 0.9 ohms. Calculate the transmission efficiency and load-end line voltage given that the sending end line voltage is 11 kV.**

Ans. Sending end line voltage, $V_{S(L)} = 11$ kV

Delivered Power, $P = 4000$ kW

Load cos $_R$ (power factor) $= 0.82$ lagging

Therefore, $\sin_R = 0.57$

Total Line resistance of each conductor, $R_{ph} = 3 \times 0.6 = 1.8$ ohms

Total Inductive reactance of each conductor, $X_{L(ph)} = 3 \times 0.9 = 2.7$ ohms

Sending end phase voltage, $V_{S(ph)} = \frac{11000}{\sqrt{3}} = 6350.85$ volts

Let the receiving end phase voltage be V_R,

Therefore, (P) Power $= [3 . V_R . I . \cos_R]$

$$4000 \times 1000 = 3 \times V_R \times I \times 0.82$$

Load current, $I = 26016.26/ V_R$ ...(a)

Also, the sending end phase voltage be V_S

$$V_S = V_R + I . R . \cos \phi_R + I . X_L . \sin \phi_R$$

$$6350.85 = V_R + \{ I.[R.\cos\phi_R + X_L. \sin\phi_R]\}$$

$$6350.85 = V_R + I . [1.8 \times 0.82 + 2.7 \times 0.57]$$

$$V_R = 6350.85 - 3.015I \quad \text{...(b)}$$

Therefore, on solving equations (a) & (b), we get:

Receiving end-phase voltage $V_{R(ph)} = 5422$ volts

Load current, I = 308 amperes

(a) Receiving end line voltage, $V_{R(L)} = \sqrt{3} \times V_R$

$$= 1.732 \times 5422$$

$$= \mathbf{5422\ volts\ (Ans.)}$$

(b) Transmission efficiency, $\eta_T = \dfrac{\text{output power}}{\text{output power + transmission line losses}}$

$$= \frac{4000 \times 1000}{4000 \times 1000 + 3 \times (308)^2 \times 1.8} \times 100$$

$$= \frac{4000000}{4512266} \times 100$$

$$\eta_T = \mathbf{88.65\ \%\ (Ans.)}$$

12. A 3-ϕ, short power transmission line delivering a balanced load of 200 amperes at cos 0.9 lagging. Each transmission line conductor resistance (R) is 0.7 ohms and inductive reactance (X_L) is 2.2 ohms. Find the sending end transmission line voltage necessary to maintain the transmission efficiency of 95 percent.

Ans. Load cos $_R$ (power factor) = 0.9 lagging

Therefore, sin $_R$ = 0.44

Line resistance of each conductor, $R_{ph} = 0.7$ ohms

Inductive reactance of each conductor, $X_{L(ph)} = 2.2$ ohms

Load current, I = 200 amperes

Transmission efficiency, $\eta_T = 95$ %

Let the receiving end phase voltage be V_R,

Thus, Receiving end power delivered,

$$P = 3 . V_R . I . \cos_R$$

$$= 3 . V_R . 200 . 0.9$$

$$= 540\ V_R$$

$$\text{Sending end power} = \frac{\text{Power received}}{\text{Transmission efficiency, } \eta}$$

Therefore,

$$\text{Sending end power} = (540\ V_R)\ /\ 0.9 = 600\ V_R$$

$$\text{Line losses} = \text{Sending end power} - \text{Receiving end power}$$

$$= 600\ V_R - 540\ V_R = 60\ V_R \qquad \ldots(a)$$

Also the line losses are $= 3.\ I^2.\ R$

$$= 3\ .\ 200^2\ .\ 0.7$$

$$= 84000 \text{ watts} \qquad \ldots(b)$$

$$60\ V_R = 84000$$

Therefore, $V_R = 1400$ volts

Per phase sending end-phase voltage ($V_{S(ph)}$),

$$V_{S\,(ph)} = [(V_R \times \cos\phi_R + I\,R)^2 + (V_R \times \sin\phi_R + I\,X_L)^2]^{(1/2)}$$

$$= [(1400 \times 0.9 + 200 \times 0.7)^2 + (1400 \times 0.44 + 200 \times 2.2)^2]^{(1/2)}$$

$$= [(1400)^2 + (1056)^2]^{(1/2)}$$

$$V_S = 1753.61 \text{ volts}$$

Per phase sending end line voltage,

$$V_{S\,(L)} = \sqrt{3} \times V_{S\,(ph)}$$

$$= 1.732 \times 1753.61$$

$$\mathbf{V_{S\,(L)} = 3037.25\ volts\ (Ans.)}$$

UNSOLVED NUMERICAL

1. Calculate the line inductance per-phase of a 3-100 kilometer long transmission line. Each conductor diameter of a symmetrical power transmission line is 0.5 cm and situated at the corners of the equilateral triangle whose sides are 1.2 meter apart. (Ans: 0.129H)
2. In a 3-Φ overhead power transmission line configuration, three transmission line conductors are positioned at the vertices of a triangle with side lengths of 1 meter, 1.3 meters, and 2 meters. The diameter of each line conductor is 2 centimeters. Find
   (a) Line Inductance (L) of a power transmission line,
   (b) capacitance perphase of a power transmission line,

   when the line length is 20 km. Assume conductors are transposed regularly.

   (**Ans:** L = 21.33 mH, C = 0.219 F)
3. Find the line constants/ parameters of a 3-ϕ, 132 kV, 50 hertz overhead transmission line. The transmission line conductor has an equivalent area of 1.5 cm^2 and a diameter of 3.98 cm. The symmetrical transmission line is positioned at the vertices of an equilateral triangle with sides spaced 8 meters apart. The conductor material having resistivity (ρ) of 1.729×10^{-6} Ω-cm.
   (Ans: R = 0.115 ohms, L = 1.25 mH/phase/km, C = 0.0093 μF/phase/km)
4. An overhead power transmission line operating at 33 kV, with a frequency of 50 Hz and a 3-Φ configuration, transmits 3600 kW power with a power factor (cos Φ) of 0.8 lagging. The transmission line conductor has resistance (R) of 5.31 ohms and line inductance (L) of 0.018 henry. Find:

(a) Line current (I)
(b) (V_R) receiving end voltage
(c) Sending end cos
(d) (η_T) Transmission efficiency

(Ans: I = 81.5A, V_R = 31.9 kV, $\cos_S$ = 0.796, η_T = 97.2%)

5. A 1-ϕ, overhead power transmission line has an overall resistance (R) of 0.2 ohms and overall inductive reactance (X_L) is 0.4 ohms. Determine the sending end line voltage required to deliver 500 kVA at a receiving end voltage of 2 kV with a power factor (cos Φ) of: a) when power factor is unity, b) n power factor is 0.707 lagging.

(Ans: (a) 2052.44 volts, (b) 2106 volts)

6. A 11 kV 3-ϕ, over-head power transmission line delivers 5000 kVA load at cos ϕ = 0.8 lagging. The overall resistance (R) of a transmission line is 1.5 ohms and total inductive reactance (X_L) is 4 ohms. Find:
(a) %age Voltage regulation
(b) (η_T) Transmission efficiency (Ans: %V.R. = 14.88%, η_T = 92.8%)

PRACTICAL

Practical -3 : Evaluate performance parameters of a given transmission line.

Objective:

The objective is to calculate the transmission efficiency (η_T) and voltage regulation (V.R.) of a power transmission line from line parameters.

Equipment required:

- Model of a three-phase short transmission line.
- Model of a three-phase transmission line.
  - T- Model
  - π- Model
- Voltmeters, ammeters, and watt meters (of proper range as per hardware model)
- Variac
- Connecting wires

Theory:

Evaluating performance of a transmission line means to calculate voltage current and power at any point on a transmission line e.g. if we know these values at the sending end of a power transmission line we should be able to find out these values at the receiving end of the power transmission line or any other point in between sending and receiving end of the power transmission line. The performance of any power transmission line depends upon its line parameters / constants i.e series inductance and resistance and shunt capacitance in case of medium power transmission lines . As discussed in this unit the conductance is generally neglected in short and medium transmission lines. Evaluating the performance of the transmission line means we want to know the efficiency transmission line voltage regulation of transmission line and values of voltage current and power factor at either receiving or standing and of transmission line when values for the other and are known. mainly we know the sending and values and want to find out the receiving and values of voltage current and power factor so that we can verify that these values are within the specified limits. The formula for calculating the efficiency and voltage regulation are already discussed in this unit; the same may be referred to.

Circuit Diagram:

Procedure:

- Connect the power supply to the working lab model of the transmission line.
- Make the connections as per circuit diagram
- Make proper Earth connections.
- Choose values of resistance and inductance as the selected line model
- Select T or - Model for evaluation of medium line
- Before switching on the main MCB bring the variac to zero position
- Loads are kept in off position at start.
- Set the sending end voltage from variac
- Record the receiving end values as per table given below.
- Take multiple reading varying values of line parameters.
- Calculate efficiency and regulation as per the table.

Observation Table:

Sr. No	Sending end values			Sending end values			Efficiency	Regulation
	V	I	P	V	I	P		

KNOW MORE

Students are advised to visit following websites to understand the transmission and distribution system in India and the latest developments going on more deeply:

- Ministry of power, Govt of India - https://powermin.gov.in/
- Central Electricity Authority, Govt of India - https://cea.nic.in/?lang=en
- Ministry of new and renewable energy -https://mnre.gov.in/
- Any state electrical transmission utility.

REFERENCES AND SUGGESTED READINGS

- https://nptel.ac.in/courses/108102047
- https://nptel.ac.in/courses/108107112
- https://nptel.ac.in/courses/108105104

❑❑

3 Extra High Voltage Transmission

UNIT SPECIFICS

Through this unit we will discuss the following aspects:

- Significance of Extra High Voltage AC (EHV AC) transmission lines?
- Primary components of EHV AC transmission lines.
- Limitations of EHV AC transmission and EHV AC transmission system in India.
- Different types of High voltage DC (HVDC) transmission systems and their components.
- Concept of Flexible AC Transmission System (FACTS) and wireless transmission of electric power.

The necessity of Extra High Voltage AC (EHVAC) transmission and High Voltage DC (HVDC) transmission lines are discussed in detail in this unit. Also, the various components of EHV AC transmission such as transformers and other switchgear are discussed in detail. Corona and Ferranti effects, as discussed in the previous unit, become predominant at extra high voltages. Their effect on the performance of the transmission lines and methods of reducing the effects have been discussed in this unit. The EHV AC transmission system in India and associated challenges have also been illustrated.

Further, the different types of HVDC transmission lines operational in India are shown through a map, giving the need and benefits of HVDC transmission over EHV AC transmission lines. The concept of flexible AC transmission, its advantages, and various types of controllers known as FACTS controllers are also given in this unit. A brief about new trends in transmission systems such as wireless transmission of electrical power has also been discussed.

The correlation of these theoretical concepts with practical work for better understanding of the readers is done through laboratory experiments given at the end of this unit. This unit will establish the foundation for a thorough understanding of the EHV AC and HVDC transmission lines and their limitations. Solved problems, unsolved problems, exercise questions, multiple choice questions, fill-in-the-blank questions, are also given at the end of this unit to further strengthen the learning of the students. The links for further learning are also provided.

RATIONALE

This unit becomes even more important to make the students understand what the need is of transmitting electrical power at extra high voltages particularly in the Indian context. After understanding the need, a comparison of EHV AC and HVDC will help readers to choose a particular system for transmission of electrical power considering their limitations and other economic aspects. The types of FACTS controllers and their use for controlling the power flow and for improving the system stability will help the readers to understand the operation and control of EHV AC systems.

Key features of this unit include a full-length explanation of EHV power transmission systems. Precise explanations are supported by solved numerical examples of EHV AC and HVDC. A photo that allows the student to visualize the components of her EHV transmission system. Unsolved problems, Short answer questions, fill-in blanks, true-false questions are given at the end of the unit for practice and to enhance the learning process.

PRE-REQUISITES

Basic subject of power systems. No prerequisite is required.

UNIT OUTCOMES

The students will be able to:

U3-O1: Justify the need for EHV AC and HVDC transmission systems.

U3-O2: Compare EHV AC and HVDC transmission systems on a technical and economical basis.

U3-O3: Understand the limitations of EHV AC and HVDC transmission

U3-O4: understand the concept of flexible AC transmission and wireless transmission of electricity

Unit-3 Outcome	EXPECTED MAPPING WITH COURSE OUTCOMES (1 - Weak Correlation; 2 - Medium Correlation; 3 - Strong Correlation)				
	CO-1	CO-2	CO-3	CO-4	CO-5
U3-O1	3	2	1	-	3
U3-O2	2	3	3	-	1
U3-O3	2	1	2	-	1
U3-O4	3	2	3	-	3

3.1 INTRODUCTION

Electrical energy demands are escalating day by day due to increasing industrialization, growth of the agriculture sector and other commercial institutions. The major consumption of electric energy is in the industrial sector which are located near the urban areas, whereas the generating plants are located away from cities due to various reasons such as availability of land and resources. Hence it becomes necessary to transmit a bulk amount of power from the generating station to end consumers. In the previous units we have seen the advantages of transmitting power at high voltages. With the development of Extra High Voltage (EHV) AC and High Voltage DC (HVDC) systems, transmitting power over very long distances has become more economical.

3.2 NECESSITY OF EHV-AC TRANSMISSION LINE (ADVANTAGES)

The necessity and purpose of EHV/ UHV transmission are as follows:

1. Increased transmission efficiency due to reduction in transmission line losses (due to inverse proportionality of the power transmission line voltage is inversely proportional to the transmission losses).
2. More economical due to reduction in cross-sectional conductor material (since the square of power transmission line-voltage is inversely proportional to the conductor material) result in less conductor material.
3. Power station construction for bulk power transmission i.e., EHV/ UHV is more reliable/ economical than that of low power transmission.
4. Due to robustness, safety, and ecological conditions, generally, the bulk power generating stations (Hydro, thermal, and nuclear power stations) are situated far away from actual load centres. Therefore, EHV/ UHV transmission is necessary for transmission of power in bulk (hundreds of MW level) over long distances from the power plants to the load centres.
5. Capacity of power transmission line increases: Expression for power transfer is given by equation 3.1

   $$P = (V_S \cdot V_R \cdot \sin\delta) / X \quad \dots (3.1)$$

   Here,

   V_S = Magnitude of the voltage at the sending end

   V_R = Magnitude of the voltage at receiving end

   δ = load angle

   X = equivalent reactance of transmission line

   Thus, as per the above expression, with the increase in the power transmission voltage there is an increase in power transfer capacity of the power transmission line. Also, the cost of power transmission decreases due to a reduction in energy losses with the increase in voltage levels. Thus, with an increase in voltage V_S, the power transfer capacity increases.
6. Power system interconnection possibility: For load sharing, development of girds and integrated transmission systems becomes necessary, without EHV power transmission systems it is not practically possible to have two or more interconnections.
7. Increase of Surge-Impedance-Loading (SIL): The load carrying capability of a power transmission line is known as Surge impedance loading. It is the line that carries power when each phase is terminated by a load equal to the surge impedance of the power transmission line.

   $$\text{Surge impedance, } Z_C = \sqrt{L/C} \quad \dots (3.2)$$

   Here, L represents the inductance per unit length in series, and C denotes the capacitance per unit length in shunt. The surge impedance loading for a power transmission line can be given by equation 3.3

   $$SIL = 3V^2/Z_C \quad \dots (3.3)$$

   Where V is phase-voltage.

   From the above expression, SIL varies as the square of operating voltage and thus with the rise in voltage level, there is a rise in SIL. Therefore, with the increase in voltage level, the power transfer capability of the line increases. The Z_C of the line depends on the configuration of the conductors of the line. For instance, the Surge impedance for lines with single double triple and quadruple conductors are 400, 300, 280 and 260 ohms.

8. Reduction in Right of way (ROW): Individuals or property managers are paid for giving the space or away or land by the organization installing the power transmission lines. There is reduction in the right of way in case of EHV/ UHV transmission which rely upon the number of conductors and width of transmission lines. Therefore, with a reduced number of circuits and requirements of land, there is a considerable increase in operating voltage.

3.3 DISADVANTAGES OF EHV TRANSMISSION SYSTEM

1. **Increased Corona loss:** The process of ionization in the air around the line conductor accompanied with hissing sound and yellowish blue glow is known as corona. The corona is a source of radio-interference and T.V. interference.

   Factors affecting the corona loss such as:

   (a) System transmission frequency
   (b) System transmission voltage
   (c) Air-density around conductor
   (d) Radius of transmission line conductor
   (e) Transmission line Conductor Surface etc.

   The problem associated with corona is more acute in EHV transmission where the electric field at the surface of the energized transmission line conductor surpasses 2-3 kV/mm, the audible or sometimes visual corona takes place.

   For Corona inception voltage gradient is an important parameter for conductor design. To limit the corona loss, it is necessary to limit the electric-stress at the surface of the conductor to 1.8 KV per mm (rms). This can be achieved by increasing the diameter of the conductor or spacing between the conductors. Further, the corona loss can be reduced by using large diameter-conductor (hollow conductor) but their use is limited due to following reasons:

   (a) manufacturing cost is high
   (b) ice-deposit and wind can affect up to much extent.
   (c) handling is difficult and costly

2. **Increased insulation requirements:** At EHV levels the insulation requirements of transmission line and switchgear are also increased. Insulation level required depends upon the magnitude of voltage surge due to internal cause (switching operation) and external cause (lightning etc.). The transmission line is protected against lightning by

   (a) Auto reclosing circuit breaker
   (b) Lightning arresters
   (c) Tower footing resistance
   (d) Ground wire

   The switching surge voltage is more dangerous as they may cause overvoltage's of two to three times the normal operating voltage.

3. **Stability Considerations:** Power transferred by synchronous machine to the transmission line is expressed as:

$$P = (V_S . V_R . \sin \delta \ / X)$$

   Here, V_S = sending-end-voltage V_R = receiving-end-voltage

δ = load angle X = reactance of transmission line

The equivalent circuit of the power transmission line shown in figure (3.1). The R, L are the series parameters and the shunt parameters or the parallel parameters G and C are the conductance and capacitance formed between the phases and neutral through some insulation like air.

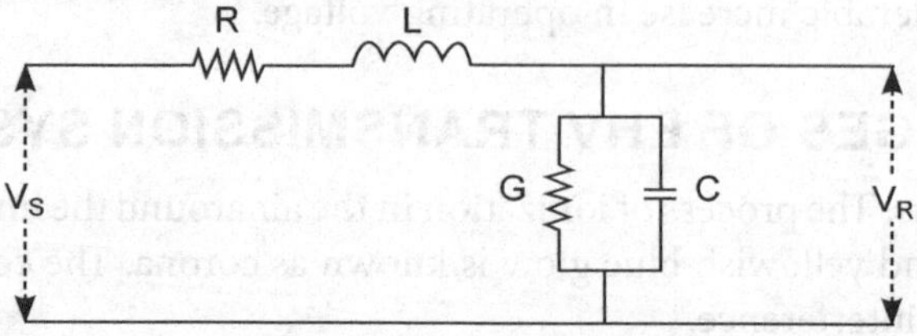

Fig. 3.1: Equivalent Circuit of Transmission Line

C is the capacitance developed in the insulating medium around the conductor.

G is the conductance whose origin is the leakage of current in the insulation.

Insulation resistance (R_i) must be infinite or $\frac{1}{Ri} = \frac{1}{\infty} = G = 0$

For lossless transmission line, the line resistance R = 0

Thus, if shunt leakage conductance (G) and resistance (R) of a power transmission line are ignored then $V_S = V_R = V$

$$P = \frac{V^2}{X}.\sin\delta \text{ Watts/ phase} = \frac{(kV)^2}{X}.\sin\delta \text{ MW}$$

When $\delta = 90$ degree, $\sin\delta = 1$ (maximum value of sine wave)

$$P_{max} = \frac{V^2}{X}$$

At $\delta = 0$, P = 0 and At $\delta = 180$, P = 0

Theoretically, the transfer of maximum power at steady state takes place at delta (δ)=90 degree but practically, δ should be kept between the limits of 20-30 degree.

4. **Heavy Supporting structures:** The transmission line towers are fabricated with steel members to give support to heavy bundled conductors of the EHV line. It bears the load of conductors, wind pressure, and weight of ice. The tower also gives the ground clearance to the conductor and air clearance between the conductors by its arms. The transmission lines are made more wind resistant as they are to bear the pressure of wind during storms and cyclones.
5. **Mechanical vibrations and oscillations:** With the rise in the number of sub-conductors in bundle conductors' transmission lines, there may be considerable effect on vibrations of conductors. Hence, the mechanical design of the system needs modification so as to counter the problem of vibrations in conductors.
6. **Audible noise:** Audible noise in the form of humming sound is created by the corona of the transmission line and transformer. It's a major problem in EHV lines. The audible noise generated by transmission lines is a function of the following:
   (a) Surface voltage-gradient across conductor
   (b) Bundle conductors (Number of sub-conductors)

(c) Diameters of transmission line conductor
(d) atmospheric conditions
(e) lateral distance between the line and point of measurement of audible noise.

7. **Interference:** The functioning of Extra High Voltage (EHV) transmission lines and substations leads to the occurrence of radio interference. The radio noise experienced at the radio receiver is linked with the phenomenon of corona. The intensity of corona primarily relies on the gradients of the conductor. As a result, radio interference, or radio noise, is intricately connected to all the factors that impact corona. Therefore, radio noise depends on:
   (a) air density
   (b) humidity
   (c) wind contaminants

   During adverse weather conditions, radio noise tends to be approximately 10 to 25 dB higher compared to radio noise levels experienced in favorable weather. The radio noise due to corona of EHV lines does not cause serious problems for frequency modulated receivers. Electromagnetic waves within the broadcast frequency range are responsible for generating radio interference and TV interference.
   (a) Radio Interference: 0.5 - 1.6 MHz
   (b) TV interference: 54 - 216 MHz

   Radio interference can be eliminated or minimized by appropriate design of line conductor. By using bundle conductor, surface voltage stress, the corona and RI can be reduced.
8. **Ferranti Effect:** As a lightly loaded/no load transmission line acts as capacitive load on the power transmission line, the voltage at the receiving end becomes higher than the sending end voltage, i.e., is $V_R > V_S$. The increase in voltage is 100% for 960 km of transmission line. Care has to be taken to control such voltage. This effect is called Ferranti effect and this effect can be controlled by using shunt reactors at the load ends.
9. **Surge impedance loading (SIL):** The Surge impedance loading for a power transmission line is given as SIL = $3V^2/ Z_C$ watts/ phase, where V is phase voltage. SIL, or Surge Impedance Loading, is also referred to as a natural load. When the line is terminated with a natural load, uniform voltage prevails across the entire line length. However, in practical scenarios, the line is not consistently operated under natural load conditions. Under such circumstances, voltage drop occurs along the line for inductive loads, while capacitive loads lead to increase in voltage. Table 3.1 shows the surge impedance and SIL of the transmission line with various voltage levels.

Table 3.1: Surge impedance and SIL of the transmission line with various voltage levels

Line Voltage (kV)	132	220	275	380	400
Surge Impedance (Z_o)	400	375	370	385	320
Natural Load (SIL) (MW)	44	130	205	430	500

3.4 COMPONENTS OF EHV AC SUBSTATION

Transmission of electric power at EHV/UHV level requires a strong network of transmission lines for bulk power transfer from remote generating stations to load centres. EHV AC substations are required at the generating end and at the receiving end of EHV lines. Special considerations are required in selecting site, switchgear, transformers etc. The step-up substations are erected at generating stations and step-down stations are installed at load ends. Switching substations are also sometimes necessary for tapping or paralleling long EHV/UHV lines.

3.4.1 Types of EHV AC Substations

EHV substations can be broadly classified into three categories as given below:

(i) Step-up substation

(ii) Step-down substations

(iii) Switching substations

Main components and equipment's of EHV AC of substations, apart from busbars and insulators, are:

(a) EHV Power transformers – to step down or to step up the voltage levels.

(b) Circuit breakers – to interrupt the circuit under normal or fault conditions. The various types of circuit breakers are Air Circuit Breaker, SF_6 circuit breakers and vacuum circuit breakers.

(c) Isolators – to isolate the circuits/ equipment

(e) Instrument transformers (CT/PT) – to measure and monitor the voltage and currents.

(e) Surge arresters – for the protection of equipment from lightning and switching overvoltage's.

(f) Earthing

(g) Series and shunt reactors

(h) Capacitor banks

3.4.2 System Interconnections Advantages

The various advantages of interconnected systems are:

(a) Lesser overall installed capacity

(b) Lesser spinning reserve

(c) Better use of energy reserve

(d) Better system support

(e) Strong grid with system stability

3.5 FERRANTI EFFECT

When a medium or long power transmission line is lightly loaded/ open-circuited, the voltage at the receiving-end becomes more than the voltage at the sending-end. This phenomenon of rise in the power transmission line-voltage at the receiving-end of the lightly loaded/ open-circuited is called Ferranti Effect. The effect was observed in 1980 on the Deptford mains laid down by S. Z. de Ferranti.

The effect of charging current in line inductances causes the voltage drop when the applied voltage is in phase with the sending end of the transmission line. Therefore, both inductance and capacitance are necessary to cause this effect. The charging current i.e., capacitance is negligible for short transmission lines but significant for the long and medium transmission lines.

Consider a long transmission line whose line constants / parameters are distributed but for simplicity it is lumped as shown in figure (3.2).

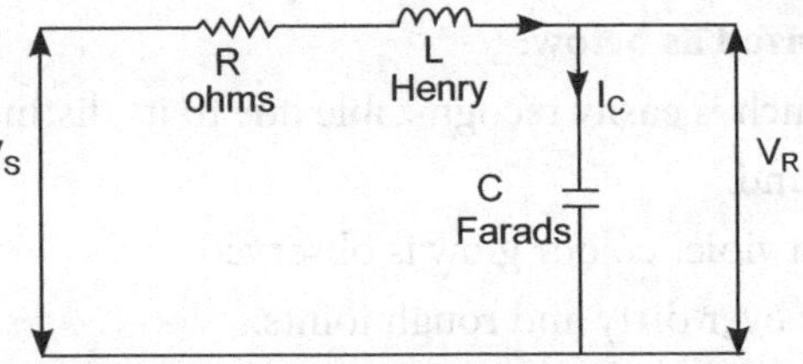

Fig. 3.2: Transmission line model at no-load condition

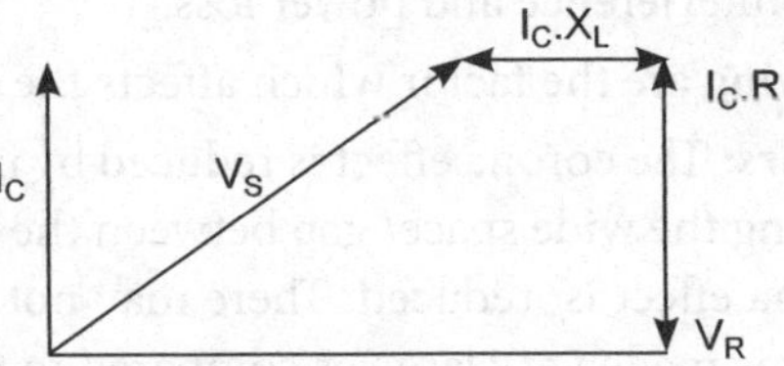

Fig. 3.3: Phasor diagram for Transmission line model at no-load condition

Normally, the capacitive reactance (X_C) of the power transmission line is relatively small as that of inductive reactance (X_L), thus the line current at no-load condition have leading cosϕ (power factor) as shown in figure (3.3). Therefore, the charging current or capacitance produces drops in the power transmission line reactance which is in-phase opposition to the voltage (V_R) at the receiving-end. Therefore, the voltage (V_R) at the receiving end is more than the voltage (V_S) at the sending end and the effect is known as Ferranti effect.

3.6 CORONA EFFECT

Across two conductors when potential difference is applied there is no actual change in the line conductor condition surrounded by atmospheric air when spacing between the line conductor is more and diameter is less for an overhead transmission line. Moreover, if there is a gradual increase in voltage, a stage will come, when violet colour glows and hissing noise occurs across the conductor. This phenomenon is known as corona and is accompanied by power losses, radio interference, and the generation of ozone gas. This violet colour glow is due to electrostatics stress in the air surrounding the conductor. More the voltage applied across the conductor, more will be the intensity of glow and sound till flashover occurs across the conductor due to breakdown in air insulation.

The phenomena characterized by a hissing sound along its span, a violet, bluish, or yellowish-blue glow, and the emission of ozone gas in an overhead power transmission line is referred to as corona.

The violet glow around the line conductor will be uniform throughout when two conductors are smooth and polished. On the other hand, flashover may take place without any glow and hissing noise when glow will be prominent at joints and rough points if the spacing between the conductors is less. This is due to lesser distance between the conductor and there is no time for glow to occur prior to breakdown of dielectric.

The visible glow of corona in the extra high voltage (EHVAC) transmission line is uniform about both the conductors but for HVDC (high voltage direct current) transmission, the positive (+ve) (substation/ pole) conductor has uniform and bright glow but has spotty glow across the negative (–ve) conductor.

The corona effect is summarized as below:

(a) It releases ozone gas, which is easily recognizable due to its distinct odor.

(b) It produces a hissing sound.

(c) Around the conductor, a violet colour glow is observed.

(d) There is maximum glow over dirty and rough joints.

(e) It induces harmonic current, therefore charging current increases

(f) It is accomplished by radio interference and power loss.

Factor affecting Corona: Following are the factor which affects the Corona:

(a) Spacing between conductors: The corona effect is reduced by increasing the distance between the line conductors. By providing the wide space/ gap between the line conductors, electrostatic stress is reduced and hence corona effect is reduced. There may not be any corona effect if the spacing between the line conductor is made very large as compared to the diameters.

(b) Conductor size: It depends on the conductor shape and conditions of the line conductor. There will be more corona effect for irregular and rough surfaces because the value of breakdown voltage reduces across roughness. With increase in diameter of the conductor, the corona decreases. A stranded conductor has more corona effect as compared to solid conductor. The corona depends upon the size(diameter), shape(stranded/ solid), condition of surface(clean/ dirty). With the increase in diameter of the line conductor, the corona decreases.

(c) Atmosphere: Corona arises due to the ionization of the surrounding air around the conductor. This phenomenon is influenced by the prevailing physical conditions of the atmosphere. Weather conditions characterized by fog and storms result in increased ion presence, leading to a more occurrence of corona as compared to drier, cleaner, and fair weather.

(d) Line voltage: Line voltage critically affects the corona. At low voltage or when the p.d. across the line conductor is low, corona is not observed. At very high electrostatic stress or at higher voltage, surrounding air gets ionized which gives rise to corona effect and it is the cause of occurrence or appearance of corona.

Merits and demerits of Corona:

In the past, the corona was something which was to be avoided because of power loss and distortion of the waveform or radio interference. But now presently it is thought of as advantageous because of the following merits:

(a) During the process of corona, an envelope of ionized air is formed which gives rise to conduction of current along with the conductor. Therefore, the virtual diameter of the conductor is increased. This reduces the potential gradient and mitigates the risk of flash-overs. Consequently, the overall performance of the system is enhanced.

(b) Corona reduces the effects of transients produced by surges due to lightning, switching etc.

Demerits: As per merits of corona, demerits are more in numbers. Thus, not required for power transmission line conductors. The following demerits are:

(a) In corona, some power is lost which is called corona loss. Due to this, the efficiency of power transmission lines is reduced.

(b) In corona, harmonics are produced.

(c) Corona currents exhibit a non-sinusoidal nature, leading to non-sinusoidal voltage drops. This phenomenon can potentially generate radio interference and TV interference in neighboring communication lines.

(d) During the formation of corona, Ozone gas is produced. This gas reacts with the material of the conductor and causes corrosion.

Methods to reduce corona-effect: Normally, at a voltage of 33kV or higher corona effects are observed. Thus, to avoid corona on the power substations or busbars rated for 33kV and higher voltages careful signs should be made, otherwise flashover in the insulator or between the phases due to highly ionized air may cause considerable damage to the equipment.

Following are the methods by which corona effect can be reduced:

3.7 LINE COMPENSATION

3.7.1 Series Compensation

Series compensation is a very important method to increase the performance of EHV transmission lines. A transmission line has distributed series reactance. Thc series compensation consists of capacitors connected in series at suitable location.The series capacitors oppose the effect of series inductive reactance of the transmission line. It improves the power handling capacity and voltage regulation.

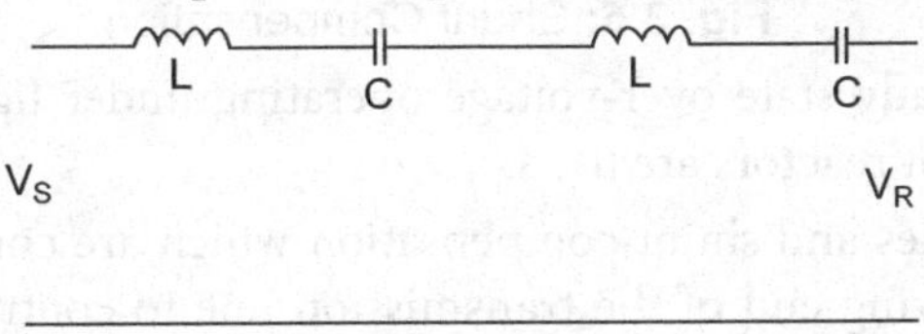

Fig. 3.4: Series Compensation

In figure (3.4), the inductive reactance of line conductors has been shown by L. To neutralize the effect of series inductance, capacitors are connected in series with the line which are shown by C. The capacitors draws the leading current from the line which balances the lagging current drawn by the inductances.

Power handling capacity is given as

$P = (V_S.V_R.\sin\delta \ / X_L)$

Capacitive reactance of series compensation = X_C

Net reactance of line = $X_L - X_C$

Now,

$P' = [(V_S.V_R.\sin\delta) /(X_L - X_C)]$

Increased power handling capacity is given as

$$P'/P = [X_L / (X_L - X_C)]$$

$$= \{X_L / [X_L(1-(X_C/X_L)]\}$$

$$= \{1 / [(1-(X_C/X_L)]\}$$

$$= \frac{1}{1-X}$$

Here, X is called the degree of compensation.

3.7.2 Shunt Compensation

Shunt compensation is of two types, namely shunt capacitor compensation and shunt reactor compensation. The shunt compensation with capacitive VARs is used to inject reactive power and control the receiving end voltage. Shunt reactor compensation is used to neutralize the raised voltage due to the Ferranti effect. For shunt compensation, static compensation employing static capacitors and reactors or synchronous compensation using synchronous phase modifier may be employed. Static compensation is being preferred to the synchronous compensation because of its inherent advantage of:

(a) higher speed response
(b) Absence of faults infeeds
(c) Low maintenance
(d) Greater stability
(e) Low cost
(f) Simpler erection

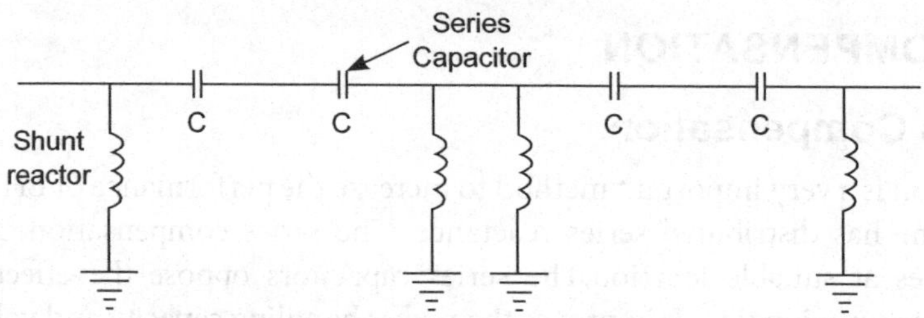

Fig. 3.5: Shunt Compensation

Thus, to control the steady state over-voltage operating under light load or energizing the long transmission EHV lines, shunt reactors are used.

Figure (3.5) shows a series and shunt compensation which are connected in parallel between the line and earth near the receiving end of the transmission line to control the overvoltage produced by Ferranti effect.

3.8 HVDC TRANSMISSION LINES

The first transmission line erected to supply power was the direct current transmission line. Later on due to various advantages AC transmission became popular in the 20th century as large no of induction motors used in industries. Now with the development of the power sector the need to transfer bulk power over long distances for which DC Transmission now became more economical. Power transfer through sea using cables over long distances DC transmission is the favourite choice. With the development in the field of power electronics converters for high power ratings become available which are the main components of a power transmission line. Over the time the costs of these solid state power electronics devices are reduced which further lead to development of DC transmission lines.

3.9 SOME IMPORTANT HVDC TERMS

(a) **HVDC transmission system:** Transfer of electric energy from one place to another in the form of HVDC.

(b) **Two terminal (2T) HVDC:** Two power transmission substations and connecting DC power transmission line.

(c) **MTDC System:** More than two power transmission substations and connecting DC power transmission lines.

(d) **HVDC coupling:** Transfer energy between AC buses (Back to Back HVDC)
(e) **HVDC Terminal Substation:** Having one or more converter units together with building, reactor, filter, reactive power supply, control monitoring, protective measuring, AC, DC yard, Valve.
(f) **Monopolar:** Only one pole and earth as return
(g) **Bipolar:** With two poles of opposite polarity
(h) **Converter unit:** Operative unit comprising one or more converter bridge together with one or more converter transformer, converter unit control equipment protective and switching devices. (Note: if a converter unit comprises two 6 pulse converter bridges connected in series with phase displacement of 30 degree then the converter unit is a 12 pulse unit .)
(i) **Valve:** A complete operative controllable array (Thyristor + other devices)
(j) **Rectifier operation:** Energy transfer from AC to DC, with delay angle kept less than 96 electrical degree
(k) **Inverter Operation:** When energy transfer from DC to AC, with delay angle kept above 90 degree electrical.

3.10 CHOICE OF HVDC POWER TRANSMISSION SYSTEM

The information presented in Table 3.2 provides guidance for the selection of HVDC for the transmission of electrical power.

Table 3.2: Choice of HVDC power transmission system

Sr. No.	Type of DC link (Type of DC Transmission lines)	Criteria of choice	Features
1	Long High-Power transmission by overhead lines: 1000 km ± 400 kV - 1000 MW ± 500 kV - 1500 MW ± 600 kV - 2200 MW	Lower total cost Better control on power flow • Less number of line conductors • No need of intermediate substation • Simple and economic • Line cost per km is lower • Break even above 800 km	Normal mode Bipolar Two terminals Can be monopolar Power flow rapid and accurate
2	System Interconnections Overhead line Underground cable/ Submarine Back-to-Back MTDC system	Technical Superiority • Provides asynchronous ties • Power flow quickly control • Improve stability • Fault level remain unchanged • Frequency conversion possible • ROW is of lesser width	Two terminals Overhead line - Monopolar or Bipolar Coupling station - no transmission line MTDC
3	Submarine Cables ± 100 kV - 500 MW ± 400 kV - 2000 MW	No continuous charging current No limit of power or distance	Two terminal Recently Bipolar

3.11 HVDC PROJECTS IN INDIA

Table 3.3: List of HVDC projects in India [7]

Sr. No.	Project Name	Connecting Region	Commissioned on	Power Rating	AC Voltage	DC Voltage	Mode of Operation	No. of Poles / Blocks	Length of line
1	Rihand - Dadri	ER-WR	December 1991	1500 MW	400 kV	500 kV	Bipole	2	816 km
2	Talcher - Kolar	ER-SR	June 2003	2000 MW	400 kV	500 kV	Bipole	2	1369 km
3	Ballia - Bhiwadi	ER-NR	Pole 1 - March 2010 Pole 2 - March 2011	2500 MW	400 kV	500 kV	Bipole	2	780 km
4	Chandrapur-Padge	CR-WR	1999	1500 MW	400 kV	500 kV	Bipole	2	752 km
5	Mundra - Mohindergarh	WR-NR	2012	1500 MW	400 kV	500 kV	Bipole	2	986 km
6	Bishwananth - Agra	NER-ER	2015	6000 MW	400 kV	800 kV	Multi Terminal	2	1728 km
7	Vidyanchal	WR-NR	April 1989	2x250 MW	400 kV	70 kV	Back-to-Back	2	
8	Chandrapur	WR-SR	December 1997	2x500 MW	400 kV	205 kV	Back-to-Back	2	
9	Sasaram	ER-SR	September 2002	500 MW	400 kV	205 kV	Back-to-Back	2	
10	Gazuwaka	ER-SR	March 2005	2x500 MW	400 kV	Block 1 - 205 kV Block 2 - 177 kV	Back-to-Back	2	

3.12 MAIN COMPONENTS OF HVDC TRANSMISSION LINE

It consists of following parts:

(i) Each terminal has an HVDC substation and an AC network.

(ii) HVDC line interconnection

(iii) Earth Electrodes and Electrode Lines

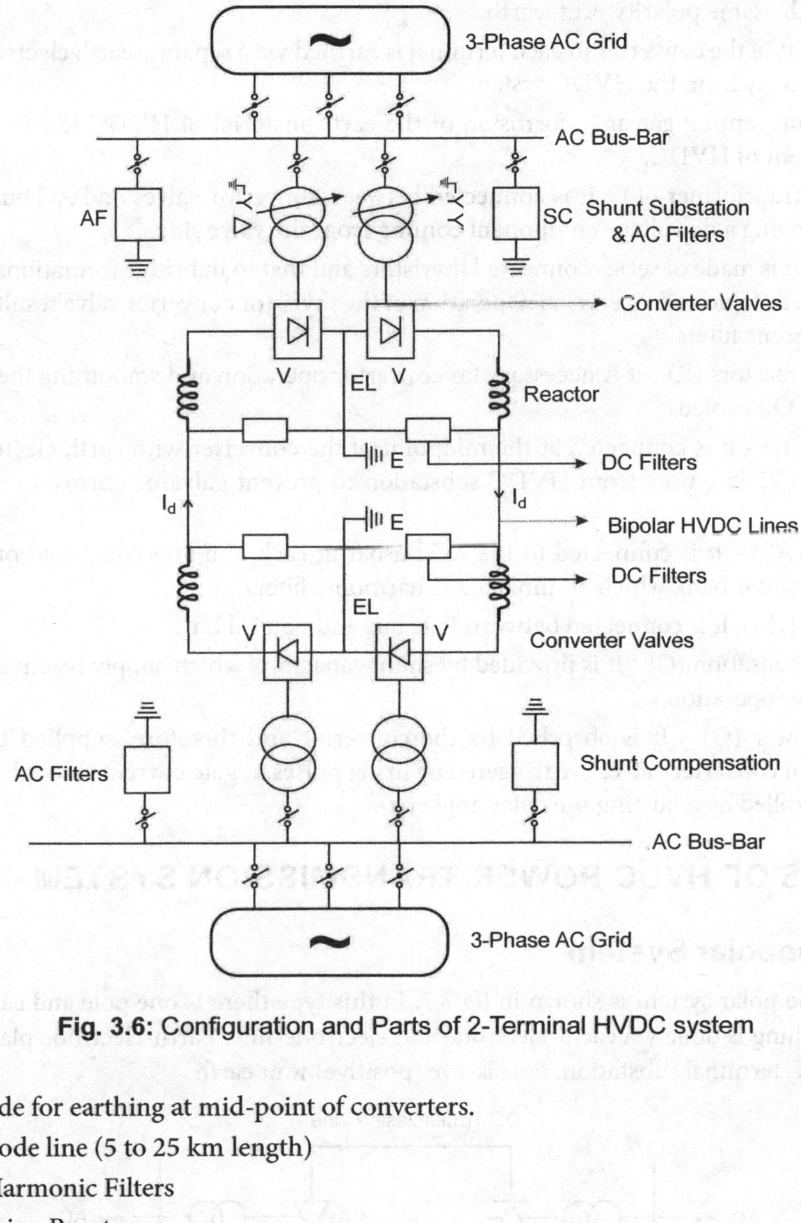

Fig. 3.6: Configuration and Parts of 2-Terminal HVDC system

Where;

E - Electrode for earthing at mid-point of converters.

EL - Electrode line (5 to 25 km length)

DF - DC Harmonic Filters

R - Smoothing Reactors

F - Filters for AC Harmonics, shunt capacitors and DC Filters

T - Convertor Transformers

V - Converter Valves

SC - Shunt Capacitors

The functions and details of components of HVDC line are:

1. HVDC has one or two poles.

2. Poles have the same polarity w.r.t. earth
3. Neutral point of the converter in each terminal is earthed via a separate earth electrode and located 5 to 25 km away from the HVDC system.
4. Therefore, preventing galvanic corrosion of the earth material of HVDC terminal due to earth return current of HVDC.
5. Converter Transformer (T) - It is connected between convertor valves and AC bus. Thus, special design as having a dc voltage component coming from the valve side.
6. Valve (V) - It is made of series connected thyristors and that to in bridge formation, which transfer power from ac to dc and vice-versa. Operation of the thyristor converter valve results in generation of AC harmonic filters.
7. Smoothing reactors (R) - It is necessary for convertor operation and smoothing the DC current. It is generally Oil cooled.
8. Electrode Line - It is connected at the midpoint of the converter with earth electrode (E) and is located 5 to 25 km away from HVDC substation to prevent galvanic corrosion of station earth material.
9. AC Filters (AF) - It is connected to the AC busbar at each end and composed of resistor bank, reactor, capacitor bank which eliminates AC harmonic filters.
10. DC Filters (DF) - It is connected between Pole bus and neutral bus.
11. Shunt Compensation (C) - It is provided by shunt capacitors which supply reactive power needed for converter operation.
12. Reactive power (Q) - It is absorbed by the converter and therefore, supplied to the AC bus. Thyristors in converter valves are triggered by firing pulses to gate current through DC valves. DC line is controlled by adjusting the delay angle (**α**).

3.13 TYPES OF HVDC POWER TRANSMISSION SYSTEM

3.13.1 Monopolar System

The HVDC Mono polar system is shown in fig 3.7. In this type there is one pole and earth is used as a return path. Earthing is done via earth-electrode and electrode-line. Earth-electrode placed 5 to 25 km away from HVDC terminal substation. Pole is +ve (positive) w.r.t earth

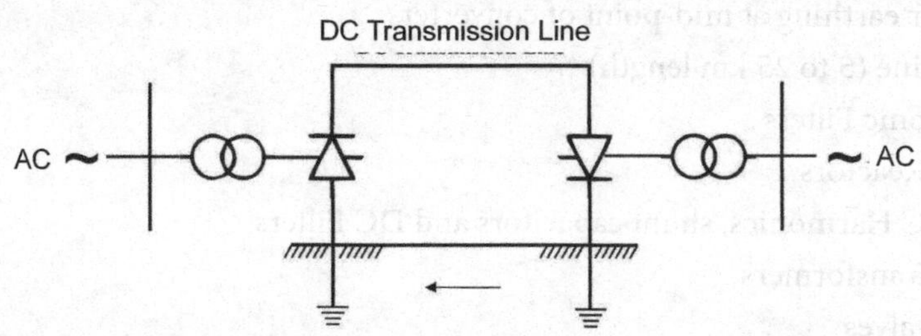

Fig. 3.7: Monopolar system

Features of monopolar HVDC system

(a) Power rating almost half

(b) Used for HVDC submarines cables

(c) Monopolar extended to Bipolar lines

3.13.2 Bipolar System

The HVDC Bipolar system is shown in fig 3.8. In this system there are two poles, one pole +ve(positive) w.r.t earth and other is -ve(negative).

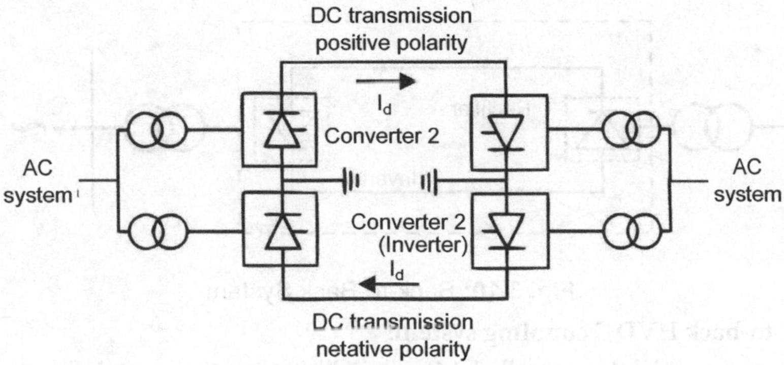

Fig. 3.8: Bipolar System

The Pole may be either a substation pole or transmission line pole. The mid-point of bipoles is earthed via earth-electrode and electrode-line. Earth-electrode is situated about 5 to 25 km away from the HVDC terminal substation.

Features of Bipolar HVDC system

(a) Normal mode - Bipolar

(b) Power transmission flow through transmission line conductor and negligible through earth i.e. current

(c) At fault - Bipolar converted to Monopolar, therefore power flow through one pole and earth return

3.13.3 Homopolar systems

The HVDC Homopolar system is shown in fig 3.9 In this system two (substation / transmission) poles are of same (negative) polarity and earth is used as the return path. This type of system is used earlier for overhead transmission lines and combination of cables.

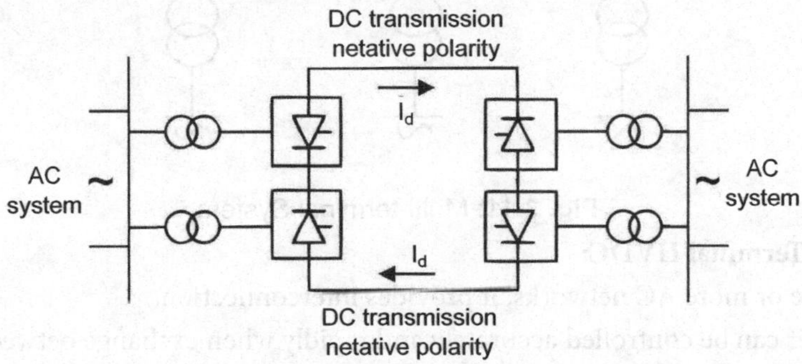

Fig. 3.9: Homopolar System

3.13.4 Back-to-Back HVDC coupling:

The HVDC Homopolar system is shown in fig 3.10 This system is normally, bipolar HVDC system without earth in return. This type is used for protection, controls and measurements reference earth. Both converters i.e. rectifiers and inverters are in the same HVDC terminal substations. There are no HVDC transmission lines in this system. Two AC systems are linked by a single HVDC back-to-back coupling station.

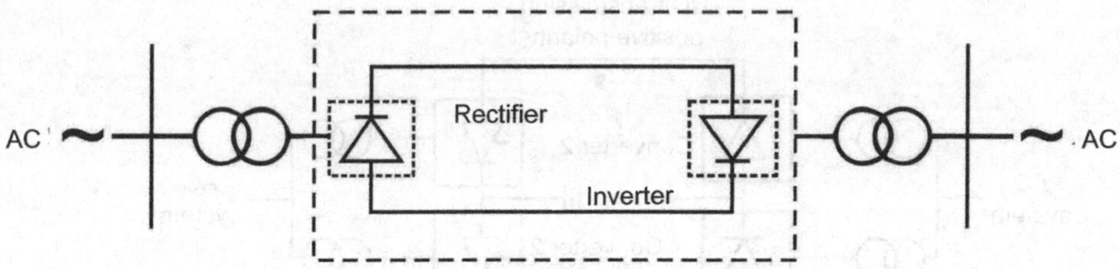

Fig. 3.10: Back-to-Back System

Features of Back-to-back HVDC coupling system:

(a) Between two independently controlled AC networks, it provides asynchronous ties.
(b) Improve system stability
(c) Transmission power transfer in either direction depending upon control characteristics.
(d) Transmission of power exchange can be rapidly changed
(e) Popular interconnection between adjacent AC network

3.13.5 Multi-Terminal HVDC:

The HVDC Homopolar system is shown in fig 3.11 This system normally has three or more HVDC terminal substations. It is a Bipolar HVDC terminal system in which some feed power in HVDC terminal buses and some receive power from HVDC buses.

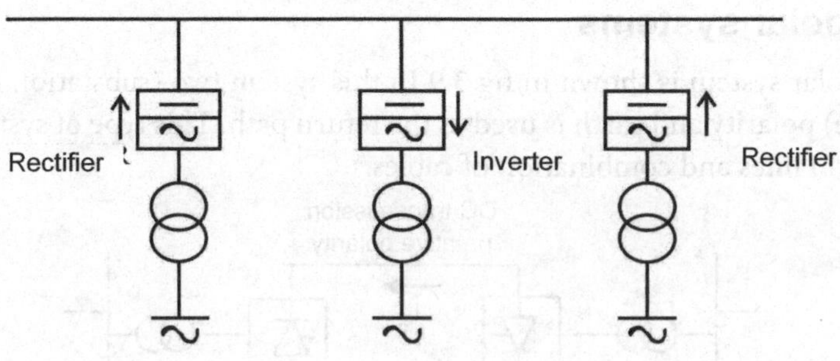

Fig. 3.11: Multi-terminal System

Features of Multi-Terminal HVDC:

(a) Between three or more AC networks, it provides interconnection.
(b) Power transfer can be controlled accurately and rapidly when exchange between AC networks.
(c) Power transmission system stability is improved.

3.14 APPLICATIONS OF HVDC POWER TRANSMISSION SYSTEM

The various applications of HVDC transmission are given below:

(a) High power transmission for long distances by overhead transmission lines.
(b) Submarine or underground cables for medium and long high-power transmission.
(c) Transmission system interconnections
(d) Multi-Terminal HVDC transmission for three or more than three phase A.C. transmission systems.
(e) Conversions of frequency is possible
(f) Incoming line in Megacities.

3.15 ADVANTAGES AND LIMITATIONS OF HVDC LINES

The various advantages of HVDC power transmission systems:

(a) Cheaper cost: Unlike EHV-transmission lines, HVDC systems require two-pole conductors, in EHV systems, three conductors and one ground conductor are used to transfer the power. All types of clearances (phase-to-phase), phase to grow are lesser dc systems. Tower design is simpler, and its size is smaller. The weight of conductors on the tower in the dc system is lesser. Hence, the need for right-of-way (ROW) is reduced compared to an AC line with equivalent power transfer capability. Additionally, when operating at the same voltage, the DC system demands less insulation. Hence insulation cost is lesser than that of ac systems. EHV transmission systems require intermediate substations containing capacitor banks and reactors etc for compensation purposes at an interval of 300 km. This increases the cost of the EHV system, but the HVDC system does not require any intermediate substations.

(b) No Skin effect: Skin effect relevant to an ac system reveals that current density is maximum on the peripheral surface of conductor. Current distribution is not uniform over the cross section of conductor. But in the dc system, current is uniformly distributed, thus there is complete utilization of conductors in the dc system.

(c) Voltage regulation: There are no inductances in the dc system conductor. So, there is no voltage drop in inductive reactances in dc systems. Therefore, voltage regulation in a dc system is better than a system.

(d) Line Loading: The allowable capacity utilization of an Extra High Voltage (EHV) AC line is constrained by the transient stability limit. In contrast, HVDC lines do not face such limitations.

(e) Surge impedance loading (SIL): EHV-AC power transmission line is loaded up to less than 80% of natural load which is equivalent to . No such cases exist in HVDC lines.

(f) Lesser dielectric loss: We know in HVDC lines, insulation required is considerably low. Therefore, less dielectric loss comes into picture. Due to less dielectric loss, current carrying capacity is higher.

(g) Negligible Sheath loss: In case of dc lines, only leakage current flows through the insulation but in ac systems, charging current and eddy current flow through the sheath of cables. Thus, sheath loss in the HVDC line is negligible.

(h) Corona loss: According to Peek's formula, it is directly proportional ($\propto$) to (f+25); where, f is the power transmission line frequency of an ac supply. In the case of the dc system, frequency is zero. Therefore, (f+25) will be lessened. So, it can be said that in an HVDC system, corona loss is lesser than in an EHV system for the same conductor diameter and operating voltage. Corona is accomplished with hissing sound and audible noise. An audible noise is the source of radio interference. Radio interference in the case of dc is less as compared to ac. Also, in the rainy season, foul weather radio interference decreases in the dc system whereas in ac system , it increases.

(i) Reactive power compensation: In a very long distance of an ac transmission line, it is very essential to use series and shunt compensation for its feasibility. The series compensation is provided for stability purposes or to neutralize the inductive reactance.

For stability, we know, $P = (V_S.V_R.\sin\delta / X_L)$ To absorb the line charging VARs (Q) shunt compensation is required. In the case of HVDC transmission lines, it does not require any reactive power compensation (Q). It is because HVDC operates with the absence of charging current and unit power factor.

(j) No stability limit: There is no limit in the dc system. In a system, the stability limit is linked with the expression $P = (V_S.V_R.\sin\delta / X_L)$. There is no term like reactance (X) in the dc system. So, the transmission line may be of any length. In an ac system, reactance X is proportional to length of line. In ac system, the length of the line is mostly 500 km. However, the length of the line can be increased by using series compensation.

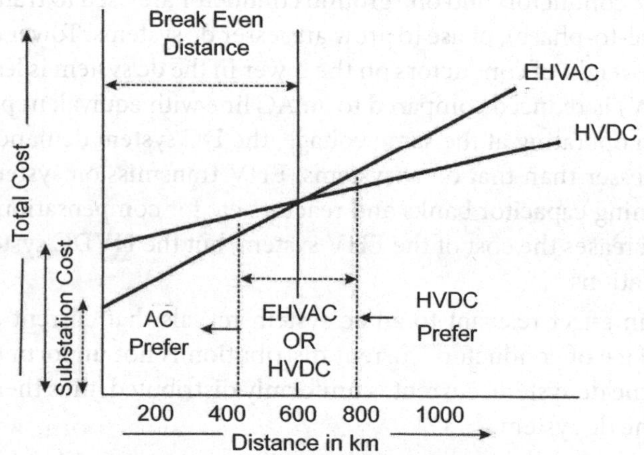

Fig. 3.12: Economical comparison of long-distance High power HVDC transmission and EHV AC transmission system

Limitations of HVDC power transmission systems:

The various limitations of HVDC transmission lines are:

(a) Generally, used for point-to-point transmission and does not have parallel lines, T-off's, mesh networks etc.

  (i) because of not having step-up or step-down power transformer

  (ii) because of not having suitable HVDC circuit breaker

(b) Can't be economically used for primary transmission, Sub-transmission and distribution transmission (used for only long-distance power transmission).

(c) Substation cost of HVDC terminal is more (due to additional equipment like converters, valves, earthing electrode etc.)

(d) Required continuous firing of thyristor valves, which makes the network complex.

(e) Required additional harmonic filters and shunt capacitors.

(f) Additional losses occur across converter transformers and valves (continuous losses) therefore necessary cooling is required to dissipate heat.

3.16 PREFERENCE CHART OF EHV-AC AND HV-DC OVERHEAD TRANSMISSION SYSTEMS

Table 3.4 provides a comparative reference chart for EHV-AC and HVDC overhead transmission systems, outlining their respective preferences across multiple parameters.

Table 3.4: Preference chart of EHV-AC and HVDC overhead transmission systems based on various parameters

Sr. No.	Characteristics	HVDC transmission link	EHVAC transmission Link	Preference
1	Transmission Power transfer Stability	High stability	Low stability (limited by power angle and Inductive reactance)	HVDC is preferred
2	Control of Power flow	Bi-directional Fast Accurate	Difficult Slow	HVDC is preferred
3	Transient performance	Excellent	Poor	HVDC is preferred
4	Transmission Frequency disturbance	Reduced	Transfer to other	HVDC is preferred
5	Transmission System support	Excellent power flow through line quickly modulated for damping oscillations	Poor oscillations continue	HVDC is preferred
6	Fault level	Remain unchanged after interconnection	Gets added after interconnection	HVDC is preferred
7	Transmission line Power swing	Quickly Damped	Long time continuation	HVDC is preferred
8	Submarine Cables	No charging current, high rating possible	Charging current set a limit on length and power	HVDC is preferred
9	Multi Terminal	Very expensive	Very economical	EHV AC is preferred
10	Reactive power flow through line	Not Possible	Occurs	HVDC is preferred
11	Cascade tripping (Black out)	Avoided	Likely	HVDC is preferred

Sr. No.	Characteristics	HVDC transmission link	EHVAC transmission Link	Preference
12	Back-to-back coupling	Possible	Not Possible	HVDC is preferred
13	Power Frequency conversion	Possible	Not Possible	HVDC is preferred
14	Spinning reserve	Reduced	Not much reduced	HVDC is preferred
15	Power Transient stability limit	Very high (upto thermal limits)	Less than half (of thermal limits)	HVDC is preferred

3.17 COMPARISON CHART OF EHV AC AND HVDC OVERHEAD TRANSMISSION SYSTEMS

Table 3.5 gives comparison of EHV AC and HVDC systems

Table 3.5: Comparison of EHV AC and HVDC systems

Sr. No.	Characteristics	EHVAC systems	HVDC Systems	Remarks
1	Capital Cost Number of circuits Substation cost Line cost Intermediate substations	 More Lower Higher Required	 One Higher Lower Not required	As per choice based on economics , the HVDC transmission systems become more economical at above 800 MW.
2	Voltage control	Due to shunt capacitance and series inductance, it is difficult for long power transmission lines.	Easier	----------
3	Power Transfer	Line inductive reactance and power angle limits are imposed	No limit	Single HVDC link adequate upto 3000 MW
4	Skin Effect	Present	Absent	----------
5	Corona Effect and Radio Interference	More	Less	----------
6	Line Losses	High	Low	HVDC substation has power losses

Sr. No.	Characteristics	EHVAC systems	HVDC Systems	Remarks
7	Earth Return	Not possible	Possible	Only single bipolar HVDC link adequate in most cases
8	Compensation Requirements	Series and shunt compensations are necessary	Not required any compensation	---------
9	Short Circuit currents	Large	Small	---------
10	Reliability	Lesser	More	---------
11	Stability of AC networks	Very low due to line inductive reactance	Much higher	D.C. line is loaded upto 90% of its thermal-rating While A.C. line is loaded upto 50% of its thermal-rating
12	Control system	Cheaper Simpler limitation of control	Costlier Difficult but accurate and fast control	For interconnections, HVDC system is advantageous due to superior control

3.18 FLEXIBLE AC TRANSMISSION SYSTEM (FACTS)

The IEEE definition for FACTS controller is stated as , "it is a power electronic based system and other static equipment that provides the control of one or more AC transmission parameters (such as voltage, impedance, phase angle and power)". Flexible AC Transmission System (FACTS) refers to an EHV AC System whereby controlling parameters of the transmission line certain limitations of static and dynamic capacity of transmission lines are overcome. In FACTS power electronic devices are used as static controllers to increase the power transfer capacity and for more effective control of transmission lines. The FACTS devices are used to provide reactive power to meet the reactive power requirements as quickly as possible. This helps in improving the efficiency, capacity and quality of the power transmission system. The power electronics devices act as fast switches and provide inductive and capacitive power to meet the particular requirements. The existing transmission lines networks can be better utilized to its maximum capacity by incorporating FACTS. This also both dynamic and transient network stability, improves reliability and availability of transmission line networks substantially. Hence performance of existing lines is significantly improved.

3.18.1 Features of Flexible AC Transmission Systems (FACTS)

(a) Using FACTS fast voltage regulation is achieved.

(b) The power transfer over long AC lines is increased.

(c) Effective dumping of power oscillations can be achieved.

(d) Load flow control is controlled in meshed systems using FACTS

3.18.2 Types of FACTS Controllers

The FACTs controllers can be classified according to the type of connection of the FACTS Controller in the power system. The various types of FACTS controllers are listed below;

(a) Series FACTS Controller
(b) Shunt FACTS Controller
(c) Combined Shunt-Series FACTS Controller
(d) Combined Series-Series FACTS Controller

3.19 WIRELESS TRANSMISSION OF ELECTRICAL POWER

The purpose of wireless transmission is to transmit electrical energy without using electrical wires, it is not the transmission of electrical signals containing information such as mobile signals or wifi transmission. With the advancements in technology it has become possible to transmit electrical energy without electrical wires over small distances. It is generally used where it is not possible or inconvenient to use wires for transmission or where it is hazardous or complicated to use wired transmission of electrical energy. Presently wireless transmission is possible for a small amount of power transfer for applications like charging of electronic equipment/ devices, health care sector, wearable devices and EV industry. Wireless transfer of energy can be done via electromagnetic induction or electromagnetic radiations.

Nikola Tesla presented the idea of transferring electric power without wires, around late 1890s by lighting an electric bulb wirelessly using electrodynamic induction. The developments in the field of high frequency power electronics devices made it possible to transfer power via high power inductive coupling. The use of wireless technology will reduce the use of metal wires which is presently a conventional method of power transfer. The most common technique used to transmit power without wires is via inductive coupling.

3.19.1 Wireless Energy Transfer Methods

The energy transfer methods are categorized based on the distance at which the energy is to be transmitted. It can be broadly classified into two categories:

(a) Short distance transfer or non-radiative method
(b) Long distance transfer or radiative method

3.19.1.1 Short Distance Transfer or Non-radiative Method

In the case of short distance or non-radiative methods, energy transfer takes place by inductive coupling between magnetic fields of two or more coils. Also, electric fields using capacitive coupling between metal electrodes can be used for energy transfer. This method finds application in wireless phone charging, or other small electronic devices such as RFID tags, medical equipment, electric toothbrushes, and EVs. In it two coils coupled magnetical are required to transfer power. Wireless transfer of electric energy in a transformer without electrical connection between primary and secondary winding is a perfect example of inductive coupling between two coils. The efficiency of power transfer depends upon the iron core and the distance between the cores. This method is already in use for wireless charges.

The maximum range for wireless transfer with this method is up to a few meters and power in a few watts. This method of power transfer is safe for human beings as the human body is non-magnetic and not affected by magnetic fields. Also, almost no interference with wifi, TV or radio signals. But only AC power can be transferred via this method.

3.19.1.2 Long Distance Transfer or Radiative Method

This method is used to transfer energy over long distances in the form of beams. Beams can be in the laser beams or microwaves.

(a) Power transfer through Laser beams: The electric power can be transferred over long distances by converting electricity in a laser beam. The Photovoltaic cells are then used to convert this laser beam back to electric power. The laser beam falls at a photovoltaic cell and is converted into electric power, this method is known as 'power beaming' technology. The special photovoltaic cells are used for conversion which are optimized for monochromatic light conversion. This type of power transfer method finds application in aerospace applications.

(b) Power transfer through Microwaves: In this method of transfer of electric power over long distances; Electromagnetic waves are used. Electromagnetic waves of different bands are used in different methods of power transfer. Initially experiments were conducted with microwaves and radio waves. Large size antennas required to transmit bulk power. Wavelength of the antenna must be longer to achieve sufficient directionality. Shorter wavelengths are generally used to transfer energy to smaller objects. The electromagnetic wave uses the waveband of radio, TV, cell phone and Wi-Fi, with a signal intensity of several orders of magnitude.

3.19.2 Applications of Wireless Power Transmission

The various applications of wireless power transmission are:

(a) Wireless charging
(b) Wireless charging of electric vehicles
(c) Wireless power powering of home appliances etc.

UNIT SUMMARY

This unit highlights the need of EHV AC transmission and HVDC transmission for transfer of bulk power over long distances. The various components, advantages and disadvantages of both types of system are discussed in detail. The Ferranti and skin effects appearing in EHV AC systems are discussed and methods of reducing them are also given in this unit. The layout and features of various types of HVDC lines are also given for the readers. The fundamental principles of Flexible AC Transmission Systems (FACTS), encompassing their characteristics, diverse types of FACTS controllers, and emerging trends in wireless transmission, are comprehensively explored and elucidated.

UNIT Highlights

1. Reduced transmission line conductor material, high transmission line efficiency, future system growth flexibility, reduced power transmission line losses, increase in surge impedance loading, transmission capacity of line increases and reduction in right of way are the advantages of electric power transmission for adopting EHV/ UHV transmission lines.
2. The corona effect is summarized as below:

(i) It produces ozone gas, which is easily detectable due to its distinct smell.
(ii) It emits a hissing sound.
(iii) Around the conductor, a violet colour glow is observed.
(iv) There is maximum glow over dirty and rough joints.
(v) It induces harmonic current, therefore charging current increases
(vi) It is accomplished by radio interference and power loss.

3. Factor affecting Corona are:
   (i) Spacing between conductors
   (ii) Conductor size
   (iii) Atmosphere
   (iv) Line voltage
4. During light loading or open-circuit conditions in a medium or long power transmission line, the voltage at the receiving end surpasses the voltage at the sending end. This phenomena of increase in voltage at the receiving end of the lightly loaded or open-circuited is called Ferranti Effect.
5. With increase in voltage level, there is increase in surge impedance loading. Surge impedance loading varies as the square of operating voltage i.e. $(3.V^2 / Z_C)$.
6. Series compensation artificially decreases the series reactance of the power transmission line which results in enhancement of transmission efficiency, system stability and voltage regulation.
7. When two or more sub conductors forming a power transmission line are called bundled conductors and categorised as one-phase conductors. The self GMD of power transmission line $L = 2 \times 10^{-7} [\log_e (Dm / DSA)]$ H/m
   Therefore, with bundling of line conductors, the self GMD is increased, thus increase in critical disruptive voltage(V_{CD}) and thus reduction in corona loss.
8. Series compensation have some difficulties as summarized below:
   (i) It introduces a sub-synchronous frequency which is proportional($\propto$) to the square root of the line compensation in the transmission system. Therefore, this sub synchronous frequency may interrelate with turbo-generator shafts and cause high torsional stress.
   (ii) It may lead to unnecessary tripping due to maloperation of the protection system.
   (iii) Large recovery voltage may occur across the circuit breaker contacts
   (iv) It produces ferro resonance when there is switching in of an unloaded transformer. Due to these problems, shunt compensation in the transmission line is preferred over series compensation
9. To artificially minimize the series reactance of a power transmission line, series compensation is provided in an extra high voltage line which results in improvement of transmission efficiency, stability and voltage regulation.
10. For a 400 kV power transmission line, 350m to 400m is the economical value of span.
11. In the case of a dc system, due to the absence of inductance (L), voltage regulation is better. Also, due to absence of charging station, there is no limit on the length of cable
12. Optronics employing a light guide system is the method of modern triggering of thyristor.
13. Synchronous condensers, static shunt capacitors, Active filters, Static VAr compensators etc. are the equipment used for supplying reactive power in HVDC transmission systems.

14. In a HVDC transmission system, the current levels and voltage levels are too high that a single SCR (thyristor) can't meet the requirements. Therefore, it is required to connect more than one SCR in parallel to meet the higher current needs and in series to achieve higher voltages.

EXERCISES

1. The cost of transmission decreases with the increase in power transmission line voltage. Justify mathematically.
2. Explain the term "Surge impedance loading".
3. State "Right-of-way" (ROW).
4. In the EHV transmission line, how Galloping is controlled.
5. Define Ferranti Effect.
6. Explain the usefulness of FACTS devices in a transmission system along with its operating principle.
7. What are the advantages of using bundled conductors in an extra high voltage transmission system?
8. Compare long distance overhead EHV AC and HVDC transmission systems.
9. Explain the different types of HVDC links.
10. Mention how problems in EHV ac transmission systems are overcome in HVDC transmission systems.
11. Explain the necessity of the EHV AC transmission system.
12. Explain the requirement of series compensation in an EHV AC transmission system.

Multiple Choice Questions

1. The power transmission line voltage are .... to the line losses.
   (a) directly proportional
   (b) inversely proportional
   (c) both (directly and inversely proportional)
   (d) independent
2. With the decrease in power transmission line voltage, the cost of power transmission ....
   (a) remain same (b) decreases
   (c) increases (d) increase or decrease
3. The surge impedance loading (Zo) is given by
   (a) $Zo = 2 . \pi . \sqrt{L/C}$ (b) $Zo = 1 / (2 . \pi . \sqrt{L/C})$
   (c) $Zo = 2 . \pi \ / \ \sqrt{L/C}$ (d) $Zo = \sqrt{L/C}$
4. Surge impedance(Zo) of a power transmission line is almost equal to ....
   (a) 1 ohm (b) 200 ohms
   (c) 400 ohms (d) 1000 ohms
5. As per the power transmission systems having less number of transmission line conductors, Right of way (ROW) is .... in case of a large number of power transmission line.
   (a) reduced (b) same
   (c) more (d) independent

6. Transmission line power transferred by a synchronous generator is given by $P = [(P_S \cdot P_R \cdot \sin \delta) / X]$ Here δ is known as ....
   (a) load / torque angle
   (b) phase angle
   (c) power transmission line coefficient
   (d) reflection coefficient
7. The receiving end voltage rises in case of long power transmission line due to Ferranti effect and this can be controlled by using .... at the load end.
   (a) series reactor (b) shunt reactor
   (c) series capacitor (d) shunt capacitor
8. In an ac system, due to .... effect, the conductor surface has maximum current density on the outer peripheral.
   (a) Hall (b) Proximity
   (c) Ferranti (d) Skin
9. System stability of power transmission line is not affected by
   (a) Reactance(X) of a line (b) Transmission line losses
   (c) Generator reactance (d) Generator excitation
10. Power flows in a HVDC link from
    (a) the terminal connected to the inverter.
    (b) the inverter end to the rectifier end.
    (c) the terminal connected to the rectifier.
    (d) the rectifier end to the inverter end

ANSWERS															
1.	(b)	2.	(c)	3.	(d)	4.	(c)	5.	(a)	6.	(a)	7.	(b)	8.	(d)
9.	(b)	10.	(a)												

Fill in the Blanks

1. Resonant vibrations have frequency lies between the range of ____________.
2. For EHV overhead power transmission lines, the insulation level of 400 kV is on the basis of ________________.
3. ____________ and ___________ is used to improve by shunt compensation for an EHV power transmission line.
4. In distribution lines, series capacitors are used to provide ______________.
5. For HVDC converters, the capital cost is _______ than ac substation.
6. Corona inception voltage ____________ with bundled conductors.
7. The voltage ranges between 400 kV to 765 kV means ____________ transmission.
8. ____________ converters are required for HVDC transmission.
9. HVDC required filters for ____________ on a.c. transmission side and ____________ on d.c. transmission side.
10. There is neither skin effect nor charging current in case of ________ transmission system.

ANSWERS							
1.	50 - 100 Hz	2.	switching over-voltage	3.	voltage profile, stability	4.	reactive power compensation
5.	more	6.	increases	7.	Extra high voltage	8.	Pulse
9.	voltage harmonics, current harmonics	10.	HVDC				

True or False

1. To reduce voltage, a Back-to-back HVDC system is used.
2. A DC power transmission line is capable of carrying a greater power load compared to an AC power transmission line.
3. To reduce line losses in distribution lines, series capacitors are used.
4. On the basis of RI interference and corona, the conductor of the EHV transmission line is selected.
5. When the load is below the surge impedance loading, the voltage at the receiving end exceeds the voltage at the sending end.
6. For both a.c. as well as d.c. transmission lines, Skin effect exists.
7. In a transmission line, corona loss is depending upon the height of the conductor.
8. Owing to the corona effect, presence of ozone gas corrodes the conductor material.
9. To improve the power system stability and compensation for inductance reactance, shunt capacitors are used.
10. In the HVDC transmission line, corona loss is lesser than the EHV transmission line.

ANSWERS									
1.	**False**	2.	**True**	3.	**False**	4.	**True**	5.	**True**
6.	**False**	7.	**False**	8.	**True**	9.	**False**	10.	**True**

Short and Long Answer Type Questions

1. Define Ferranti effect.

Ans. When a medium or long power transmission line is lightly loaded or open-circuited, the voltage at the receiving end becomes greater than the voltage at the sending end. This phenomena of increase in voltage at the receiving end of the lightly loaded or open-circuited is called Ferranti Effect.

2. For adopting extra high voltage(EHV) / ultra-high voltage(UHV) transmission systems, mention the basic advantages for transmission of electric power at EHV?

Ans. Reduced transmission line conductor material, high transmission line efficiency, future system growth flexibility, reduced power transmission line losses, increase in surge impedance loading, transmission capacity of line increases and reduction in right of way are the advantages of electric power transmission for adopting EHV/ UHV transmission lines.

3. Mention the difficulties arises with an EHV(extra high voltage) power transmission line.

Ans. The difficulties arising with EHV(extra high voltage) power transmission lines are heavy supporting structures requirement, corona loss, insulation requirements, radio interference and erection problems.

4. What will be the effect on Surge impedance loading when there is an increase in voltage level?

Ans. With increase in voltage level, there is increase in surge impedance loading. Surge impedance loading varies as the square of operating voltage i.e. $(3.V^2 / Z_C)$.

5. How bundled conductors in EHV transmission lines reduce corona loss?

Ans. When two or more sub conductors forming a power transmission line are called bundled conductors and categorised as one-phase conductors. The self GMD of power transmission line

$L = 2 \times 10^{-7} [\log_e (Dm / DSA)]$ H/m

Therefore, with bundling of line conductors, the self GMD is increased, thus increase in critical disruptive voltage(V_{CD}) and thus reduction in corona loss.

6. For overhead power transmission lines conductors, which material is universally employed?

Ans. Aluminium core steel reinforced conductors (ACSR)are universally employed.

7. What do you mean by transmission line compensation?

Ans. Reactive power compensation or neutralization of power transmission lines is called transmission line compensation.

8. Define series and shunt compensation.

Ans. When a compensating device is attached in series with the power transmission line it is known as series compensation and when a compensating device is attached across the power transmission line, it is known as shunt compensation.

9. Justify that shunt compensation in the transmission line is preferred over series compensation?

Ans. Series compensation have some difficulties as summarized below:

(i) It introduces a sub-synchronous frequency which is proportional ($\propto$) to the square root of the line compensation in the transmission system. Therefore, this sub synchronous frequency may interrelate with turbo-generator shafts and cause high torsional stress.

(ii) It may lead to unnecessary tripping due to maloperation of the protection system.

(iii) Large recovery voltage may occur across the circuit breaker contacts

(iv) It produces ferro resonance when there is switching in of an unloaded transformer.

Due to these problems, shunt compensation in the transmission line is preferred over series compensation

10. Mention the advantages of Series compensation in power transmission lines.

Ans. Series compensation artificially decreases the series reactance of the power transmission line which results in enhancement of transmission efficiency, system stability and voltage regulation.

11. Why is (Q)reactive power compensation not required in HVDC transmission systems?

Ans. Due to unity (cos power factor and absence of charging current operation.

12. For high voltage transmission of electric power, d.c. is preferred. Why?

Ans. Due to the effect of surge impedance loading(SIL) there is a limit to the distance of a.c. transmission lines which cause high voltage at the receiving end. Thus as an alternative, d.c. is used for high voltage for an electric power transmission.

13. Mention the equipment in HVDC converter stations which supply reactive power.

Ans. Static shunt capacitors, a.c. filters, static VAR compensators, synchronous condensers, etc.

14. Can corona loss in HVDC power transmission lines be ignored?

Ans. No

15. Why does iron and graphite not be used as material for earth electrodes?

Ans. When earth electrodes are buried in earth it causes a large amount of loss of material because of the high rate of corrosion in case of iron and graphite.

PRACTICAL

Prepare a PowerPoint presentation on any of the following:

(i) Transmission of electricity using Extra High Voltage AC Transmission lines.

(ii) Transmitting electricity through High Voltage DC Transmission lines.

(iii) Implementing Flexible AC Transmission lines for enhanced control and efficiency.

(iv) Exploring novel advancements in wireless transmission methods for electrical power.

KNOW MORE

Students are advised to visit following websites to understand the transmission and distribution system in India and the latest developments going on more deeply:

- Ministry of power, Govt of India - https://powermin.gov.in/
- Central Electricity Authority, Govt of India - https://cea.nic.in/?lang=en
- Ministry of new and renewable energy -https://mnre.gov.in/
- Any state electrical transmission utility.

REFERENCES AND SUGGESTED READINGS

- https://nptel.ac.in/courses/108102047
- https://nptel.ac.in/courses/108107112
- https://nptel.ac.in/courses/108105104

REFERENCES

1. P. Eekshita, N. S. V. Narayana and R. Jayaraman, "Wireless Power Transmission System," 2021 International Conference on Computer Communication and Informatics (ICCCI), 2021, pp. 1-4, doi: 10.1109/ICCCI50826.2021.9402575.
2. Mohammad Etemadrezaei, "Wireless power transfer", Power Electronics Handbook (Fourth Edition), 2018, Pages 711-722.
3. Sumi FH, Dutta L, Sarker F (2018) Future with Wireless Power Transfer Technology. J Electr Electron Syst 7: 279. doi: 10.4172/2332-0796.1000279.

4. https://www.allaboutcircuits.com/technical-articles "Introduction to Wireless Power Transfer".
5. Vishvendra Singh, Akhand Pratap Singh, Sachin Kumar, "Introduction to Wireless Power Transmission" HCTL Open Int. J. of Technology Innovations and Research HCTL Open IJTIR, Volume 8, March 2014 e-ISSN: 2321-1814 ISBN (Print): 978-1-62951-499-4.
6. Farhana Haque Sumi1, Lokesh Dutta, Dr. Farhana Sarker, "Future with Wireless Power Transfer Technology", J Electr Electron Syst, an open access journal Volume 7 • Issue 4 • 1000279 ISSN: 2332-0796.
7. Report On Operation and Maintenance Of HVDC Stations, Praveen Ranjan, PGCIL, 2011.

❑❑

4 AC Distribution System

UNIT SPECIFICS

Through this unit we will discuss the following aspects:

- The components and working of an AC electric power distribution system.
- The various necessary requirements of a perfect distribution system.
- The classification of the AC distribution system into primary and secondary distribution?
- What are feeder and distributor and their design considerations
- Different types of distribution schemes and their advantages and disadvantages.
- Classification, components, and selection of sites for distribution substations.
- Single line diagrams, symbols, and their functions.

The theory topics related to the AC distribution system are explained to invoke critical and innovative thinking among the readers.

This unit highlights the AC distribution system for the delivery of electric power to end consumers. Unit summary and main highlights are given at the end of the unit for quick revision of the unit contents. The exercise questions are designed following revised bloom's taxonomy keeping in view fast and slow learners. For self-practice of the student's Multiple-choice questions, true-false options, and fill-in-the-blanks are also given at the end of the unit. Links for further reading on the topics are also provided under the section know more.

Solved numerical problems, formula summaries, and unsolved numerical questions are provided for the users of this book for reference and practice. The practical associated with the unit have been painstakingly constructed to give a comprehensive comprehension of the concepts presented in unit IV. Finally, a fundamental grasp of the AC distribution system is formed, connecting the topic to applications in daily life or/and industry.

RATIONALE

Understanding the ac distribution system is very important for power engineers as most of the time they need to deal with the distribution part of the power system. Critical questions such as "Why is the AC system adopted for distribution and what are its advantages and limitations?" are needed to be answered by a power system engineer. After understanding the need, the various components of the distribution system, their functions, and design considerations are discussed in detail. The different distribution schemes such as radial, ring, and grid are discussed along with the advantages and disadvantages of each scheme with a focus on the cost and maintenance of regular uninterrupted power supply to end users. How to select a site for distribution substations; components of distribution substations?

Comprehensive information on the AC Distribution System utilized for the distribution of electric power, feeders, and distributors as well as an in-depth discussion of distribution substations along with their components are the main highlights of this unit . Single line diagrams of 33 kV / 11 kV substation, 11 kV / 415V substation - various symbols and their functions are given in this unit will help the readers to understand the topic more clearly. . Exact explanations that are backed up by examples; pictures that help students see the Ac distribution system's parts.

PRE-REQUISITES

Basic subject of power systems. No prerequisite is required.

UNIT OUTCOMES

The students will be able to:

U4-O1: Classify the AC distribution system and its components.

U4-O2: Choose an AC distribution scheme as per the requirement of the end consumers.

U4-O3: Understand the layout/ single line diagrams of distribution substations

U4-O4: Select the site and components for the distribution substation.

Unit-4 Outcome	EXPECTED MAPPING WITH COURSE OUTCOMES (1 - Weak Correlation; 2 - Medium Correlation; 3 - Strong Correlation)				
	CO-1	CO-2	CO-3	CO-4	CO-5
U4-O1	3	3	3	1	1
U4-O2	1	1	1	1	1
U4-O3	1	1	1	3	1
U4-O4	-	-	-	3	2

4.1 INTRODUCTION

Previously, electricity was produced, transmitted, and used in the form of direct current (DC) supply. The major disadvantage of DC was that it can't be stepped up or stepped down easily. Whereas it is convenient to generate AC voltage at higher voltage levels as compared to DC voltage and it's easy to change the voltage level (step-up or step-down) in AC systems with the help of transformers. This is the major reason that the AC system was generally adopted by the world for transmission and use of electric power. Presently, a major part of the electric supply system works on AC systems. The large network of power supply systems uses AC for generation, transmission, distribution and utilization of electrical energy. The bulk electrical energy is transmitted via 3-phase 3-wire high-power overhead transmission lines. This power is received at receiving substations for distribution to end consumers.

An AC distribution system is a part of the electric supply system that distributes electricity to end consumers for utilization. The section of the electrical supply system between the distribution substation and the consumers' terminals is generally referred to as the distribution system. The AC distribution system is mainly divided into two parts i.e., primary distribution and secondary distribution, based on the operating voltage levels. A typical ac electric distribution system consists of feeders, distributors, and service mains. It can be an overhead system or an underground system. Further, it can be classified according to the scheme of connection such as radial, ring or grid system. The advantages, disadvantages and limitations of these connection schemes are also discussed in detail in this unit. The feeder and distributor are designed considering the voltage drop and variations in receiving end/consumer end voltage. The voltage at the consumer terminals must be kept within the limits as specified by the Indian standards. At distribution stations, the voltage levels are stepped down to 415 V. A 3-phase, 4-wire system is used to distribute power to final consumers at 415/230 V. We'll concentrate on the various facets of AC distribution in this chapter.

4.2 DISTRIBUTION SYSTEM

The arrangement of supplying electric power from a distribution substation to the various consumers as per their requirements is called an electric supply distribution system. The feeder, distributor, and service mains together forms a distribution system. Figure (4.1) shows the single line diagram of a typical Low Tension (LT) distribution line.

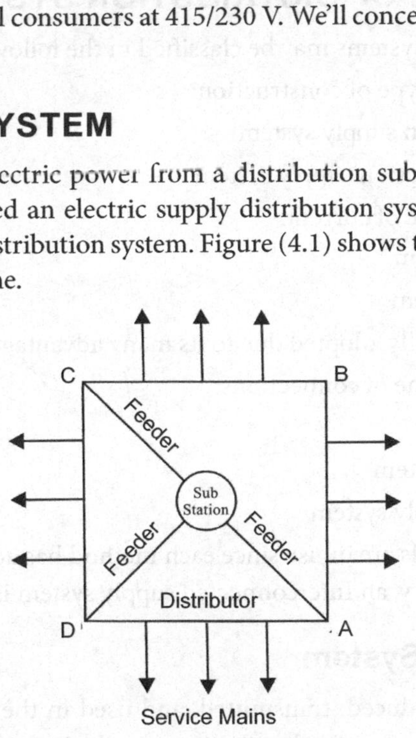

Fig. 4.1: (Distribution System)

Various components of a distribution system are described as:

(a) Feeder: A feeder is that section of the distribution system which is used to establish a connection between the substation station and the intended distribution area. Large currents are carried to the feeding points by conductors of very high ratings along with the towers. Figure (4.1) - "S" shows substation and SA, SC and SD are the feeders. The feeder's current remains constant as no tapping are taken from it. The feeder's current carrying capacity is the primary factor to be taken into account while designing the feeder.

(b) Distributor: A line or conductor which is used to connect various consumers through service main is known as distributor. The function of this section of the distribution system is to distribute electric power to end consumers. Figure (4.1) sections AB, BC, CD and DA are shown as the distributors. Current flowing through a distributor is not constant throughout its length because there are several tappings taken from it. Voltage drop along a distributor's length is the primary factor to be taken into account while designing the distributor. As the voltage drop in the distributor depends upon the loading done on it by the consumers, the limit for variation of the voltage at any point is ± 5% of the rated voltage at the user's terminal.

(c) **Service mains:** A small cable known as a service main links the consumer's terminal to the distributor. The cable is supported by an earth wire from the nearest pole to the consumer's energy meter.

4.3 CLASSIFICATION OF DISTRIBUTION SYSTEM

The electric supply distribution systems may be classified in the following ways:

A. Depending on the nature/type of construction:
   (a) Overhead distribution supply system
   (b) Underground distribution supply system

B. Depending upon the nature of current:
   (a) AC distribution system
   (b) DC distribution system

   AC distribution is universally adopted due to its many advantages over DC distribution systems.

C. Depending upon the scheme of connections:
   (a) Radial supply system
   (a) Ring main supply system
   (c) Inter-connected supply system

Nevertheless, all the methods are in use since each method has advantages and disadvantages of its own. But for service dependability, an Interconnected supply system is preferred.

4.3.1 AC Distribution System

Nowadays, electric power is produced, transmitted, and used in the form of alternating current. The primary reason for using an AC system for distribution over the DC system is because alternating voltage can be easily altered in magnitude using a transformer. In accordance with our needs, the AC voltage level can be increased or decreased.

The AC distribution system is classified into:

(a) HT or Primary distribution system
(b) LT or secondary distribution system

HT or Primary distribution: The bulk consumers or big consumers are supplied at HT voltage. A step-down transformer is installed at their premises to step down the voltage as per their requirements. Generally, a 3-phase, 3-wire system is used for primary distribution. A typical primary distribution system is shown in figure (4.2).

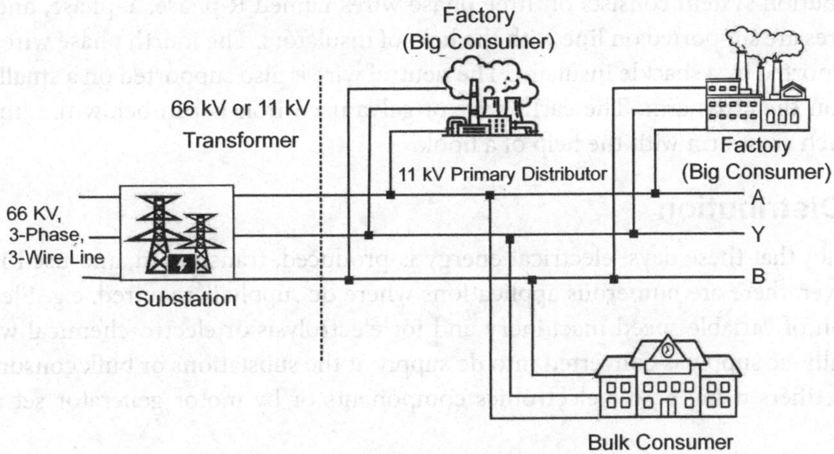

Fig. 4.2: (Primary Distribution)

Electrical power from generating stations is received by the receiving substation at a high voltage, nearly 66 kV or 33 kV, and is reduced to 11 kV. The 11 kV primary distribution line connects the distribution substation to the different localities of the city. The bulk consumers and low-voltage distribution transformers located in residential localities are supplied by the primary distributor or primary distribution line.

LT or Secondary Distribution: The small and domestic consumers are supplied at low voltages (normally 415/230V) and the supply system by which they are supplied electricity is known as a secondary distribution system. It is carried out by a 3-phase, 4-wire system where the line voltage is 415V and the phase voltage is 230 V.

Figure (4.3) demonstrates a secondary power distribution network. The primary power distribution lines deliver power to a distribution substation or distribution transformer where the voltage is stepped down from 11 kV to 415 volts. The LT distribution lines (3-phase, 4-wire) are run along the roads and streets. Domestic loads and other single-phase loads are connected between any one phase and the neutral. The motive or three-phase loads are supplied by three phases and a neutral wire. The 3-phase, 4-wire connections are given to the commercial and big domestic consumers.

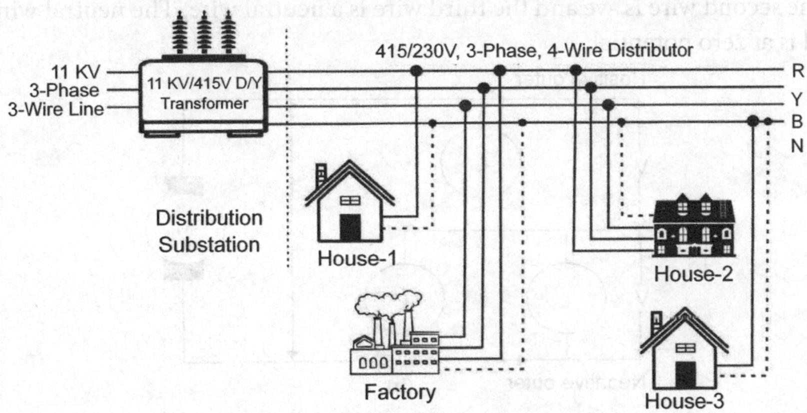

Fig. 4.3: (Secondary Distribution)

This distribution system consists of three phase wires named R-phase, Y-phase, and B-phase. All three phases wires are supported on line with the help of insulators. The fourth phase wire, named street light, is also supported by a shackle insulator. The neutral wire is also supported on a small size insulator which is fixed on the cross arm. The earth wire of galvanized iron is run below the line conductors, supported on each cross arm with the help of a hook.

4.3.2 DC Distribution

There is no doubt that these days, electrical energy is produced, transmitted, and used in the form of ac supply however, there are numerous applications where dc supply is required. e.g. Electric traction, for the operation of variable speed machinery and for electrolysis or electro-chemical works. For this purpose, generally, ac supply is converted into dc supply at the substations or bulk consumers premises by means of rectifiers using power electronics components or by motor generator set and then it is distributed by:

(a) Two-wire system

(b) Three-wire system

DC Two wire System: In this system, dc power is distributed using two conductors. One conductor is positive (outgoing) and the second is negative (return) conductor. The motor load or lamp load is connected between +ve and -ve line as shown in figure (4.4).

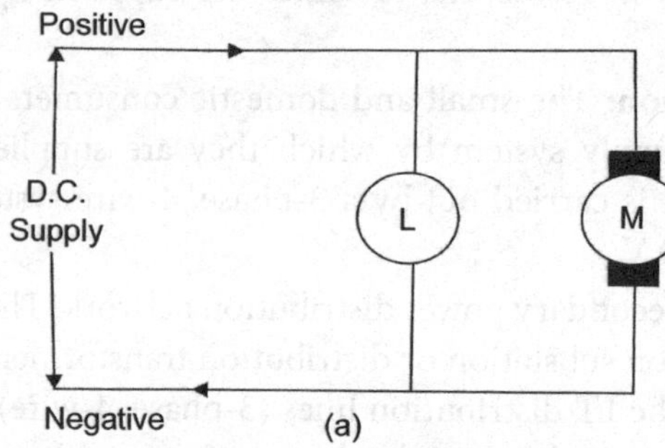

Fig. 4.4: DC Two wire system

DC Three wire System: In this distribution system, three wires are used to distribute electric power. One wire is +ve, the second wire is -ve and the third wire is a neutral wire. The neutral wire is earthed at the substation and is at zero potential.

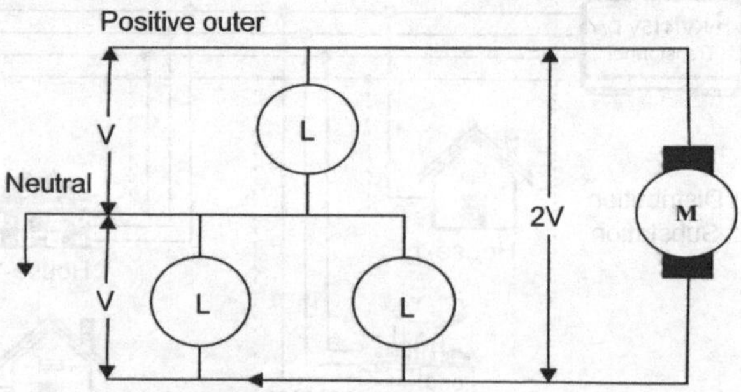

Fig. 4.5: DC Three wire system

The voltage between any one outer and neutral is V as shown in figure (4.5) and the voltage between +ve and -ve is 2V. Thus, two voltages i.e. low voltages (between +ve and neutral or -ve and neutral) and high voltage (between both the outers) are available to consumers. The lamp loads are connected across low voltage sides and the motor loads are connected across high voltage sides. Since the current flowing in the neutral is due to an unbalanced load and is generally very small, therefore the neutral wire of size half of the outer conductors is used in this type of supply system.

4.4 VARIOUS TYPES OF CONNECTION SCHEMES

In all distribution systems, the major requirement is to maintain constant voltage at the consumer terminals. The various connection schemes used for distribution of electrical energy are given below:

(a) Radial: In radial systems, several feeders start from a single substation, and they are connected to the distributors at the other end. Figure 4.6 shows a single line diagram of a radial distribution system.

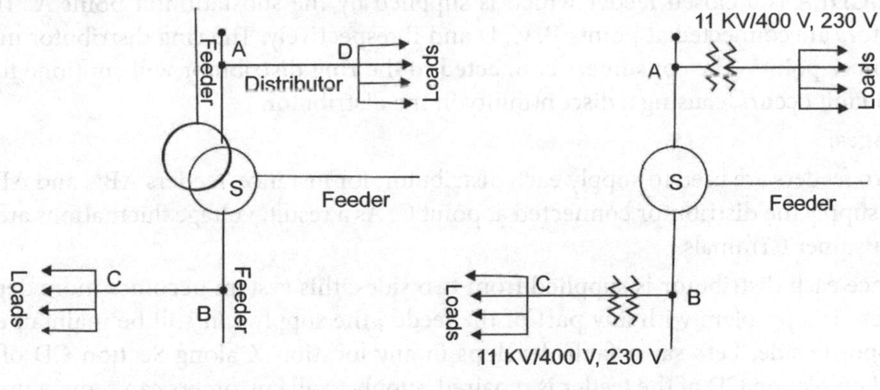

Fig. 4.6: Single line diagram of a radial distribution system

In this figure (4.6), SA and SB are the feeders, radiating from substations S and they are feeding the distributors AD and BC at their ends D and C respectively. This system is used when the substation is located at the centre of the load and power distributed is very small and

Advantages:

(i) It has a low installation cost.

(ii) This type of distribution system is simple and easily manageable.

Disadvantages:

(i) The distributor end that is closest to the feeding point will be heavily loaded.

(ii) Since consumers are dependent upon a single feeder, in case of fault there will be supply disruptions.

(iii) When the load on the distributor fluctuates, the customers at the other end would experience significant voltage swings.

This technique is only utilised over short distances because of the many disadvantages.

(b) Ring Main: In a ring main system, the distributor is supplied by two feeders. The feeder in this system creates a complete ring by closing in on itself, giving rise to the name "ring main system." Figure (4.7.a) shows a ring main system for dc distribution and figure (4.7.b) shows a ring main system with ac distribution.

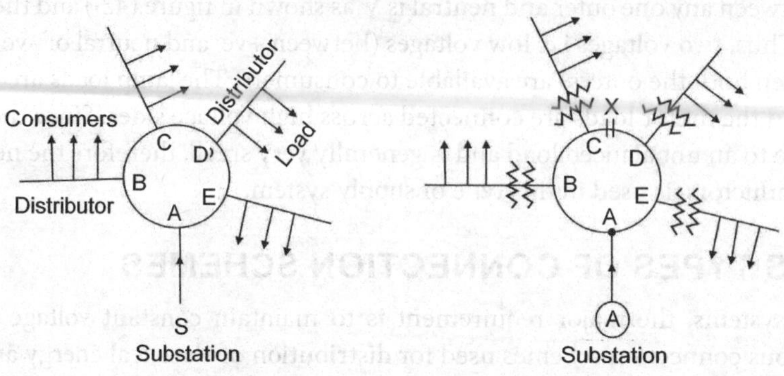

(a) - DC Distribution (b) - AC Distribution

Fig. 4.7: Ring main system

Here ABCDEA is a closed feeder which is supplied by the substation at point A. The different distributors are connected at points B, C, D and E respectively. The ring distributor may be fed at one or more points. The consumers connected to the ring distributor will continue to get supply even if a fault occurs, causing a discontinuity in the distributor.

Advantages:

(i) Two feeders are used to supply each distributor; for instance, feeders ABC and ADC are used to supply the distributor connected at point C. As a result, voltage fluctuations are reduced at consumer terminals.

(ii) Since each distributor is supplied from two sides, this system becomes more dependable. If there is a problem with any part of the feeder, the supply can still be maintained from the opposite side. Let's say a fault develops in any location X along Section CD of the feeder. When section CD of the feeder is repaired, supply to all customers can remain uninterrupted while section CD is isolated for maintenance.

(c) **Inter connected**: In an interconnected system, the feeder ring is powered by two or more than two generating stations or substation single-line diagrams of a dc and an ac interconnected system are shown in Figures (4.8.a) and (4.8.b), respectively. Two substations, S1 and S2, located at the points Q and P, respectively, supply the interconnected feeder.

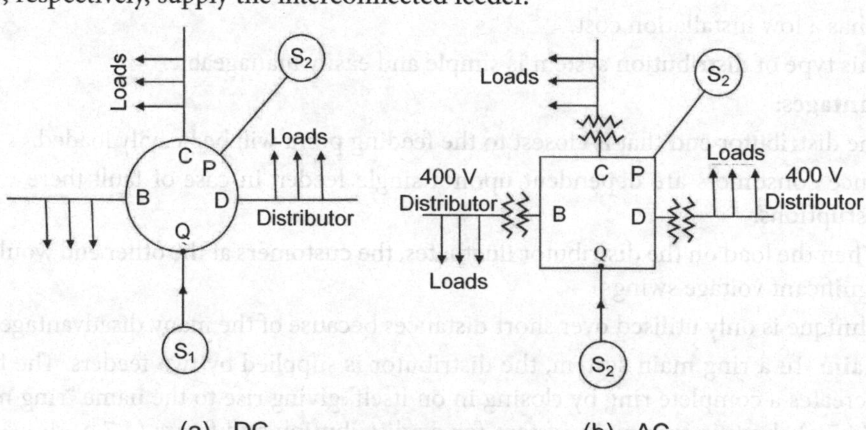

(a) - DC (b) - AC

Fig. 4.8: Single line diagram of Interconnected system

Distributors are shown connected at points B, C, and D.

Advantages:

(i) The continuity of supply can be maintained even in case any fault occurs on any section of the feeder; the supply to healthy sections can be maintained by isolating the faulty section.

(ii) During peak hours the heavily loaded area can be fed from the other generating stations. Thus, it reduces the reserved power capacity and increases the load factor and efficiency of the power system.

4.5 VARIOUS REQUIREMENTS OF THE DISTRIBUTION SYSTEM

Electric power is used by various consumers, some are bulk consumers, and some are small consumers. Every effort should be made to supply electrical power to the consumers within their requirements. A reliable distribution supply system must also have the proper voltage at the consumer terminals, be reliable, and be able to supply electricity on demand.

(a) Voltage profile: Maintaining continuous supply, and constant voltage at the consumer terminals is the most essential requirement for any distribution system. i.e., the fluctuation of voltage should be as minimum as possible. As per Indian Electricity rules the permissible limit of voltage fluctuation is $\pm 6\%$ of the rated voltage at the consumer terminals. Low voltage results in loss of revenue, poor working of electrical appliances, insufficient lighting and the possibility of heating and burning of electric motors. The voltage can be kept nearly constant by selecting the proper size of the conductor.

(b) Power availability on demand: The customer must have access to electrical power in any amount as required from time to time. This is the second most important requirement of the distribution system. For example, any consumer can turn on or off the light without first notifying the utility and also they start or stop the motors and other appliances as per their requirements. The distribution system should be able to meet the consumer's load requirement. To forecast such significant load fluctuations, the operational staff must continually monitor the load pattern.

(c) Reliability: Nowadays, electrical power is used for lighting, heating, cooling, and ventilation of industrial units, homes, offices, hospitals, etc. It requires a reliable power supply system. Unfortunately, like all other commodities, electric power can never be reliable. However, the reliability of supply can be improved by using integrated systems, automatic controls and providing additional facilities

(d) Design considerations: The most important factor in the distribution network is to deliver quality service to the consumers. The required voltage at the consumer terminals can be maintained within the limit specified by standards. This can only be achieved through proper design and selecting the right feeder and distributor.

(e) Feeder design: The main consideration is designing the feeder based on its current carrying capacity. The voltage drop considerations are relatively less important as voltage drop in a feeder can be compensated by using voltage-regulating devices.

(f) Design of Distributor: The major concern in designing the distributor is its voltage drop throughout its length. The current carrying capacity of the distributor is relatively less important. Hence, the size and length of the distributor are designed in such a way that the voltage at the consumer's terminal stays within the permissible limits.

An ac distribution supply system differs from dc distribution in the following aspects:

(a) In the DC distribution system, the drop in voltage is only due to resistance whereas, in an AC distribution system, the drop in voltage is due to the cumulated effects of resistance, inductance, and capacitance i.e., Impedance.

(b) In DC systems, all additions and subtractions of currents are made arithmetically, whereas, in AC distribution systems, all additions and subtractions of the currents are made vectorially. Therefore, in ac systems, voltage and currents are expressed in symbolic notation.

(c) At load points the phase angle between voltage and current must be considered, which means the power factor plays an important role.

(d) All the distribution methods employed in the dc distribution system hold good for ac distribution method with the only difference that, in an AC system, all impedances, voltage, and currents are expressed in symbolic notation. The reference may be taken as voltage or current.

The power factor can be referred to in two different ways:

(a) The voltage at the supply or receiving end may be used to refer to the power factor and is taken as the reference vector.

(b) It may refer to the voltage at the load point itself.

4.6 METHODS OF SOLVING PROBLEMS IN AC DISTRIBUTION - (CONCENTRATED LOADS)

There are many methods of solving ac distribution problems. The Impedances are considered in place of resistances as compared to DC distribution and voltages and currents are taken as vector sums in place of arithmetic sums. In ac distribution, the power factor of the loads plays an important part, so there are two ways of referring to the power factor.

(a) Power factor referred to receiving end voltage

(b) Power factor refers to respective load voltages

4.6.1 Power Factor Referred to Receiving End Voltage

In this method let us consider an AC distributor AB as shown in figure 4.9 having two concentrated loads connected at points C and B. The power factor and current drawn by the load connected at B are $\cos\phi_B$ and I_B respectively and the Power factor for the load connected at C is $\cos\phi_c$ and I_c. For making calculations the receiving end voltage V_B is taken as a reference. Hence the power factors of the loads connected at A and B are lagging. The current I_B and I_C lag the voltage V_B by ϕ_B and ϕ_c. The voltage drop in distributor sections AC and CB is calculated considering the impedance of that section.

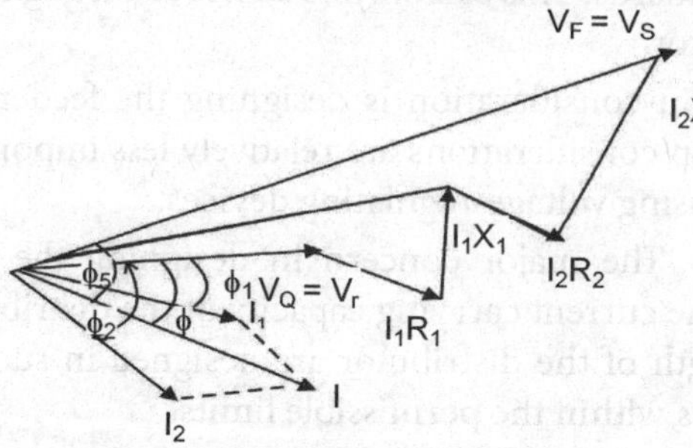

Fig. 4.9: Power factor referred to receiving end voltage

Impedance of the

section AC; $Z_{AC} = (R_{AC} + jX_{AC})$

section CB; $Z_{CB} = (R_{CB} + jX_{CB})$

The current in the section CB is I_c in complex form is $I_c\ (\text{Cos}\phi_c - j\text{Sin}\phi_c)$

Applying KCL to Node C Current in Section AC will be $I = I_c + I_B$

$I = I_c\ (\text{Cos}\phi_c - j\text{Sin}\phi_c) + I_B\ (\text{Cos}\phi_B - j\text{Sin}\phi_C)$

Voltage drop in section CB is

$V_{CB} = I_c\ (\text{Cos}\phi_c - j\text{Sin}\phi_c)\ Z_{CB}$

Voltage drop in section CA is

$V_{CA} = I\ Z_{AC}$

The voltage at the sending end (A) is $V_A = V_B + V_{CB} + V_{CA}$

4.6.2 Power Factor Refers to Load Voltages

In this case, the power factor is considered with reference to connected load point voltages. In the above case, the current I_B and I_C lag the voltage V_B by ϕ_B and ϕ_c whereas in this case I_B lags V_B by ϕ_B and I_C lags the voltage V_C by ϕ_c.

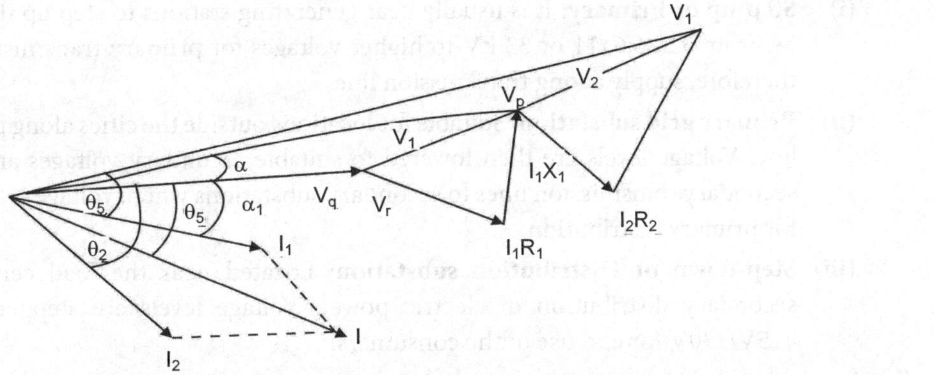

Fig. 4.10: Power factor refers to load voltages

The voltage drops in sections BC and CA are calculated to find out the sending end voltage and power factor.

4.7 SUBSTATION

Substitutions are located near the load centers for the distribution of electrical energy. Electrical power is received from generating stations or receiving substations at high voltages at distribution substations. At the distribution substation voltage level is further reduced to a value suitable for primary and secondary distribution in nearby areas. Distribution substations also provide switching facilities. Protection devices such as relays and circuit breakers are also installed at substations to disconnect equipment in the event of a fault. Power factor correction devices such as synchronous condensers or static condensers at the end of the transmission line for improving power factor are also installed at substations. Thus, the following considerations should be made while constructing a substation:

(a) **Location:** The substation should be located at or near the load centres to reduce losses and to keep the voltage profile as per requirements. Distribution substations are generally step-down substations.

(b) **Availability land:** Land should be preferably levelled and open from all sides. There should not be any water logging on the land selected for constructing a substation. The space near the aerodrome, shooting practice should be avoided. Approximately 50 acres are needed for the 415 kV, 25 acres for 220kV and 10 acres for 132kV substation respectively.

(c) It should involve minimum capital cost.

(d) **Communication facility:** The site selected should be easily accessible i.e., facilitate an easier and cheaper transport and communication facilities. It should be equipped with all the safety arrangements, such as protection from explosions or fire etc. Facilities for carrying out repair and maintenance must be there for proper operation and maintenance of substation.

(e) **Atmosphere pollution:** These conditions must be avoided i.e., metal corroding, gases, air fumes, dust, near sea coast where air is humid.

4.8 CLASSIFICATIONS OF SUBSTATION

(a) **Nature of duties:**

(i) **Step-up or Primary:** It is usually near generating stations to step up the generated voltages i.e. from 3.3, 6.6, 11 or 33 kV to higher voltages for primary transmission. Higher voltages therefore, supply a long transmission line.

(ii) **Primary grid substation:** Suitable for locations outside the cities along primary transmission line. Voltage levels are then lowered to suitable secondary voltages and therefore feed the secondary transmission lines to secondary substations where voltage is further stepped down for primary distribution.

(iii) **Step-down or Distribution substation:** Located near the load centres for primary or secondary distribution of electric power. Voltage levels are stepped down to 11kV or 415V/230V for end use of the consumers.

(b) **Service rendered:**

(i) **Receiving Substation:** To tap transmission lines from primary transmission lines and to change the voltage level to another level as per requirement.\

(ii) **Switching Substation:** without changing voltage levels, used for switching operations.

(iii) **Converting Substations:** To either convert ac to dc or dc to ac or for changing the frequency of supply voltage converting substations are used.

(c) **Operating Voltage levels:**

(i) Substations operating at voltages between 11kV to 66 kV are know as high voltage (HV) substations.

(ii) Substations having voltage levels between 132 kV to 400 kV are Extra high voltage substation (EHV):

(iii) Substations operating above 400 kV fall in the category of ultra high voltage substation (UHV)

(d) Relevance:

(i) **Grid Substation:** Handle bulk power which is transmitted from one point to another.

(ii) **Town Substation:** For further distribution of electric power in metropolis, step-down the voltages to 33 kV or 11 kV.

(e) Design:

(i) **Indoor substation:** The apparatus is installed inside the substation building only. It is usually 11 kV and can be erected to 33 kV and 66 kV when contaminants such as dust, gases, and other pollutants are present in the surrounding environment.

(ii) **Outdoor substation:** It is of two types:

A. **Pole mounted:**

- Transformer capacity of upto 250 kVA
- May be H-pole / Four-pole / single stout pole

B. **Foundation mounted:**

- Transformer capacity greater than 250 kVA
- Voltages greater than 33 kV

4.8.1 Indoor Substations

In these types of substations, the electrical apparatus is installed inside the substation building. Indoor substations are typically built to handle voltages up to 11 kV, but they may also be built to handle 33 kV or 66 kV when the air is contaminated by pollutants such conductive dust, fumes, and gases that cause the metal to corrode present at the site. While designing indoor substations, every effort should be made to minimize the fire risk, sectionalizing by fire-resisting walls, and the fire extinguishing cylinders must be installed in the indoor substation. Such type of substations are also necessary where continuity of supply is very important e.g. industrial area, cinema hall, railway station and other Commercial Complex etc.

In these types of substations, there are normally two transformers each having 500 kVA capacity. The primary voltage is 11 kV and the secondary is 415/230 V. The HT Switchgear which consists of an oil circuit breaker or ACB, is also installed near the transformer. The secondary side (LT side) is connected to the low voltage busbar. Many consumers are fed from these low voltage line busbars through controlling equipment. The panel for each feeder consists of a switch, isolator and a circuit breaker. The circuit breaker for a particular area should be so selected that in case of increased load, it may be used.

Layout of Indoor substation: Figure (4.11) depicts the typical layout design of an indoor substation and figure (4.12) shows the SLD of a 11 kV/ 415 V, Indoor substation.

This type of substation has two transformers each of 500 kVA. Normally, these are Delta/ star connected 3-phase transformers. The primary voltage of a transformer is 11kV and the secondary is 415 / 230 V. The consumers are fed from the secondary of the distribution transformer.

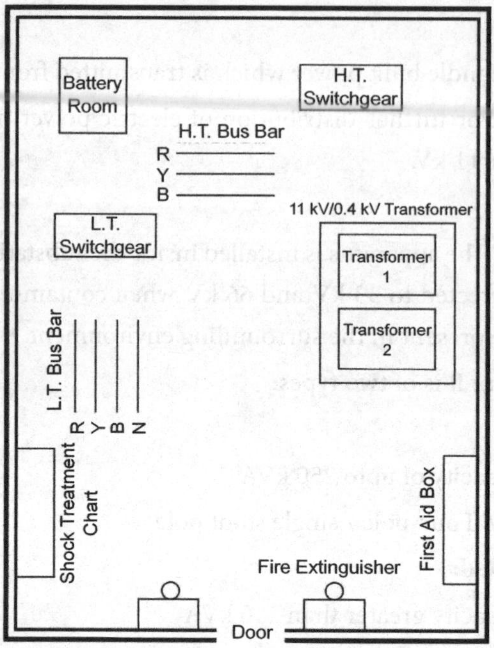

Fig. 4.11: Typical layout design of an indoor substation

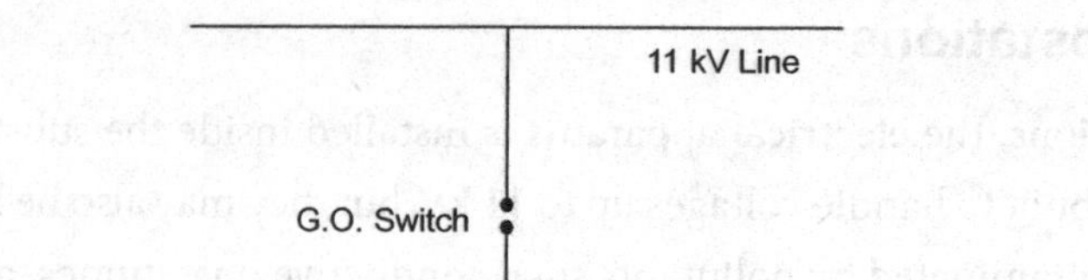

Fig. 4.12: SLD of a 11 kV/ 415 V, Indoor substation

SLD of 11 kV / 415 V Substation

The 11 kV line (3-ϕ 3-wire) is tapped and connected to input side of GOS (Gang operating switch) installed near the substation. From GOS, the 11 kV line is brought to the substation through an underground cable. It is given to the primary of the transformer via 11 kV ACB or OCB. The transformer stepped down the voltage to 415 V, three-phase four-wire. The secondary voltage of 415 V is given to LT Busbar via 415 V ACB. The voltage between lines is 415 V, whereas between phase and neutral is 230 V. Motor loads are connected across three-phase supply while single phase between one phase and neutral. Single phase loads are distributed such that the system remains in a balance condition. Current transformers are also located at suitable places, and they supply low current for metering and other indicating instruments.

Building requirements for an Indoor substation:

(a) The size of the indoor station should be such that it must accommodate transformers. HT and LT switchgear and trenches for incoming and outgoing cables.
(b) There should be good ventilation in the building so that there should be free circulation of air.
(c) There should be provisions for both fire protection and emergency lighting.
(d) The building should have sufficient height.
(e) The substation must have sufficient floor area for adequate clearance between the fire-resisting walls and equipment.

4.8.2 Outdoor Substations:

In such substations, electrical apparatus is installed in open spaces and hence named outdoor substation.

a Foundation Mounted Substation:

The substations are usually installed in the open area that is at the outskirts of the city and transmit electrical energy at 33 kV and above. These substations require huge equipment. Therefore, the locations chosen for these substations should have good road connectivity for the transport of heavy equipment. The equipment installed in foundation-mounted substations includes transformers (250 kVA and above), circuit breakers, control panel, etc. The primary and secondary transmission of electrical power is handled by these substations. At and above 132 kV, outdoor substation construction is universally employed. Figure (4.13) shows a line diagram of such a substation.

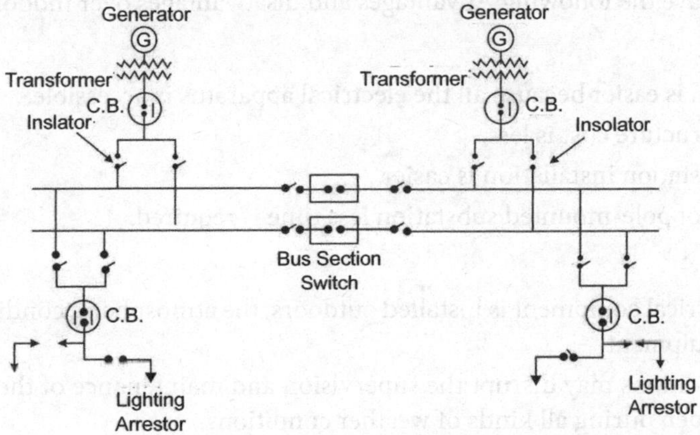

Fig. 4.13: Foundation mounted substation

b Pole Mounted Substations

These types of substations are erected for mounting transformers well above the ground level on poles.

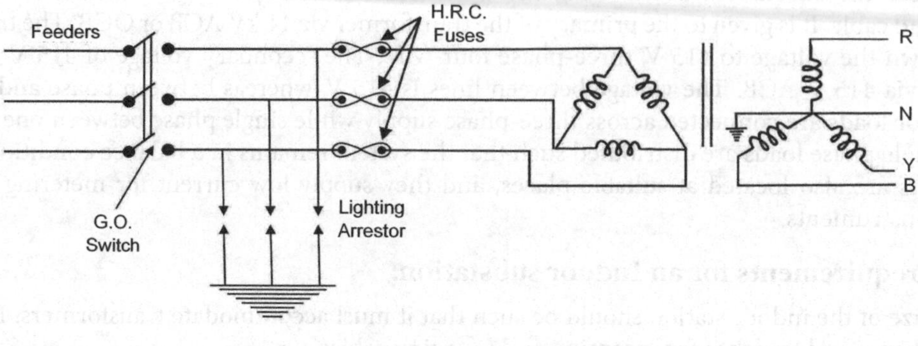

Fig. 4.14: Pole mounted substation

A transformer of Maximum 250kVA capacity is used in pole-mounted transformers. substations. Such types of substations are simply and comparatively cheaper than indoor substation. The switching, and protection equipment used in outdoor-type substations are mounted on a suitable height on the supporting structure. The primary side of the transformer is connected to a GO switch and HRC fuse of appropriate capacity. There is no need for a circuit breaker on the primary side. The LT side or secondary side is controlled by low-tension switches of suitable capacity with a fuse installed. Lightning arresters are installed on the HT side for the protection of the transformer from the surges. Double earthing is provided in these substations. Such a substation receives power at 11 kV and step-down to 415/ 230 V for distribution purposes. Figure (4.14) shows a simplified line diagram of such a substation.

Generally, transformers up to 100 kVA are mounted on double-pole H-type structures and transformers above 100 kVA but less than 250 kVA are mounted on four-pole structures with a suitable platform. These types of substations are elected in very thickly populated areas.

4.9 ADVANTAGES AND DISADVANTAGES OF OUTDOOR SUBSTATION

Outdoor substations have the following Advantages and disadvantages over indoor substations.

Advantages:

(a) The fault location is easier because all the electrical apparatus is accessible.
(b) Building/ infrastructure cost is less.
(c) Extension of substation installation is easier.
(d) For the erection of pole-mounted substation less time is required.

Disadvantages:

(a) Since all the electrical equipment is installed outdoors, the atmospheric conditions may deteriorate the life of the equipment.
(b) The weather conditions may disrupt the supervision and maintenance of the equipment as it is to be done in the open during all kinds of weather conditions.
(c) These substations require more space for installations.

4.10 COMPARISONBETWEENOUTDOORANDINDOORSUBSTATIONS

Table below gives the comparison of outdoor and indoor substations:

Table 4.1: Comparison of outdoor and indoor substations

Sr. no.	Particular	Outdoor Substation	Indoor Substation
1	Space Requirements	Higher	Lesser
2	Capital cost of Installation	Low	High
3	Fault detection	Simple; due to complete visibility of all the equipment	Tough: simply because enclosed equipment and less space for access
4	Substation Erection time	short	large
5	Substation extension	Can be done Easy	Difficult to extend
6	Operation	Difficult	Easy

4.11 LAYOUT OF 33/ 11 KV, SINGLE-BUSBAR DISTRIBUTION SUBSTATION WITH SECTIONALIZATION

A single bus-bar is split into two sections in this type of design, and the entire load is distributed evenly across all the sections. Interconnection of any two sections is done through a circuit breaker and isolator as shown in figure (4.15). The benefit of sectionalizing the busbar is that, in the event of a fault, that segment may be disconnected without affecting the supply to other parts. Another advantage of sectionalization is that if any section of the bus bar requires repair or maintenance, it may be done by de-energizing that section only, without impacting the other healthy sections. This kind arrangement is usually done for voltage up to 33 kV.

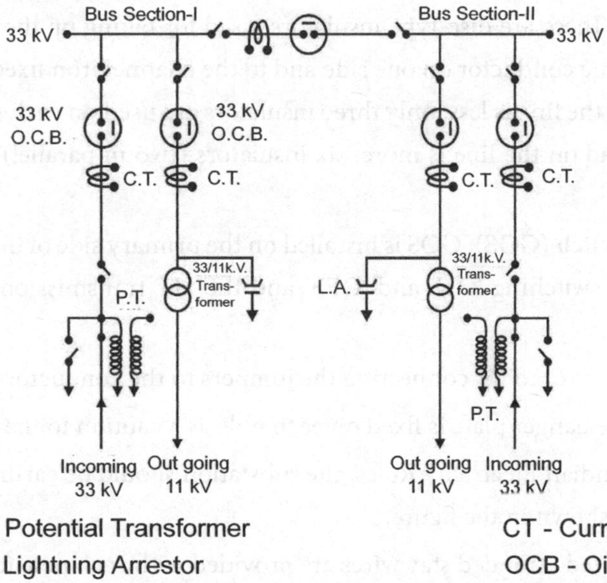

PT - Potential Transformer CT - Current Transformer

LA - Lightning Arrestor OCB - Oil Circuit breaker

Fig. (4.15): Layout of 33/ 11 kV, Distribution Substation with single Busbar system with sectionalisation

Figure (4.15) shows an arrangement of a single bus bar with sectionalization. In the figure, two 33 kV incoming lines are shown connected to sections I and II through a circuit breaker and isolator. Each 11 kV outgoing line is connected to one section of bus bar through an isolator, circuit breaker and 33/11 kV transformer. Each segment of the busbar operates independently.

4.12 COMPONENTS OF 11 KV / 415 V POLE MOUNTED SUBSTATION

A pole mounted substation is an outdoor substation and is erected in thickly populated areas for distribution of electrical power in various localities.

A pictorial view of the pole-mounted substation is shown in figure (4.16). The various components of such a substation are given below:

(a) **RCC poles:** These are reinforced cement concrete poles which give support to the transformer.

(b) **Transformer platform:** It is built up of channel iron on which the transformer is mounted.

(c) **Transformer:** For distribution purposes, a 3-Φ, 11 kV / 415 V, Delta / Star step-down transformer is used. The transformer kVA rating depends upon the connected load of the locality.

(d) **Insulators:** Normally 11 kV, pin-type insulators made of porcelain are mounted on the top of the pole structure. They also house the jumpers of the 11 kV line.

(e) **Jumpers:** These are made of ACSR conductors and are used for connecting 11 kV line conductors on either side of the pole structure.

(f) **Fuses:** One fuse is placed in each phase wire of the 11 kV, the primary side of the transformer for protection purposes.

(g) **Strain Insulators:** These are disc-type insulators, used for taking up the strain of the line and are connected to the line conductor on one side and to the channel iron fixed to the pole on the other side. If the load on the line is less, only three insulators are used on each side of the pole structure. However, if the load on the line is more, six insulators (two in parallel) are used on each side to bear the load.

(h) **Gang operating switch (GOS):** GOS is installed on the primary side of the distributed transformer and employed for switching 'ON' and 'OFF' and the HT transmission line. This is a manually operated switch.

(i) **PG clamps:** These are used for connecting the jumpers to the conductors.

(j) **Danger Plate:** One danger plate is fixed on each pole as a caution to the public.

(k) **Earthing:** As per Indian Electricity Rules, the substation should be earthed at two or more places. A pipe earthing is shown in the figure.

(l) **Stay wire:** Galvanized Stranded stay wires are provided with each pole to take up the strain of the line.

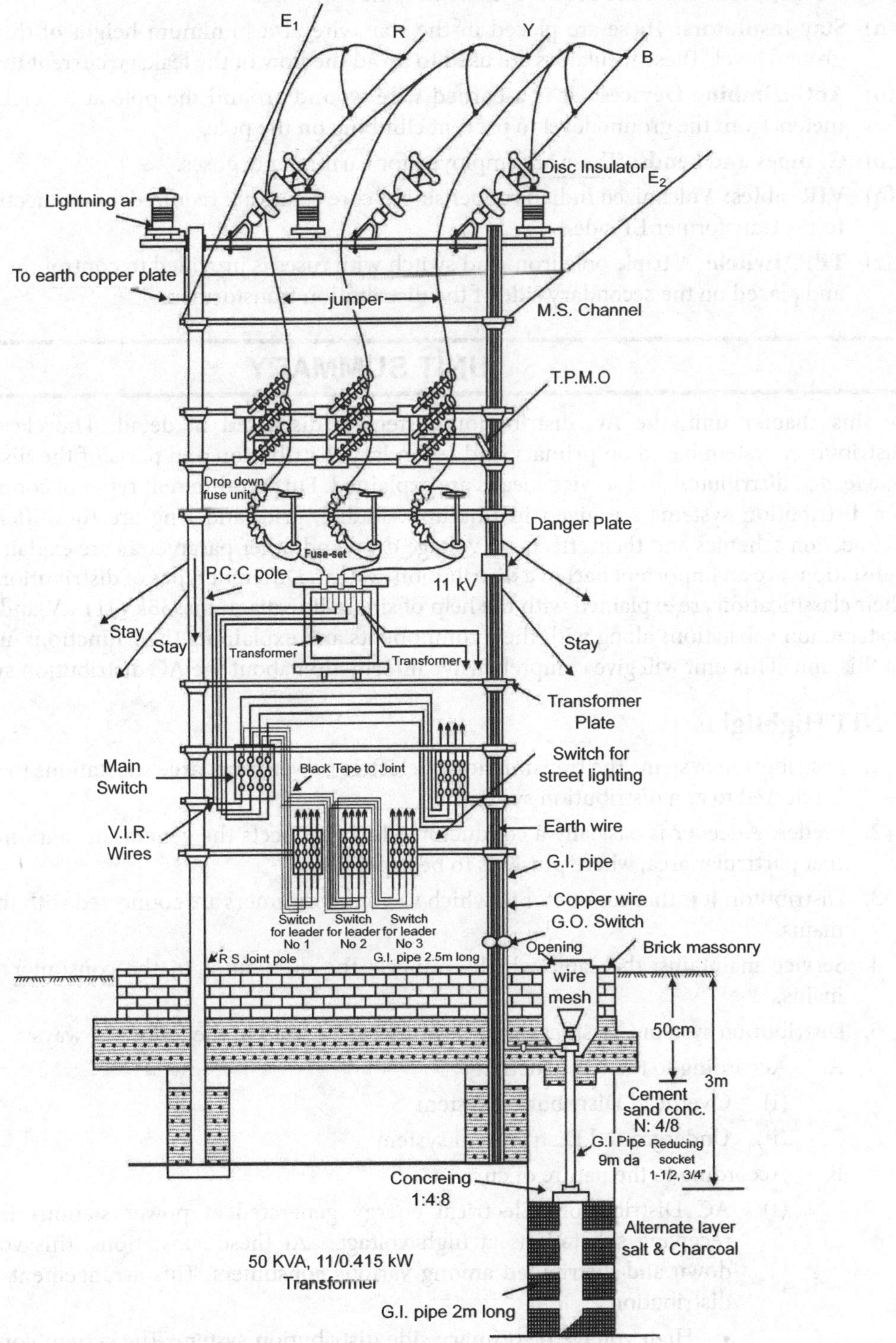

Fig. (4.16): Pictorial view of the pole-mounted substation

(m) Anchor Rod: These are used for tightening the stay wire.

(n) Stay Insulators: These are placed in the stay wire at a minimum height of three meters above ground level. These insulators are used to avoid the flow of the leakage current to the earth.

(o) Anti-climbing Devices: It is a barbed wire wound around the pole at a height of about three meters from the ground level to prevent climbing on the pole.

(p) GI pipes and bends: These are employed for earthing purposes.

(q) VIR cables: Vulcanized Indian rubber single-core cables are required for connecting the LT switch to the transformer LT side.

(r) TPIC switch: A triple pole iron-clad switch with fuses is provided to control the distribution line and placed on the secondary side of the distribution transformer.

UNIT SUMMARY

In this chapter unit, the AC distribution system is discussed in detail. The classification of the distribution system based on primary and secondary distribution and parts of the distribution system like feeder, distributor, and service means are explained. Further different types of connections schemes for distribution systems are given in this unit. Radial, grid, and ring are the different distribution connection schemes and their effects on voltage drop and other parameters are explained. Distribution substations are an important part of a distribution system. Different types of distribution substations and their classification are explained with the help of single-line diagrams. 33kV/11 kV and 11kV/ 415 volts distribution substations along with their components and explaining their functions are also presented in this unit. This unit will give comprehensive information about the AC distribution system.

UNIT Highlights

1. Distribution System: The transmission of electric power from large substations to a variety of users is referred to as a distribution system.
2. Feeder: A feeder is basically a conductor, which connects the generating station or substation to that particular area, where power is to be supplied.
3. Distributor: It is that conductor to which various consumers are connected with the help of service mains.
4. Service maintains: the cable which connects the distributor to the consumer is called service mains..
5. Distribution system Classification: These are categorized in the following ways:

   A. According to the construction

      (i) Overhead Distribution system

      (ii) Underground Distribution system

   B. According to the nature of current

      (i) AC Distribution: Electrical energy generated at power stations is transmitted to receiving substations at high voltages. At these substations, this voltage is stepped down and distributed among various consumers. This arrangement is known as AC distribution.

      - High voltage or primary side distribution system: The system consists of 3-phase, 3-wire, and the voltage level is somewhat higher than the general utilization.

- Low voltage or secondary side distribution system: The voltage level is quite low i.e., 415/230, 415 V being the line voltages and 230 V being the phase voltages.

(ii) DC Distribution: The part of the power system in which dc supply is distributed among the various consumers.

- DC two-wire system
- DC three-wire system

C. According to scheme of connections

(i) Radial system: Several feeders radiate from a single substation and further they feed the distributor at one end.

(ii) Ring main system: Feeder closes on itself in the form of a ring. The distributor is supplied by two feeders.

(iii) Interconnected system: Feeder ring is energised from two or more than two generating stations or substations.

6. The main requirements of a distribution system are proper voltage, reliability, and availability of power on demand.
7. Design of feeder: The main consideration is the current carrying capacity while designing the feeder.
8. Design of distributor: The main consideration is the voltage drop in it while designing distributor.
9. Difference in AC and DC distribution:
   (a) In a dc system there is no power factor but in ac system it plays an important role.
   (b) In a dc system, the voltage drop is only due to resistance whereas in ac, drop in voltage is due to combined effect of resistance, inductance and capacitance.
   (c) In a dc system, all addition and subtraction of currents are done arithmetically whereas in ac, all the additions and subtractions are done vectorially.
   (d) All distribution methods employed in the dc system hold good in ac systems, with the only difference that in ac, impedances, voltage, and current are expressed in symbolic notation.
10. Methods of solving problems in AC distribution:
    (a) Power factor referred to receiving end voltage or sending end voltage
    (b) Power factor refers to various load points, and voltages.
11. The comparison between outdoor and indoor substations is given below:

Sr. no.	Particular	Outdoor Substation	Indoor Substation
1	Space required	More	Less
2	Capital cost	Low	High
3	Fault location	Easier, because the entire equipment is in full view	Difficult, because the equipment is enclosed
4	Time required for erection	Less	More
5	Future extension	Easy	Difficult
6	Operation	Difficult	Easier

12. **Classifications of Substation:**
    (a) Nature-of-duties
        (i) Primary or Step-up
        (ii) Primary grid substation
        (iii) Distribution or Step-down
    (b) Service rendered
        (i) Transformer Substation
        (ii) Switching Substation
        (iii) Converting Substations
    (c) Operating Voltage
        (i) High voltage substation (HV)
        (ii) Extra high voltage substation (EHV)
        (iii) Ultra-high voltage substation (UHV)
    (d) Importance
        (i) Grid Substation.
        (ii) Town Substation.
    (e) Design
        (i) Indoor substation
        (ii) Outdoor substation
            A. Pole mounted
            B. Foundation mounted

EXERCISES

1. What is meant by the primary distribution system?
2. What is the difference between feeder and distributor?
3. Why 3-wire chosen over 2-wire dc distribution system?
4. The more reliable system is the ring main system. Why?
5. Briefly discuss the design considerations in the distribution system?
6. Explain the difference between the radial distribution system over the ring main distribution system?
7. Mention the various methods used in AC distribution.
8. For electric power, explain the 3-ϕ, 4-wire distribution system.
9. Discuss layout of distribution system.
10. Primary lines are known as feeders, why?
11. Compare the performance of a distribution system when fed at both-ends and one-end.
12. For the following, write short notes:
    (a) Radial, ring main and interconnected systems
    (b) Single-phase ac distribution system
    (c) methods of solving ac distributors

13. What is substation? Name the factors which will be kept in mind while designing and erecting a substation.
14. For a pole mounted substation, draw and explain the schematic connections and layout.
15. Give the layout of a 66/33/11 kV substation.

Multiple Choice Questions

1. A line which connects distributor to the substation is known as
   (a) Distributor (b) Feeder
   (c) Service-mains (d) Sub-transmission lines
2. While designing a____________, the main consideration is the voltage drop.
   (a) Service-mains (b) Sub-transmission lines
   (c) Distributor (d) Feeder
3. A line from which number of tapings are taken is called
   (a) Feeder (b) Service-mains
   (c) Sub-transmission lines (d) Distributor
4. When a distributed line connects a consumer to the supply it is known as _____.
   (a) Service-mains
   (b) Feeder
   (c) Distributor
   (d) Sub-transmission lines
5. While designing a feeder _________ is the main consideration.
   (a) Voltage drop (b) Power factor
   (c) Current carrying capacity (d) Energy
6. While designing a distributor_________is the main consideration.
   (a) Voltage drop (b) Power factor
   (c) Current carrying capacity (d) Energy
7. As compared to radial distribution system, a ring main system is _________reliable.
   (a) Less (b) More
8. At the consumer's terminal ______ percentage of rated voltage is the statutory limit for voltage.
   (a) ±3 (b) ±4
   (c) ±5 (d) ±6
9. In AC distribution system, addition and subtraction of currents are done __________.
   (a) Vectorially
   (b) Arithmetically
10. For __________ distribution loads, 3-ϕ with 3-wire ac systems is used.
    (a) Unbalanced (b) Balanced
    (c) Lagging cos-ϕ. (d) Leading cos-ϕ
11. For pure domestic loads, _________ ac system is employed for distribution.
    (a) 3-ϕ with 4-wire (b) 3-ϕ with 3-wire
    (c) 1-ϕ with 2-wire (d) 2-ϕ with 3-wire

12. ________ system is required for lighting load and combined load.

(a) 1-ϕ with 2-wire (b) 2-ϕ with 2-wire
(c) 3-ϕ with 3-wire (d) 3-ϕ with 4-wire

13. The cross-sectional area of any line conductor is generally ________ for neutral.

(a) Same (b) Double
(c) Half (d) triple

14. If fault occurs on any section, the supply to all consumers has to be ________ for a singly fed distributor.

(a) Shut off (b) Remain on

15. ________ connection is normally connected for pole mounted distribution transformers.

(a) delta(Δ) / star(Y) (b) delta(Δ) / delta(Δ)
(c) star(Y) / star(Y) (d) star(Y) / delta(Δ)

16. ________ substation is required when climatic conditions usually decrease the lifespan of the *equipment.*

(a) indoor (b) outdoor

ANSWERS															
1.	(b)	2.	(c)	3.	(d)	4.	(a)	5.	(c)	6.	(a)	7.	(b)	8.	(d)
9.	(a)	10.	(b)	11.	(c)	12.	(d)	13.	(c)	14.	(a)	15.	(a)	16.	(b)

Fill in the Blanks

1. ________ distribution system is more reliable because of two or more sources of supply.
2. ________ are nothing but underground armoured cables and overhead conductors carried over poles.
3. As per IER, ± ____ % voltage is maintained at the consumer end.
4. Primary distribution lines are known as ________.
5. In a dc distribution, at first cost ________ system is the simplest and cheapest.
6. For a radial distribution system, the criteria for selecting the size of a distributor is ________.
7. The loads on 3-phase, 4-wire distributors are usually ________ .
8. For a 3-wire dc distribution system the area of cross section of the neutral wire is usually the ________ of that of outer.
9. In ________ distributor, load point is the minimum potential which receives current from both sides.
10. The magnitude of current flowing through the neutral is determined by applying ________ law, for a 3-wire dc system.
11. Transmission lines and distribution lines can be discriminated by ________.
12. ________ distribution lines are known as feeder.
13. Fault location is easier in an ________ substation than in ________ substation.
14. At the generating points ________ substations are located.

ANSWERS							
1.	Ring main	2.	Feeder	3.	6	4.	Feeders
5.	Radial	6.	Voltage drop	7.	unbalanced	8.	one half
9.	ring	10.	Kirchhoff's first	11.	operating voltage	12.	Primary
13.	Outdoor, Indoor	14.	step-up				

True or False

1. The distributor does not connect the feeder and service mains.
2. For a distribution system, radial systems are less reliable than the ring main system.
3. Interconnected systems reduce the reliability of power supply.
4. Distribution transformers are usually connected in delta/star.
5. Overhead system is less flexible than the underground system.
6. In a ring distributor, the system fed at one or more than one point and forms a closed loop.
7. Three voltages are available for a 3-wire dc distribution system.
8. In singly fed distributors, in the event of fault, the supply to all consumers will have to be disconnected.
9. The cross-sectional area of neutral is generally double of either outer for a 3-wire system.
10. A ring distributor is similar to having equal voltages when fed at both ends for a distributor.
11. The transformer voltage required for a pole mounted substation, 110/11 kV.
12. For the same capacity the cost of outdoor substation is less as compared to indoor substation.

ANSWERS									
1.	**False**	2.	**True**	3.	**False**	4.	**True**	5.	**False**
6.	**True**	7.	**False**	8.	**True**	9.	**False**	10.	**True**
11.	**False**	12.	**True**						

Short and Long Answer Type Questions

1. What is the declared consumer voltage as per IER rules?

Ans. The declared consumer voltage, according to IER is 415/ 240V. [i.e. 415V between lines (RY/YB/BR), line voltage, and 240V between phase and neutral (RN/YN/BN), phase voltage] with a permissible voltage variation of $\pm$ 6 %.

2. Primary voltage depends on what factors?

Ans. For distribution, the primary voltage depends on the distance of the substation and the amount of power required to be supplied.

3. What is a feeder?

Ans. The line carrying current is known as Feeder when the current flows from secondary substation to the distribution substation.

4. Define the term distributor?

Ans. When different taps are taken for providing supply to the consumers along its length is known as Distributor.

5. Mention the merits of ring distribution over radial distribution.

Ans. The following table shows the difference between ring distribution over radial distribution.

Sr. No.	Ring Main System	Sr. No.	Radial System
1.	It is used for high voltages. It feeds the distributor with two feeders.	1.	It is used for low voltage. It feeds the distributor with one end.
2.	Initial cost is high.	2.	Initial cost is minimum.
3.	Ring main system needed less copper as it carries less current.	3.	More copper is needed because it carries more current.
4.	It increases the reliability of supply.	4.	It is less reliable.
5.	There are two feeders feeding the distributor, if one fails, the other can be used, ensuring continuity of supply.	5.	There is a single feeder on which consumers depend. In case of failure, all the consumers suffer.

6. Why is it necessary to keep voltage variation at the consumer's terminal as low as possible?

Ans. All the appliances and motors are designed to be operated at a particular or declared value of voltage. Large variations means either a too high or too low voltages. Low voltage will cause less revenue to the supplier. On the other hand, high voltage will cause the lamps or appliances to fail permanently. So, the requirements at the consumer's terminal should be the lowest possible (not more than $\pm$ 6%) of a distribution system.

7. What are the various methods of ac distribution?

Ans. There are two methods of AC distribution:

(a) High voltage or primary side distribution system (3.3kV, 6.6kV or 11kV): The generation system consists of 3-phase, 3-wire and the voltage level is somewhat higher than the general utilization.

(b) Low voltage or secondary side distribution system: The voltage level is quite low i.e. 415/230V, where 415 volts being the line-voltages and 230 volts being the phase-voltages.

8. On what parameters does the dc distribution system differ from ac distribution system?

Ans. The ac distribution differs from dc in the following manner:

(a) In a dc system there is no power factor but in ac system it plays an important role.

(b) In a dc system, resistance is the only main cause of voltage drop whereas in ac system, resistance, inductance and capacitance have the combined effect on voltage drop.

(c) In a dc system, all addition and subtraction are done arithmetically whereas in ac system, all the additions and subtractions of currents are done vectorially.

(d) All distribution methods employed in the dc system hold good in ac systems, with the only difference that in ac, impedances, voltage and current are expressed in symbolic notation.

9. In congested areas, how will you distribute electrical energy?

Ans. In congested areas, the electrical energy is distributed via underground system due to the following reasons:

(a) All cables are laid underground, so it provides better safety.

(b) Its appearance is good.

(c) Less chances of interruption of supply, so the system is more reliable.

(d) No line or bare conductor is approachable, less chances of accidents.

10. Compare the performance of a distribution system when fed at both-ends and one-end.

Ans. The performance of a distribution system when fed at both-ends and one-end is given below:

Sr. No.	Particular	Distributor fed at	
		One-end	Both-ends
	Cost and Simplicity	It is easy to design, so simple and cost is less.	It is complicated in designing and cost is also more.
	Reliability	It is less reliable.	It is more reliable.
	Efficiency	It is less efficient.	It is more efficient
	Voltage fluctuation	Voltage fluctuations at far end is more	Voltage fluctuations are less.
	Loading	Heavily loaded near the feeding end.	Distributor is lightly loaded.

Numerical Problems

Solved Numerical

1. A 500 meters cable for 1-ϕ distributed load AB is shown in figure 4.18. From the feeding point A, at a distance of 300m it supplies 100A at lagging 0.707 cos-ϕ and at a distance of 500m it supplies 150 A at lagging 0.8 cos-ϕ. The per kilometer resistance is 0.3 ohms and reactance is 0.2 ohms. Determine the cumulative voltage drop along the cable and take into account the power factors of the loads at the remote end, with regards to the voltage.

Ans. Resistance of distributor, R = 0.3 ohm/km

Reactance of distributor, X = 0.2 ohm/km

Impedance of distributor, Z = (0.3 + j0.2) ohm/km

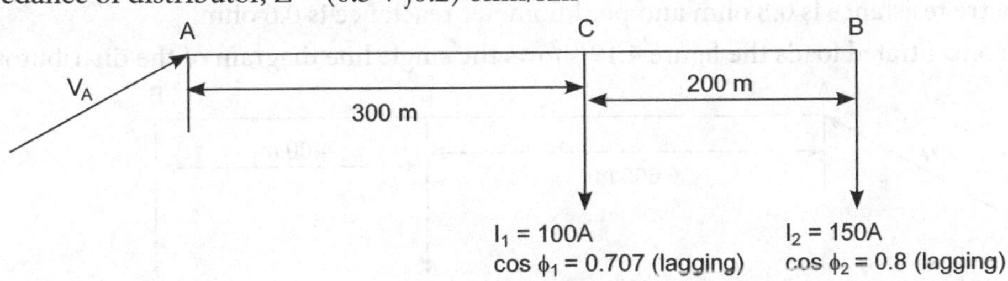

Fig. 4.17:

Section AC having impedance $Z_{AC} = \dfrac{0.3 + J0.2}{1000} \times 300 = [0.09 + j0.06]$ ohm

Section CB having impedance $Z_{CB} = \dfrac{0.3 + J0.2}{1000} \times 200 = [0.06 + j0.04]$ ohm

Taking V_B as reference vector at receiving end voltage:

At B the load current $I_2 = I_2 (\cos\phi_2 - j\sin \phi_2) = 150 (0.8 - j\ 0.6)$

$= (120 - j\ 90)$ A

At C the load current $I_1 = I_1 (\cos\phi_1 - j\sin\phi_1) = 100 (0.707 - j0.707)$

$= (70.7 - j70.7)$ Amperes

In section CB the current $I_{CB} = I_2 = 120 - j\ 90$

In section AC the current $I_{AC} = I_1 + I_2$

$= 70.7 - j\ 70.7 + 120 - j\ 90$

$= (190.7 - j\ 160.7)$ A

In section CB the voltage drop $V_{CB} = I_{CB} . Z_{CB}$

$V_{CB} = (120 - j90) . (0.06 + j0.04)$

$= 7.2 - j\ 4.8 - j\ 5.4 + 3.6$

$V_{CB} = (10.8 - j\ 10.2)$ V

In section AC the voltage drop $V_{AC} = I_{AC} . Z_{AC}$

$V_{CB} = (190.7 - j\ 160.7) . (0.09 + j\ 0.06)$

$= 17.163 - j\ 11.442 - j\ 14.463 + 9.62$

$V_{CB} = (26.805 - j\ 25.905)$ V

Total distributed voltage drop $= V_{AC} + V_{CB}$

$= 26.805 - j\ 25.905 + 10.8 - j\ 10.2$

$= (37.605 - j\ 36.105)$ volts

Magnitude of total voltage drop $= \sqrt{(37.605)^2 + (36.105)^2}$

$= \sqrt{1413.76 + 1303.21}$

= 52.124 V (Ans.)

2. In Figure 4.19, a 3-phase distributed load AB is depicted. The 3-phase, 440V, 10 HP induction motor (IM) has a power factor (cos-ϕ) of 0.707 lagging and an efficiency of 92 percent is connected at point B. At point C, the load has a power factor of 0.8 lagging, drawing 10 A per phase. The goal is to determine the voltage at point A when maintaining a voltage of 440V at point B. The per kilometre resistance is 0.8 ohm and per kilometer reactance is 0.6 ohm.

Ans. With concentrated loads the figure 4.19 shows the single line diagram of the distributor.

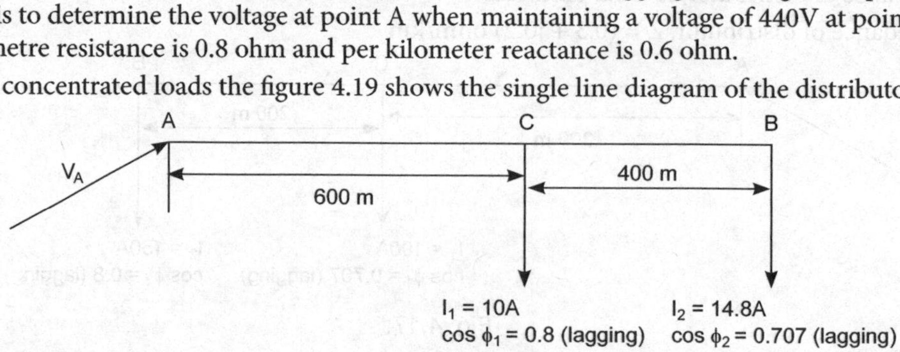

Fig. 4.18:

At point B the Phase Voltage $V_B = \frac{440}{\sqrt{3}} = 254V$

Taking V_B as reference vector for receiving end voltage:
Voltage per phase at B, $V_B = (254 + j\,0)$
Since, on point B, 440 volts i.e. the terminal voltage across the load of 10 HP for a 3-ϕ, IM.

$$\text{Per-phase load current } I_2 = \frac{10 \times 735.5}{\sqrt{3} \times 440 \times 0.707 \times 0.92} = 14.8 \text{ A}$$

$$\text{At point B the load current } I_2 = I_2(\cos\phi_2 - j\sin\phi_2) = 14.8\,(0.707 - j\,0.707)$$
$$= (10.46 - j\,10.46) \text{ Amperes}$$
$$\text{At point C the load current } I_1 = I_1(\cos\phi_1 - j\sin\phi_1) = 10\,(0.8 - j\,0.6)$$
$$= (8 - j\,6) \text{ Amperes}$$
$$\text{In section CB the current } I_{CB} = I_2 = (10.46 - j\,10.46) \text{ A}$$
$$\text{In section AC the current } I_{AC} = I_1 + I_2$$
$$= 8 - j\,6 + 10.46 - j\,10.46$$
$$= (18.46 - j\,16.46)\text{A}$$
$$\text{In section CB the voltage } V_{CB} = I_{CB} \cdot Z_{CB}$$
$$V_{CB} = (10.46 - j\,10.46) \cdot (0.32 + j\,0.24)$$
$$= 3.35 + j\,2.51 - j\,3.35 + 2.51$$
$$V_{CB} = (5.86 - j\,0.84) \text{ V}$$
$$\text{Voltage drop in section AC, } V_{AC} = I_{AC} \cdot Z_{AC}$$
$$V_{CB} = (18.46 - j\,16.46) \cdot (0.48 + j\,0.36)$$
$$= 8.86 + j\,6.64 - j\,7.9 + 5.93$$
$$V_{CB} = (14.79 - j\,1.26) \text{ V}$$
$$\text{Voltage at point A, } V_A = V_B + V_{AC} + V_{CB}$$
$$= 254 + j0 + 5.86 - j\,0.84 + 14.79 - j\,1.26$$
$$= (274.65 - j\,2.1) \text{ volts}$$

$$\text{Magnitude of } V_A \text{ per phase} = \sqrt{(274.65)^2 + (2.1)^2}$$
$$= \sqrt{75432.63 + 4.41}$$
$$= 274.6 \text{ V}$$

$$\text{Line voltage at point A} = 274.6 \times \sqrt{3}$$
$$= \mathbf{475.7\ V\ (Ans.)}$$

3. To maintain a voltage of 230 V at the far end, determine the sending end voltage and the phase angle voltage between the two ends. The distributor, with a length of 2 kilometers, has a per-kilometer (go and return) resistance of 0.05 ohms and a reactance of 0.1 ohms. At the far end, a lagging load of 120 A at 0.8 power factor is supplied, and at the midpoint, an 80 A load at 0.9 power factor is present. Both loads are referred to at the far end.

Ans. In figure 4.20 the SLD of distributor 2km long is shown.

Taking V_B as reference vector for receiving end (far end) voltage :

$$V_B = 230 + j\,0$$

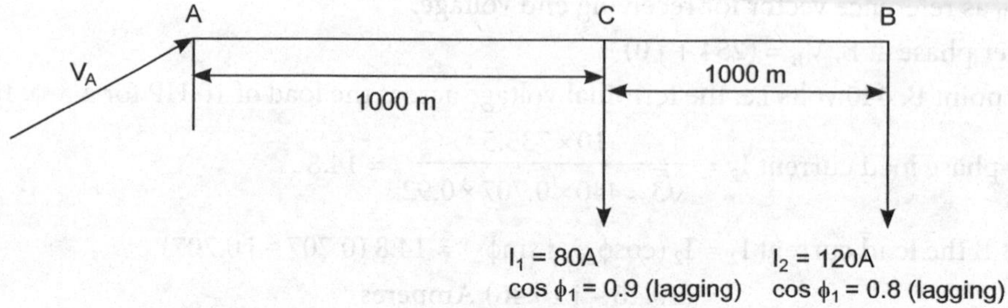

Fig. 4.19:

For section AC the impedance $Z_{AC} = (0.05 + j\,0.1)$ ohm

For section CB the impedance $Z_{CB} = (0.05 + j\,0.1)$ ohm

At point B the load current $I_2 = I_2\,(\cos\phi_2 - j\,\sin\phi_2) = 120\,(0.8 - j0.6)$

$$= (96 - j\,72)\text{ A}$$

At point C the load current $I_1 = I_1\,(\cos\phi_1 - j\,\sin\phi_1) = 80\,(0.9 - j0.436)$

$$= (72 - j\,34.88)\text{ Amperes}$$

In section AC the current $I_{AC} = I_1 + I_2$

$$= 72 - j\,34.88 + 96 - j\,72$$

$$= (168 - j\,106.88)\text{ A}$$

In section CB the voltage drop $V_{CB} = I_{CB} \,.\, Z_{CB}$

$$V_{CB} = (96 - j\,72)\,.\,(0.05 + j\,0.1)$$

$$V_{CB} = (12 + j\,6)\text{ V}$$

Voltage drop in section AC, $V_{AC} = I_{AC} \,.\, Z_{AC}$

$$V_{AC} = (168 - j\,106.88)\,.\,(0.05 + j\,0.1)$$

$$V_{AC} = (19.08 + j\,11.45)\text{ V}$$

At point A the voltage $V_A = V_B + V_{AC} + V_{CB}$

$$= 230 + j\,0 + 12 + j\,6 + 19.08 + j\,11.45$$

$$= (261.08 + j\,17.45)\text{ volts}$$

At point A, the magnitude of V_A per phase $= \sqrt{(261.08)^2 + (17.45)^2}$

$$= \sqrt{68162.76 + 304.50}$$

$$= \mathbf{261.67\ V\ (Ans.)}$$

The Phase angle between voltage (V_A) and voltage (V_B) is given by :

$$\tan\theta = \frac{17.45}{261.08} = 0.0668$$

$$\theta = \tan^{-1}(0.0668)$$

$$\theta = \mathbf{3.82^o\ (Ans.)}$$

4. For a 1-ϕ, ABCA-ring distributor which is fed at A. The total impedance of the section Z_{AB}=(2+j1), Z_{BC} = (2 + j3) and Z_{CA} = (1 + j2) ohms. Point A as referred to the voltage , the lagging load at point B is 40 A at 0.8 power factor and at point C is 60 A at 0.6 power factor. Find the current in I_{AB} , I_{BC}, I_{CA} section.

Ans. A ring distributor in figure 4.21 shows the SLD(single line diagram).

At point A, Let V_A be the reference vector:

At point B the current $I_1 = I_1(\cos\phi_1 - j\sin\phi_1) = 40\,(0.8 - j\,0.6)$

$= (32 - j\,24)$ Ampers

At point C the current $I_2 = I_2(\cos\phi_2 - j\sin\phi_2) = 60\,(0.6 - j\,0.8)$

$= (36 - j\,48)$ Ampers

Assuming in section AB the current $I_{AB} = (x + j\,y)$

In section BC the current $I_{BC} = I_{AB} - I_1 = (x + j\,y) - (32 - j\,24)$

$= (x - 32) + j\,(y + 24)$

similarly, in section CA the current $I_{CA} = I_{BC} - I_2 = [(x - 32) + j\,(y + 24)] - [36 - j\,48]$

$= (x - 68) + j\,(y + 72)$

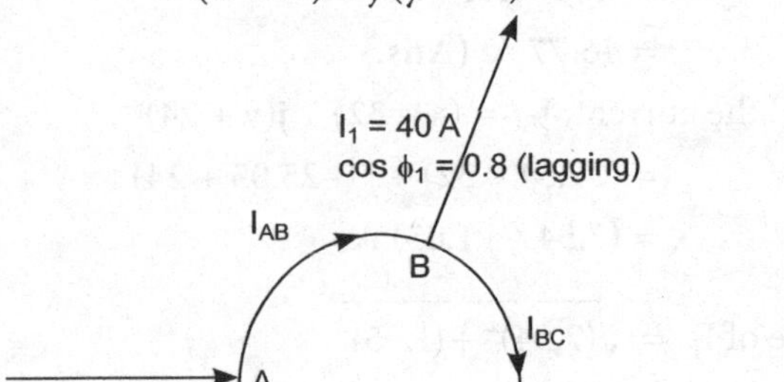

Fig. 4.20:

Impedance of section AB, $Z_{AB} = [2 + j\,1]$ ohm

Impedance of section BC, $Z_{BC} = [2 + j\,3]$ ohm

Impedance of section CA, $Z_{CA} = [1 + j\,2]$ ohm

Voltage drop in section AB, $V_{AB} = I_{AB} \cdot Z_{AB}$

$V_{AB} = (x + j\,y)\,.\,(2 + j\,1)$

$V_{AB} = [(2x - y) + j\,(x + 2\,y)]$ V

Voltage drop in section BC, $V_{BC} = I_{BC} \cdot Z_{BC}$

$V_{BC} = [(x - 32) + j\,(y + 24)]\,.\,(2 + j\,3)$

$V_{BC} = [(2x - 3y - 136) + j\,(3x + 2\,y - 48)]$ V

Voltage drop in section CA, $V_{CA} = I_{CA} \cdot Z_{CA}$

$V_{CA} = [(x - 68) + j\,(y + 72)]\,.\,(1 + j\,2)$

$V_{CA} = [(x - 2y - 212) + j\,(2x + y - 64)]$ V

As per KVL(kirchhoff's voltage law), in a ring (closed) circuit ABCA the algebraic sum of emf and the voltage drops is equal to zero.

i.e. $V_{AB} + V_{BC} + V_{CA} = 0$

$$[(2x - y) + j (x + 2 y)] + [(2x - 3y - 136) + j (3x + 2 y - 48)] + [(x - 2y - 212) + j (2x + y - 64)] = 0$$

$$[(5x - 6y - 348) + j (6x + 5 y - 112)] = 0$$

$$5x - 6y - 348 = 0 \qquad \ldots (a)$$

$$6x + 5 y - 112 = 0 \qquad \ldots (b)$$

By solving equation (a) and (b) we have,

$$x = 39.54 \quad \text{and} \quad y = -25.05$$

(i) Now in section AB the current, $I_{AB} = (x + jy)$

$$= (39.54 - j\,25.05)\text{ A}$$

$$\text{Magnitude of } I_{AB} = \sqrt{(39.54)^2 + (25.05)^2}$$

$$= \sqrt{1563.41 + 627.50}$$

$$= \mathbf{46.77\ A\ (Ans.)}$$

(ii) Now in section BC the current, $I_{BC} = (x - 32) + j(y + 24)$

$$= (39.54 - 32) + j\,(-25.05 + 24)$$

$$= (7.54 - j\,1.05)\text{ A}$$

$$\text{Magnitude of } I_{BC} = \sqrt{(7.54)^2 + (1.05)^2}$$

$$= \mathbf{8.23\ A\ (Ans.)}$$

(iii) Now current in section CA, $I_{CA} = (x - 68) + j\,(y + 72)$

$$= (39.54 - 68) + j\,(-25.05 + 72)$$

$$= (-28.46 + j\,46.95)\text{ A}$$

$$\text{Magnitude of } I_{CA} = \sqrt{(28.46)^2 + (46.95)^2}$$

$$= \mathbf{54.92\ A\ (Ans.)}$$

Unsolved Numerical Problems

1. Consider a 1-phase distributed load AB with a total resistance (R) of 0.2 ohms and a reactance (X) of 0.3 ohms. At the midpoint C, the lagging load current is 100 A at a power factor (cos-ϕ) of 0.6. The load is also tapped at the far end, where the current is 100 A at a power factor of 0.8 lagging. We need to determine the midpoint voltage, the voltage at the sending end, and the phase angle of the load current, assuming the voltage at the far end is 200V.

   Given that the respective load points of cos-ϕ are w.r.t the voltages.

   (Ans: 217.1V, 252.36V, 36.87°, 35.29°)

2. A 1000-meter 2-wire distributor is supplying load of lagging power factor (cos-ϕ) when referring to the voltage at its respective load points. At the far end, it supplies a load of 100 A with a power

factor of 0.8, while at the midpoint, it supplies a load of 60 A with a power factor of 0.85. The distributor has a per kilometer resistance of 0.08 ohms and a reactance of 0.12 ohms respectively. Given that a voltage of 250V is to be maintained at the far end, determine the supply end voltage and phase angle at both ends. **(Ans:** 267V, 1°26')

3. For a 1-ϕ, ABCA-ring distributor which is fed at A. The total impedance of the section Z_{AB}=(1+j1), Z_{BC}=(1+j2) and Z_{CA}=(1+j3) ohms. As referred to the voltage point A, the lagging load at point B is 20 A at 0.8 power factor and at point C is 15 A at 0.8 power factor. Find the current in I_{AB}, I_{BC}, I_{CA} section. (**Ans.** 23.1 ∠-32°, 3.01 ∠30° 1', 13.1 ∠-60° 8', 31.6 ∠-31° 8')
4. As illustrated in figure 4.21 is a 3-phase distributor AB. The 3-phase induction motor (IM) having power output of 10 HP at 415V with a lagging power factor of 0.85 and an efficiency of 90 percent is connected at point B. At point C, the load demand is 5 A per phase with a lagging power factor of 0.8. Given that the voltage is upheld at 415V at point B, determine the voltage at point A. The distributor features a per kilometer resistance of 1 ohm and a per kilometer reactance of 0.5 ohms. (**Ans.** V_A = 433 V)

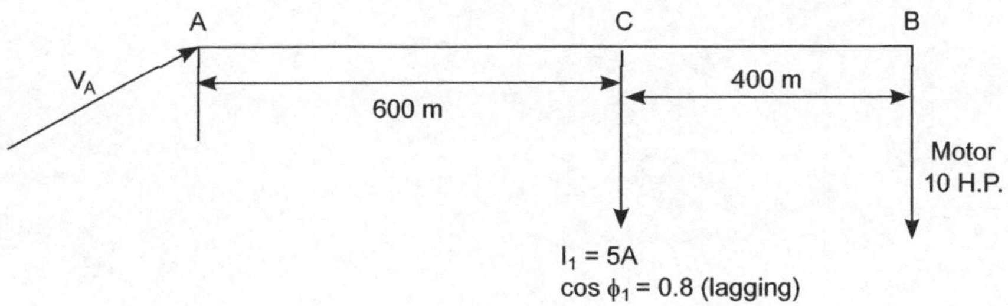

Fig. 4.21:

PRACTICAL

Visit to 33 kV / 11 kV substation and 11 kV / 415V Distribution Substation and write a report.

The report should contain the following:

1. Title page
2. Acknowledgement
3. Introduction
4. Purpose of the visit
5. Single line diagram of the substation
6. Learnings from the visit.
7. Conclusion

KNOW MORE

Students are advised to visit following websites to understand the transmission and distribution system in India and the latest developments going on more deeply:

- Ministry of power, Govt of India - https://powermin.gov.in/
- Central Electricity Authority, Govt of India - https://cea.nic.in/?lang=en
- Ministry of new and renewable energy -https://mnre.gov.in/
- Any state electrical transmission utility.

REFERENCES AND SUGGESTED READINGS

- https://nptel.ac.in/courses/108102047
- https://nptel.ac.in/courses/108107112
- https://nptel.ac.in/courses/108105104

❑❑

5 Components of Transmission and Distribution Lines

UNIT SPECIFICS

Through this unit we will discuss the following aspects:

- Different types of conductors and conductor materials used in transmission and distribution lines.
- Various types of line support structures and methods of erection of support structure for transmission and distribution.
- The properties of insulating materials used for making line insulators.
- Causes of failure of line insulators.
- Concept of string efficiency.
- Classification of cables used for transmission and distribution of electric power.
- Comparison of overhead and underground systems of power transmission.

Components of lines and cables used for the transmission and distribution of electrical power are discussed in detail. The most important component of a transmission line is overhead conductors; in this unit various types of conductor materials used in overhead transmission lines along with their properties are presented. Another important component are the line supports used for supporting the live conductors above ground level. Various types of support structures, their specification, and the method of erection are discussed in detail using pictorial explanations for a better understanding of the students. The line conductors are at higher potential and the support structure (steel poles) is at ground potential. Hence, it is very important that the live conductor and support structure should not come in direct contact. So, the live conductors are supported on steel towers with the help of line insulators. Different types of insulation material, their properties, and different types of insulators used in overhead transmission and distribution are presented. The concept of string efficiency and the causes of insulator failures are also discussed. In the end, the cables used for underground transmission of electrical power, the method of laying, and a comparison with the overhead system are presented.

RATIONALE

Knowledge of the transmission and distribution line components is crucial for fully comprehending the power transmission and distribution system. The three major components of overhead transmission lines are conductors, the support structure (towers/poles), and insulators. The knowledge of the material and properties of the material used for making the components is essential for selecting the proper components. The knowledge of specifications will help select these components according to a voltage level. The major cause of faults in transmission and distribution lines is the failure of insulators. The concept of string efficiency, causes of failure, and methods to avoid the failure of insulators are explained in detail. Generally, the distribution of electrical power in congested areas is done via underground cables. The types and construction of cables for various applications and methods of laying cables are also presented.

Some key features of the Unit include comprehensive details on three major components of overhead transmission lines i.e., Conductors, line supports, and insulators. In the case of transmission and distribution of electrical power via underground cables, the classification construction and methods of laying power cables are presented. The cable jointing process is also presented to enhance the learning of students. Precise explanations backed up by examples, pictures that help students envisage the parts of transmission systems, and solutions to problems at the end of each course unit to help students learn more effectively will be of interest to learners.

PRE-REQUISITES

Basics of power systems.

UNIT OUTCOMES

The students will be able to:

U5-O1: Select the material and specification of the components of the transmission and distribution line as per the requirement of different voltage levels of transmission and distribution.

U5-O2: perceive the causes of failure of insulators and methods to avoid it.

U5-O3: select line supports for transmission and distribution lines

U5-O4: choose power cables depending upon classification, construction, and requirements, comparing with overhead lines.

Unit-5 Outcome	EXPECTED MAPPING WITH COURSE OUTCOMES (1 - Weak Correlation; 2 - Medium Correlation; 3 - Strong Correlation)				
	CO-1	CO-2	CO-3	CO-4	CO-5
U5-O1	2	2	2	1	3
U5-O2	1	-	1	-	3
U5-O3	1	-	1	-	3
U5-O4	1	-	1	-	3

5.1 INTRODUCTION

Transmission and distribution of electrical power is performed using overhead lines and/or underground cables. The primary function of a transmission line is to transport electric power in bulk from the generating power plants to the load centres, and the distribution system enables further distribution of power at appropriate power and voltage levels to the end consumers. The transmission and distribution of power is done at different voltage levels ranging from 800kV to 415V.

Transmission lines are made up of many components such as poles, lattice structures, conductors, cables, insulators, foundations, and earthing systems. This unit goes into further information about each of these components.

5.2 COMPONENTS OF OVERHEAD TRANSMISSION LINE

The major components of overhead power transmission lines are given below:

(a) **Line supports(towers/poles):** These can be poles or towers to maintain the conductors at a safe distance from the ground.

(b) **Line Conductors:** They carry electricity from the transmitting substation to the receiving substation. The size and type of line conductor depend on the amount of current to be carried and the length of the power transmission line. The material of line conductors is generally aluminium (Al) or aluminium-cored steel reinforced (ACSR).

(c) **Insulators:** These are fastened to line supports and provide insulation to the conductors which are at higher potential from the line support which is at ground potential. The Insulators can be pin type, suspension type, or strain type.

(d) **Cross-arms:** These are attached to line support on one end and other ends provide support to insulators. These are either made of wood or steel angle sections.

(e) **Phase plates**: These are provided to distinguish the various phases.

(f) **Lightning arrestors:** These are used to discharge unwanted excessive voltage built in the line to earth because of lightning.

(g) **Barbed wire:** It is wound around over some portion of the pole or tower as an anti-climbing device.

(h) **Bird-guards:** These prevent flashovers caused by birds pecking on conductors. These are made of ebonite and have rounded tops. It is attached near the insulator on the cross-arm.

(i) **Earth wire:** This protects the line against lightning discharge. It is attached to the top of the tower.

(j) **Fuses & insulating switches**: These are used to isolate various parts of the overhead transmission line.

(k) **Miscellaneous items:** These include danger plates, guys, stay and Vee guards, etc.

5.3 LINE SUPPORTS (POLES AND LACTIC TOWERS)

Transmission and distribution line conductors support is provided by poles and towers. The various line supports are made of wooden/ steel/ RCC poles or steel towers. These poles/ towers must have the following characteristics:

(a) They must be mechanically strong

(b) They must be cheap in cost

(c) They must have the least number of parts

(d) They must have a longer life

(e) They must be light in weight

(f) The shape should bc pleasing

(h) Their maintenance cost should be minimum

(i) They should be easily accessible for paint and the erection of the line.

5.3.1 Wooden Poles

Small-capacity overhead electrical wires are supported by these poles at a secure height from the ground. Due to the low initial cost as well as the inherent insulating qualities of wood, wooden poles are utilized most frequently in earlier days. These poles should be highly sound and clear of huge nodes and should be available in that area or the neighbouring jungles. The clearance above the ground, the total number of cross-arms, and other equipment that must be attached are taken into consideration while determining the length of the wooden pole. The wooden pole typically ranges in length from 10 to 12 meters.

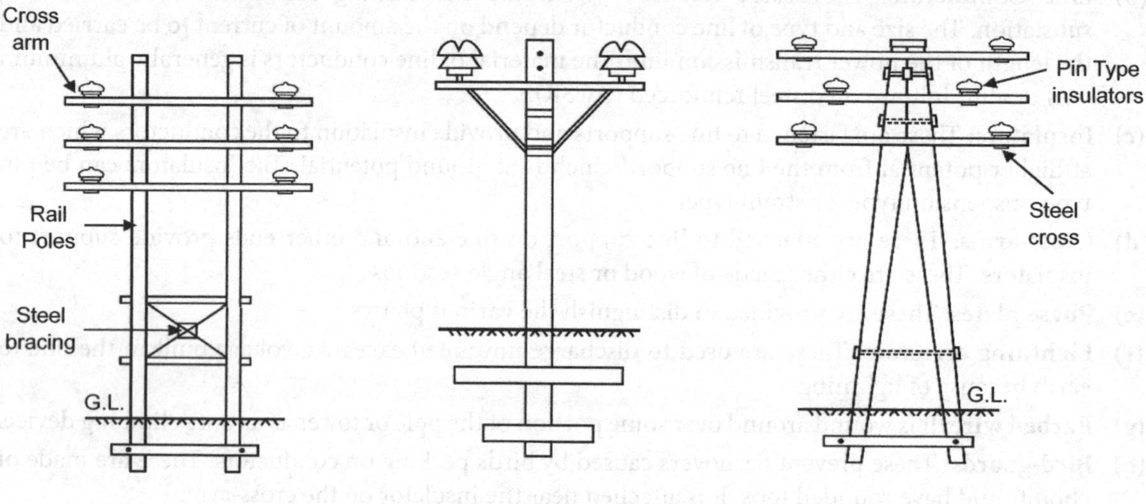

Fig. 5.1: Wooden Poles

The pole must be strong to bear the pressure of wind, ice, and snow along with the weight of the equipment and conductors. The depth of the pole in-ground depends upon the height of the pole, soil condition, weight, and pull factor if any. For a pole, having a length of 10 meters, the setting depth should not be less than 1.5 in case of normal soil conditions and 2 meters in case of poor soil conditions. The more the length of the pole, the deeper the setting length will be. After setting the pole, it is permeated with oil of creosote or any preservative that has a life between 25- 30 years. By permeation with the oil of creosote, they become free from climatic effects and insects. The wooden poles in service must be inspected in their routine check-ups.

5.3.2 Steel Poles

Steel poles are of the following three types:

(i) Tubular poles (ii) Rail poles (iii) Rolled steel poles

Tubular poles are circular, rail poles are formed like rail tracks, and steel pole joints are I-shaped. The steel poles are suitable for distribution lines such as for street lighting etc.

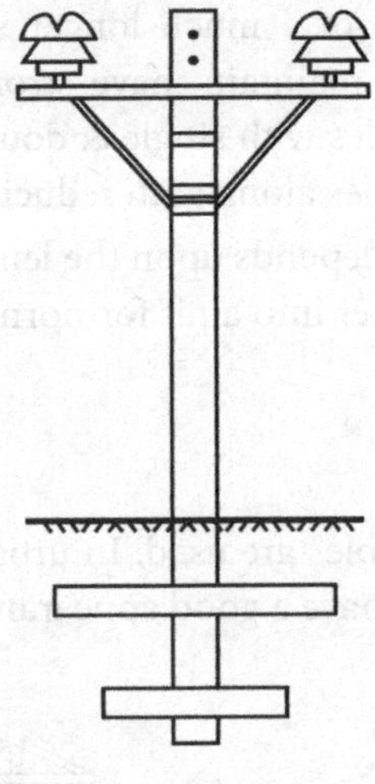

Fig. 5.2: Steel Poles

When compared to hardwood poles, these poles offer far higher mechanical strength, and longer shelf life, and may be used for much longer periods. The pros of tubular poles are their lightweight and easy installation, even though their actual cost is a bit more than the wooden poles. The distance between the pole and the ground is determined by the length of the pole, the quality of the soil, and the number of conductors that must be supported.

The other steel pole used is rolled steel of 'H' cross-section or Girder shape pole. The girders are set in concrete foundations. The advantage of this type of section is that it occupies less space. The poles are painted at regular intervals of time. These are extensively used for 3-phase, 4-wire systems.

5.3.3 RCC Poles

The concrete poles made of reinforced cement concrete have been in demand for the past few years.

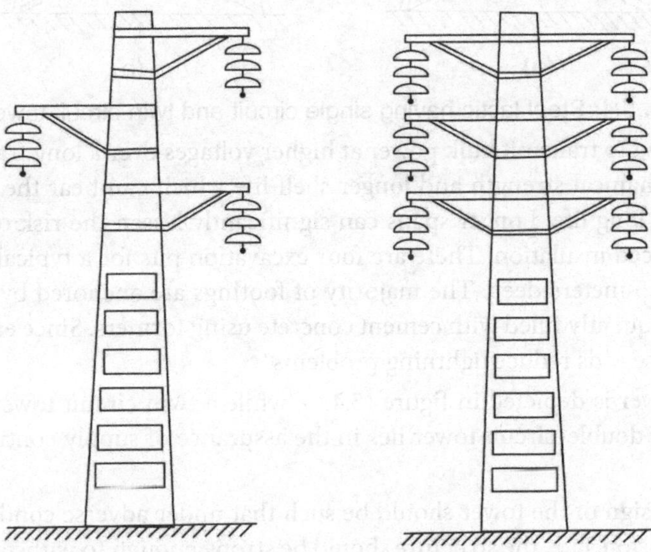

Fig. 5.3: RCC Poles

The RCC Poles have the advantage of a much longer shelf life free from insects and harmful environmental effects. They are easy to maintain, have strong insulating qualities, and have a nice appearance. Figure (5.3) shows R.C.C. poles with single & double circuit lines. The function of holes in the poles is to facilitate the climbing of poles along with reducing the weight of these line supports.

The depth of the pole in the ground depends upon the length of the poles. Normally for a length of 10 meters of the pole, 1.6 meters will be set into a pit for normal soil conditions and 2 meters for poor soil conditions.

5.3.4 Steel Lacttic Towers

For distribution in rural areas, wooden poles are used. In urban areas, the steel tubular/RCC poles are utilized for distribution purposes as they have a good appearance too.

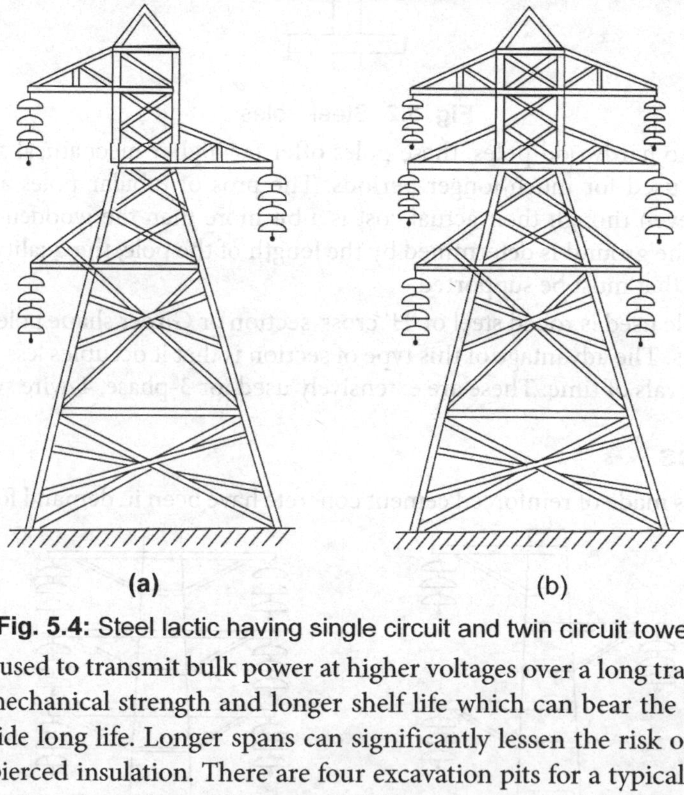

(a) (b)

Fig. 5.4: Steel lactic having single circuit and twin circuit tower

Steel towers are used to transmit bulk power at higher voltages over a long transmission line. These towers have better mechanical strength and longer shelf life which can bear the harshest atmospheric conditions and provide long life. Longer spans can significantly lessen the risk of service interruption due to damaged or pierced insulation. There are four excavation pits for a typical 132 kV transmission line, each of which is 3.5 meters deep. The majority of footings are anchored by driving rods into the ground. The pit is subsequently filled with cement concrete using formers. Since each tower functions as a lightning arrestor, these rods reduce lightning problems.

A single circuit tower is depicted in figure (5.4.a), while a twin circuit tower is depicted in figure (5.4.b). The benefit of a double-circuit tower lies in the assurance of supply continuity provided by the second circuit.

The mechanical design of the tower should be such that under adverse conditions of wind, storm, ice, snow, conductor tension, etc., the structure should be strong enough to withstand all such effects. To get durability, the tower is kept free from rust by galvanizing the structure.

5.3.5 Conductors

The conductor material used for electrical energy transmission and distribution should have the following properties.:

(a) High conductivity.
(b) High tensile strength to bear mechanical stress.
(c) The conductor material should not be brittle.
(d) It should have low specific gravity hence less per unit weight.
(e) It should not be too costly to be used over long distances.

Conductor Materials

One of the few most necessary items in the transmission & distribution of electrical power is the choice of conductor material. Since most of the capital investment in the outlying of line is spent on the purchase of conductor material, Therefore, it is crucial to select the right conductor material and size.

Materials: Steel, copper, aluminum, cored aluminum, galvanized steel, and cadmium copper are the most often used materials for overhead lines.

Overhead line wires are purposefully stranded to increase their flexibility. Most stranded conductors feature a central wire around which additional layers of 6, 12, 18, 24, etc. wires are coiled. The total number of individual wires after n layers will be 3n [n+1] + 1. According to theory, the conductor will have an overall diameter of (2n+1)d if each strand has a diameter of "d". To hold the successive wire layers together, stranded conductors are made by twisting or spiralling the wires in opposing directions.

(a) **Copper:** Due to its excellent tensile strength & great electrical conductivity, copper is the perfect material for overhead wires. Hard-drawn copper conductors are universally used for the transmission and distribution of electrical energy because it is twice soft-drawn as soft drawn copper. The main characteristics of the copper conductor are given below:
   (i) The conductivity of copper conductor is best as compared to other metals used for the purpose.
   (ii) High current density i.e. the current per unit area is very large. It has two main advantages – firstly, a very small cross-sectional area is required & secondly, line supports required for supporting the line will be less stronger.
   (iii) It has low specific resistance.
   (iv) Copper does not corrode in a normal atmosphere.
   (v) Durability and good scrap value.

   Copper is unquestionably the best material for transmission and distribution, but it is rarely utilized since it is expensive and not readily available in large enough quantities. Hence, the shift is to use aluminum above copper.

(b) **Aluminum:** Aluminum conductors are much in use these days because of the higher cost of copper. The aluminum conductors are next to copper conductors in order of merit.
   (i) It is comparatively more economical than copper.
   (ii) Lightweight.
   (iii) Aluminum has 60.6% of the conductivity of copper. The conductor cross-sectional area required in case of aluminium conductors will be greater than copper's due to lower conductivities for the same transmission efficiency.

(iv) Diameter of the Aluminum conductor is approximately 1.27 times of copper for the same ohmic resistance.

(v) Aluminum conductors are light and amount to greater swings. Therefore bigger cross-arms are needed.

(vi) The melting point of aluminum being low, there is more damage to aluminum conductors during short circuit faults.

(vii) Jointing of aluminium is much more difficult than copper.

(c) Aluminum Conductors Steel reinforced (ACSR): Copper conductors are very uneconomical; steel conductors have very poor conductivity and aluminum conductors have less tensile strength. Therefore, the ACSR conductors were developed to get the finest possible combination.

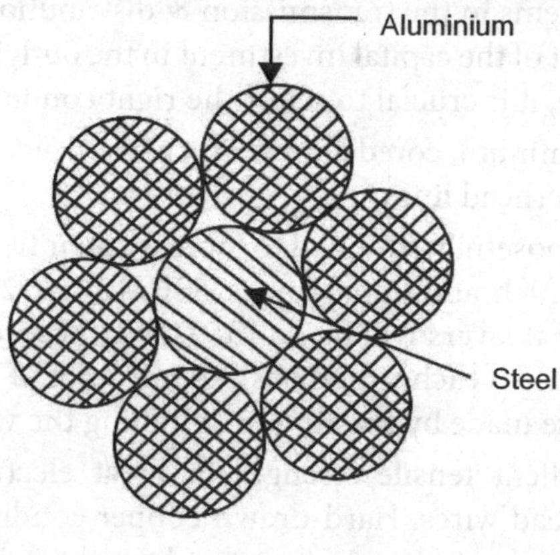

Fig. 5.5: Aluminum conductor steel reinforced

An aluminum conductor with galvanized steel wire as the core is utilized for the high-voltage power transmission. This is done to enhance the tensile strength of aluminum conductors. Generally, the diameter of steel and aluminum wire is equal. The cross-section of these two metals is typically in the ratio of 1:6, whereas the ratio is 1:4 for conductors with greater strengths. A steel-cored aluminium conductor with six aluminium wires around one steel wire is seen in Figure (5.5). The combination produces a steel core with a higher percentage of mechanical strength and aluminium conductors that carry the majority of the current load. Longer spans may be employed with an ACSR conductor since it has a lower weight and better tensile strength, which results in little sag. There is reduction in corona loss because of the greater diameter of ACSR conductors. Such conductors are utilized generally for high-voltage power transmission where longer spans are required.

(d) Galvanized steel conductors: The tensile strength of these conductors is greater. Galvanized steel conductors may therefore be used for incredibly great lengths. These are found most satisfactory for rural areas, where cost is the major contemplation. As the conductivity is poor, about 13% of the copper is mixed with these conductors. These conductors are inadequate for sending more power over a longer distance. However, they can be used to transfer lower power over shorter distances when the economically necessary copper conductor size is often smaller than 8 S.W.G. and cannot be used because of its weak mechanical strength. To transfer significant amounts of electricity, these conductors are incompatible with E.H.T. lines.

(e) **Cadmium-copper conductor:** Now-a-days in certain cases, an alloy of copper and cadmium is utilized as conductor material. Adding 1% to 2% of cadmium results in around 50% improvement in tensile strength; whereas pure copper's conductivity is lowered to 15%. Hence, cadmium-copper conductors can be convenient for exceptionally longer spans. However, because cadmium is quite expensive, these conductors can be cost-effective for lines with small cross sections where the cost of conductor material is somewhat lower than the cost of supports.

5.3.6 Insulators

The function of the insulator is to provide insulation between the conductor and the supporting arm of the pole or tower in the overhead transmission line so that currents from bare conductors don't flow to the earth via line supports. To do this, insulators are positioned in between the conductors and the line support. As a result, the line insulators' quality and maintenance are crucial for the transmission system's efficient operation. The line insulators should have the following characteristics:

(a) Their di-electric strength should be very high.
(b) There should be no internal impurities.
(c) The insulating material should be non-porous.
(d) Insulators should be robust and mechanically strong.
(e) They should have high insulation resistance to leaking current.

Insulators break down because of a puncture or flashover. Between the line conductor and the earth, the flashover may occur due to many reasons such as polluted environmental conditions. The most frequently used material for insulators is **Porcelain**, although glass, steatite, etc. are also used to a little extent.

(a) Porcelain is preferred over glass because of the following properties:
(b) Mechanically much stronger.
(c) Its insulating properties remains unaffected even after dirt deposits on the insulator.
(d) It has high dielectric strength up of to 60 kV/cm.
(e) It has a high compressive strength of about 7000 Kg/cm^2.
(f) It has a high tensile strength of about 500 Kg/cm^2.

Types of insulators: Most frequently used insulators in an overhead line are

(a) Pin type insulators
(b) Suspension type insulators
(c) Strain insulators
(d) Shackle insulators
(e) Egg/stay insulator

a Pin Type Insulator

These insulators are used in telephone lines and low-voltage overhead lines. To ensure that the conductor stays intact during storms and high-pressure winds, it is inserted into the top semi-circular groove and tied along its neck with the aid of a separate wire made of the same material as the conductor. The insulator is built up in various curved surfaces facing downward to increase the surface area to remain dry even during rain. The rain sheds (projection facing downward) are designed in a way that even when insulators get wet, a sufficiently dry space is provided by those inner sheds to avoid flashover and leakage current.

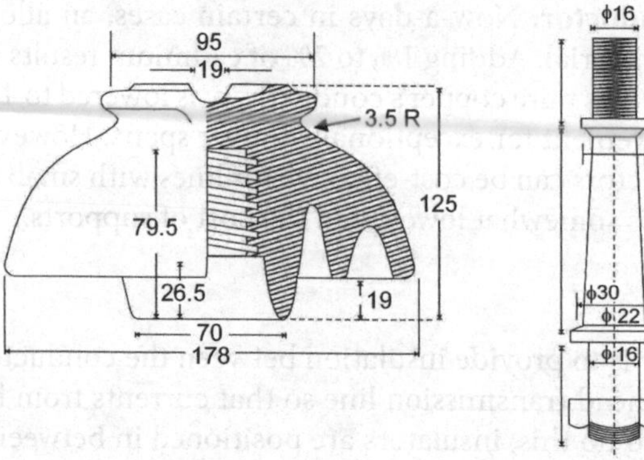

Fig. 5.6: (a) Pin type insulator

At higher voltage, the material thickness needed for insulation purposes should be more but on account of manufacturing difficulties, a single-piece insulator cannot be manufactured in very large sizes. Hence, for higher voltages 2 or 3-piece insulators are designed. Insulators are designed up to 50 kV as they become uneconomical for higher voltages.

These insulators can be used for up to 33 kV. For lower voltages, generally, a single piece type of an insulator is used. Figure 5.6(a) shows a pin type insulator and galvanised steel bolt. To avoid leakage of surface current, the insulators are given a long leakage path by providing two or more petticoats or sheds or projections facing downward.

b Suspension Type Insulators

Beyond 33kV transmission voltage, pin type insulators become expensive. As a result, it is common practice to use suspension type insulators for voltages greater than 33 kV. These consist of a series of porcelain discs connected by metal links in the shape of string, as shown in figure (5.7).

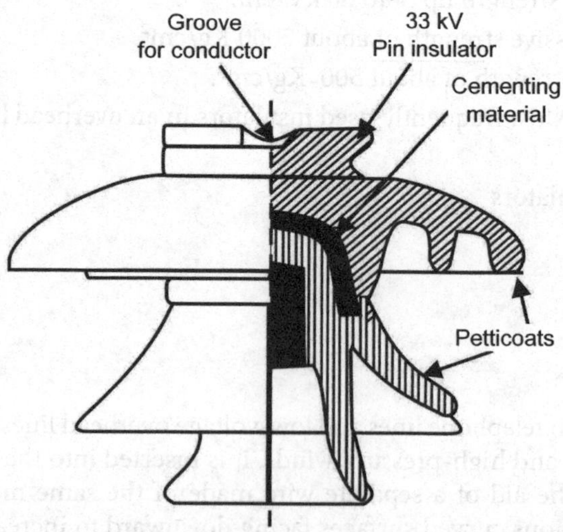

Fig. 5.6: (b) Suspension type insulator

The conductor is suspended at one end of this string, while the other end is secured to the tower's cross arm. The suspension type insulator provides much more flexibility to the line and reduces mechanical stresses. Each unit or disc is rated for 11 kV, and the number of discs connected in series is determined by the operating voltage. For example, if the line's operating voltage is 66 kV, the string will have six discs connected in series.

The suspension-type insulators have the following advantages:

Suspension type insulators are less expensive than pin type insulators for voltage above 33kV.

Every insulator & disc is designed for 11kV and insulation required for any line voltage can be drawn by using a suitable number of such insulators in the string.

When any insulator or disc gets damaged, it is not required to change the whole string; rather only damaged discs are required to be changed.

In case of a rise in voltage level, the same string can be utilized by adding one or two more discs.

Suspension type insulators placed on steel towers, also protect the line conductors partly from the effect of lightning, since these conductors run beneath the earthed cross arm.

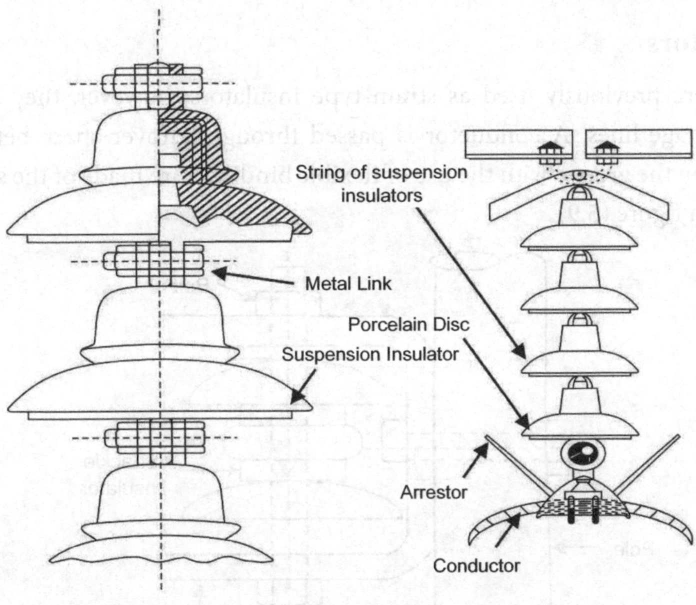

Fig. 5.7: String of suspension insulators

Following are the disadvantages of suspension-type insulators:

The spacing required between the conductors is large as compared to pin-type insulators because the swing amplitude of conductors becomes large.

It is costlier than pin-type insulators, so is generally not used below 33 kV, transmission voltage.

c Strain Insulators

The strain insulators are used either at the line's dead end, at steep curves, at river crossings, or corners. As illustrated in figure (5.8), these are used for the high-voltage lines forming an assembly of suspension insulators. When the pull applied on the string of suspension insulator is high, as, in the case of long spans across the river, two or more strings are employed in parallel.

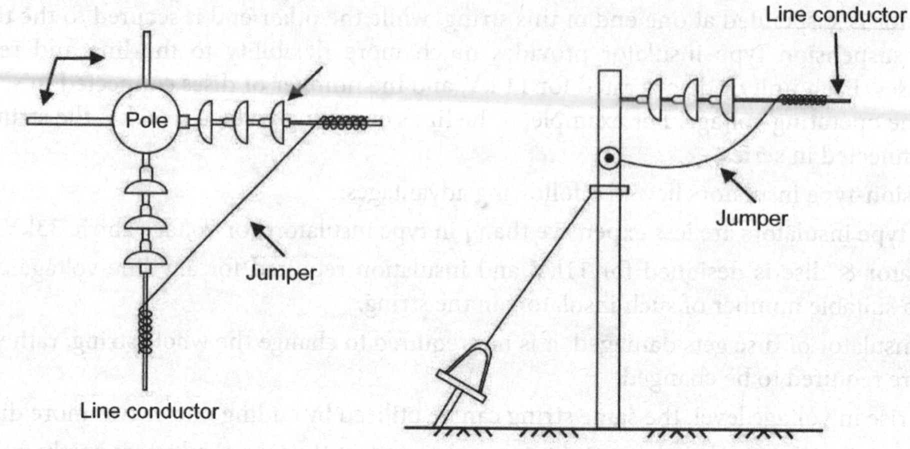

Fig. 5.8: Strain insulators

d Shackle Insulators

Shackle insulators were previously used as strain-type insulators; however, they are now frequently employed for low-voltage lines. A conductor is passed through leftover space between the clamp & insulator & is tied along the groove with the use of flexible binding wire made of the same material as the conductor as shown in figure (5.9).

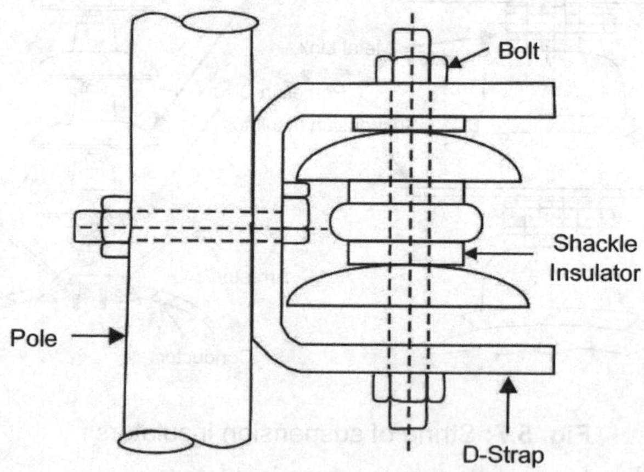

Fig. 5.9: Shackle insulators

e Egg or Stay Insulators

Stay insulators are used for stay wire to provide insulation between the pole and the stay clamp as shown in figure (5.10). Stay wires on low voltage lines are insulated at a height of at least 3 meters above the ground. It has two perpendicular holes from which two ends of these stay wires are looped so that when the insulator breaks, the stay wire does not tend to fall on the ground.

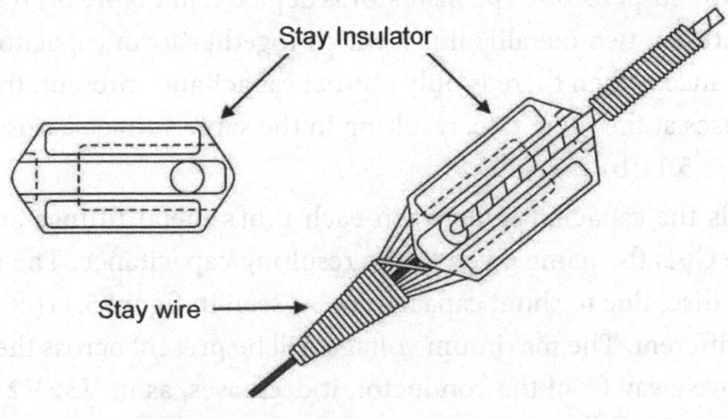

Fig. 5.10: Egg or stray insulators

5.4 POTENTIAL DISTRIBUTION ALONG A SUSPENSION INSULATOR STRING

For overhead lines operating at high voltage i.e., higher than 33 kV, a string of the suspension type insulator consisting of multiple porcelain discs is used as shown in figure (5.11).

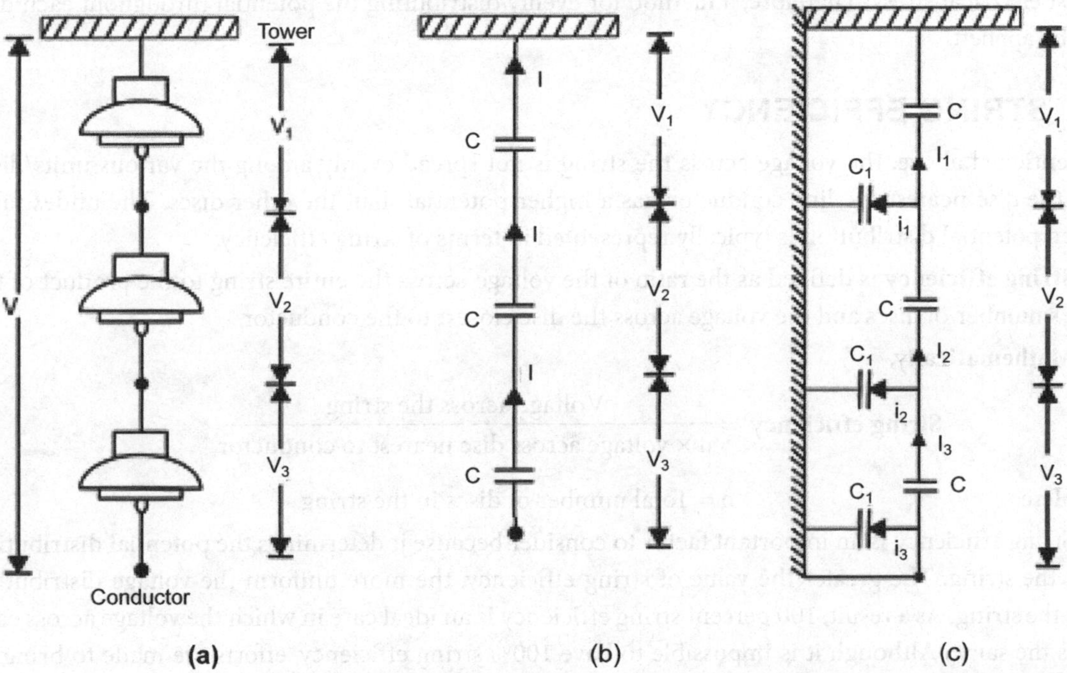

Fig. 5.11: Three-disc string of suspension insulators

Metal links connect these discs in series. The string of insulators is a unit formed by connecting several discs in series. The line conductor is secured at the string's very bottom disc, while the top disc is connected to the cross-arm of the pole/tower.

The 3-disc string of the suspension-type insulator is depicted in Figure 5.11(a). Each disc's porcelain section is sandwiched between two metallic links, which together form capacitor C. This is referred to as self- or mutual capacitance. When there is only mutual capacitance present, the charging current will flow through all of the discs at the same rate, resulting in the same voltage across each disc (or unit), or V/3, as illustrated in figure 5.11(b).

Additionally, there is the capacitance between each unit's metal fittings and the earthed pole or tower. Shunt capacitance C_1 is the name given to the resulting capacitance. The charging current is not equal in all of the string's discs due to shunt capacitance, as seen in figure 5.11(c). As a result, the voltage across each disc will be different. The maximum voltage will be present across the disc closest to the line conductor, and as we move away from the conductor, it decreases, as in V3>V2>V1. If a string has "n" discs, then Vn>Vn-1>....V2>V1 follows. It's important to note the following details regarding possible potential distribution over a string of suspension-type insulators:

Due to the presence of a shunt capacitance, the voltage applied to the string of suspension insulators does not automatically distribute uniformly over each disc.

Maximum voltage is present at the disc closest to the conductor. As we move closer to the cross arm, the voltage across each disc decreases.

The disc that is nearest to the conductor is most likely to fail first because it is experiencing the highest electrical stress. Therefore, a method for evenly distributing the potential throughout each disc must be applied.

5.5 STRING EFFICIENCY

As mentioned above, the voltage across the string is not spread evenly among the various units/discs since the disc nearest the line conductor has a higher potential than the other discs. The undesirable uneven potential distribution is typically represented in terms of string efficiency.

String efficiency is defined as the ratio of the voltage across the entire string to the product of the string's number of discs and the voltage across the disc closest to the conductor.

Mathematically,

$$\textbf{String efficiency} = \frac{\text{Voltage across the string}}{n \times \text{voltage across disc nearest to conductor}}$$

Here, n = Total number of discs in the string

String efficiency is an important factor to consider because it determines the potential distribution along the string. The greater the value of string efficiency, the more uniform the voltage distribution along the string. As a result, 100 percent string efficiency is an ideal case in which the voltage across each disc is the same. Although it is impossible to have 100% string efficiency, efforts are made to bring its value as close to the ideal value as possible.

Mathematical Expression for String Efficiency:

An equivalent string circuit, as shown in figure 5.12, can be used to determine the voltage distribution across different insulator string units and the string efficiency.

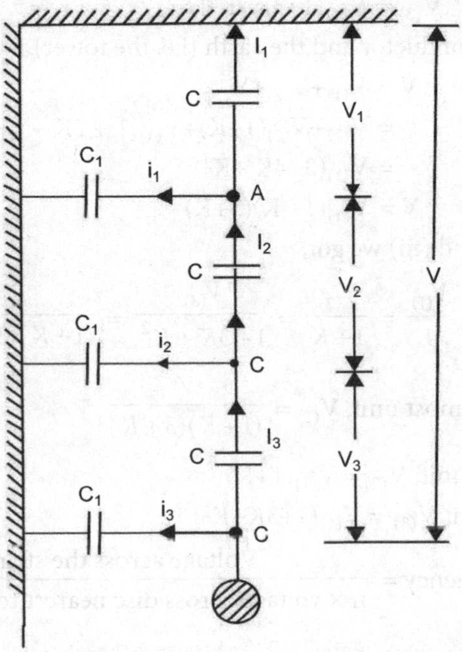

Fig. 5.12: Equivalent of the string for string efficiency

Considering an equivalent of a string consisting of 3-disc insulators as shown;

Let, C = Mutual capacitance of every disc

$C_{(1)}$ = Shunt capacitance which is the function of mutual capacitance

$$\therefore \qquad C_{(1)} = KC$$

Currents in various branches are marked as shown in figure 5.12. The voltage across each unit starting from the cross-arm or tower is V_1, V_2, and V_3, respectively.

At node 'A' apply KCL, we get:

$$I_{(2)} = i_{(1)} + I_{(1)}$$

$$\therefore \qquad V_{(2)}\omega C = V_{(1)}\omega C_{(1)} + V_{(1)}\omega C$$

$$\therefore \qquad V_{(2)}\omega C = V_{(1)}\omega KC + V_{(1)}\omega C$$

$$\therefore \qquad V_{(2)} = V_{(1)}(K+1) \qquad \text{... (i)}$$

At node 'B' apply KCL,

$$I_{(3)} = i_{(2)} + I_{(2)}$$

$$\therefore \qquad V_{(3)}C = (V_{(1)}+V_{(2)}).(C_{(1)}) + V_{(2)}C$$

$$\therefore \qquad V_{(3)}C = (V_{(1)} + V_{(2)}).(KC) + V_{(2)}C$$

$$\therefore \qquad V_{(3)} = (V_{(1)} + V_{(2)}).K + V_2$$

$$= KV_{(1)}+V_{(2)}(1+K)$$

$$= KV_{(1)}+V_{(1)}(1+K)^2$$

$$= V_{(1)}[K+(1+K)^2]$$

$\therefore \quad V_{(3)} = V_{(1)}[1+3K+K^2]$ ... (ii)

The voltage between the conductor and the earth (i.e. the tower) is as follows:

$$V = V_{(1)}+V_{(2)}+V_{(3)}$$
$$= V_{(1)}+V_{(1)}(1+K)+V_{(1)}[1 + 3K + K^2]$$
$$= V_{(1)}(3+4K +K^2)$$
$$V = V_{(1)}(1+ K)(3+K) \quad \text{...(iii)}$$

From expressions (i) (ii) and (iii) we got,

$$\frac{V_{(1)}}{1} = \frac{V_{(2)}}{1+K} = \frac{V_{(3)}}{1+3K+K^2} = \frac{V}{(1+K)(3+K)} \quad \text{... (iv)}$$

$\therefore$ Voltage across the topmost unit, $V_{(1)} = \dfrac{V}{(1+K)(3+K)}$

Voltage across the second unit, $V_{(2)} = V_{(1)}(1+K)$

Voltage across the third unit, $V_{(3)} = V_{(1)}(1+3K+K^2)$

$\therefore$ percentage String efficiency $= \dfrac{\text{Voltage across the string}}{\text{n} \times \text{voltage across disc nearest to conductor}}$

$\therefore$ String efficiency $= \dfrac{V}{3xV_{(3)}}$

The following points should be noted from the preceding expression:

(a) The voltage distribution across different units is not consistent. It is greatest across the disc closest to the conductor and decreases as we move toward the cross-arm or tower.

(b) The voltage distribution across different discs depends on the value of K i.e. $K = \dfrac{C_{(1)}}{C}$. Lesser the value of K, the more uniform will be the voltage distribution over the string and string efficiency will be higher. It can be achieved by keeping the string away from the towers by using longer cross arms.

(c) As the number of discs in the string increases, so does the inequality in voltage distribution. As a result, shorter strings are more efficient than longer ones.

5.6 METHODS FOR IMPROVING STRING EFFICIENCY

The voltage distribution across an insulator string is nonuniform. Maximum voltage appears across the insulator closest to the line conductor and decreases as we move toward the cross-arm. If the insulation of the lowermost disc fails or a flashover occurs, the remaining insulator units will fail in sequence. To improve string efficiency, it is necessary to make the uniform potential across different units of string.

The following are the various methods used to improve string efficiency:

(a) Using long cross-arms

(b) Insulators grading

(c) Use of guard-ring

(a) **Using long cross-arms:** The value of string efficiency depends on the value of K because string efficiency = $\frac{(1+K)(3+K)}{3(1+3K+K^2)}$ and further the value of the K = $\frac{C_{(1)}}{C}$ i.e. the ratio of shunt capacitance to the mutual capacitance. The expression for string efficiency shows that smaller the value of K, greater is the string efficiency and more uniform potential distribution exists across the string. To decrease the value of K, the value of $C_{(1)}$ must be reduced, which can only be accomplished by increasing the distance between the metallic links of the string and the support. This can be accomplished by employing longer cross-arms. However, cost and support strength constraints prevent the use of much longer cross-arms. In practice, K = 0.1, which is the upper limit that this method can achieve.

(b) **Insulators grading:** This method involves selecting insulators of different sizes so that each one should have a different capacitance and placing them in the string in such a way that the top unit typically has the lowest capacitance and the bottom unit has the highest. This method more evenly distributes potential among the units in a string because the voltage is inversely proportional to the capacitance. The biggest problem with this method is that a lot of different-sized insulators are required for the majority of the strings. Due to economic constraints, this practice is not followed below 220 kV.

(c) **Use of guard ring:** In this case, a metallic guard ring is attached to the conductor electrically. This ring surrounds the lowermost insulator as depicted in figure (5.13). The capacitance between the line conductor and the metal fittings of the string is equipoised by introduction of the metallic guard ring. This increases capacitance for the lower unit more than the other units. Thus, it improves the uniformity of potential distribution across the different units of the string. Although it is impossible to obtain an equal voltage distribution using this method, however, significant improvements are made.

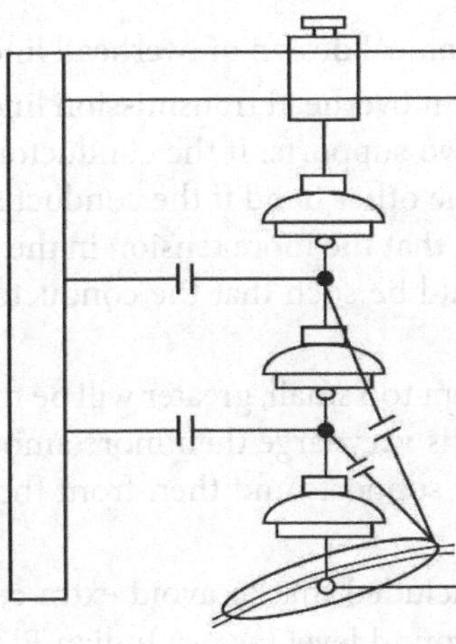

Fig. 5.13: Guard ring surround the lowermost insulator

5.7 SAG

It is very important to remember that conductors supported on towers must be under safe tension while erecting an overhead line. They should not be stretched too far between the supports, as this may cause them to reach an unsafe value and, in some cases, break due to high tension. So, to maintain safe tension in the conductors, they are never fully stretched but are allowed to have a dip/ sag. Sag is the difference in levels between the points of support and the lowest point on the conductor.

When the sag/dip is very small in comparison to the span length, the catenary is nearly identical to the parabola.

Figure (5.14) shows a conductor hung between two supports A & B. The supports are at the same height. This conductor forms a catenary and is not completely stretched. "O" is the conductor's lowest point, then by definition;

Sag or Dip = OD

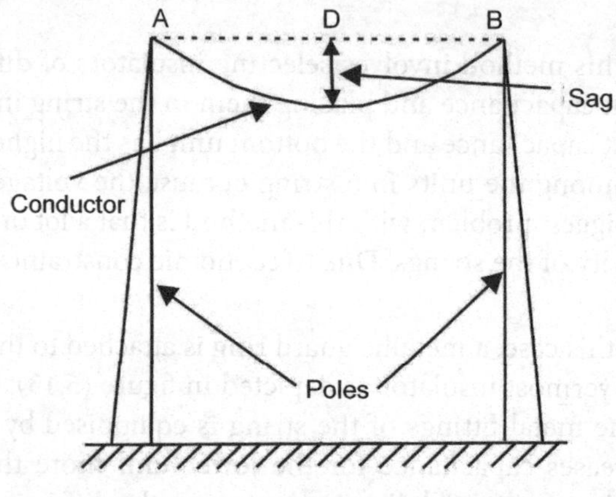

Fig. 5.14: Conductor hung between two supports A and B

5.7.1 Significance of Sag

Sag has the following effects on the mechanical design of overhead lines:

(a) **Tension in conductors:** The sag in an overhead transmission line can be adjusted by adjusting the stretch of the conductor between two supports. If the conductors are stretched too much, the sag will reduce i.e. it will be small on the other hand if the conduct stretch is lesser the sag in the line will be higher. Hence, it is observed that the more tension in the conductors, the lesser the sag and vice-versa. Therefore, line sag should be such that the conductor's tension should be within safe limits.

(b) **Height of tower:** When the sag is kept too small, greater will be the tension in overhead conductors and online supports. But if the sag is very large then more amount of conductor material will be needed & more weight on the line supports and then from the point of safety, higher poles are necessary.

From the above discussion, it is concluded that to avoid extra conductor material needed & pole height, the proper clearance above the ground level (as per Indian Electricity Rules), the sag should be kept as small as possible.

The factor which affects the sag in overhead lines are given under

(a) **Weight of conductor:** This has a direct impact on sag. The sag will increase as the conductor weight increases. The sag will also get worse at the location where the ice starts to accumulate on the conductor.

(b) Span Length: Sag is proportional to the square of the total span length. If all other conditions remain constant, such as conductor type, working tension, temperature, and so on, a section with a longer span will have much more sag.

(c) Tensile strength of conductor: The working tensile strength of the conductor has an inverse relationship with sag. Suppose all other factors, such as temperature and span length, remain constant. In that case, the safe or working tensile strength of the conductor is calculated by multiplying the ultimate stress by the cross-sectional area and dividing by the safety factor.

(d) Temperature: Each metal body expands with an increase in temperature, therefore as the temperature rises, the conductor's length also increases and the sag deepens.

5.7.2 Calculation of Sag

a When Supports are at the Same Level

Consider a conductor suspended in still air between supports A and B, with 'O' representing the lowest point, as shown in figure (5.15).

Let, L = span length in metres

W = weight per metre length of the conductor in Kg

T = tension in the conductor

Let us consider a point P having coordinates x and y from the origin 'O' i.e lowest point on the conductor. Assuming that there is very little curvature and curved length OP is equal to the horizontal projection, OP = x.

The OP portion of the conductor will be subjected to the following two major forces.

At a distance of x/2 metres from point O, the conductor's weight Wx is acting in the downward direction.

Tension T acting at point O at y metres from point P gives a horizontal moment.

Equating the moments about point P;

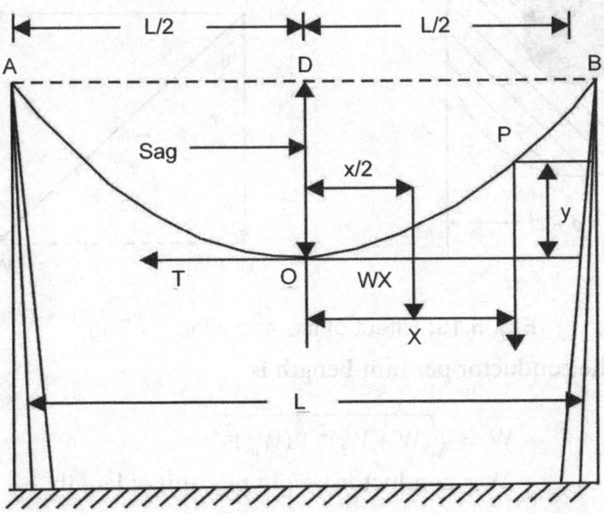

Fig. 5.15: Conductor suspended in still air between supports A and B

$$T.y = Wx.\frac{x}{2}$$

or $$y = \frac{Wx^2}{2T}$$

At point B, y = S (sag) and x = L/2

$$\text{Sag, } S = \frac{W.(L/2)^2}{2T}$$

or $$\text{Sag, } S = \frac{WL^2}{8T}$$

b Effect of Ice and Wind

At normal temperatures with still air, sag is due to the weight of the conductor. But at some mountainous places such as Jammu and Kashmir and Himachal Pradesh, a conductor may have a coating of ice and consecutively be subjected to the wind pressure. The weight of ice (W_i) will act vertically downward i.e. in a similar direction in which the weight of the conductor acts, however the wind load (W_w) will act horizontally i.e. at the right angle to the projected surface of the conductor. Hence, the total amount of force on the conductor will be the vector sum of horizontal & vertical forces as shown in figure (5.16).

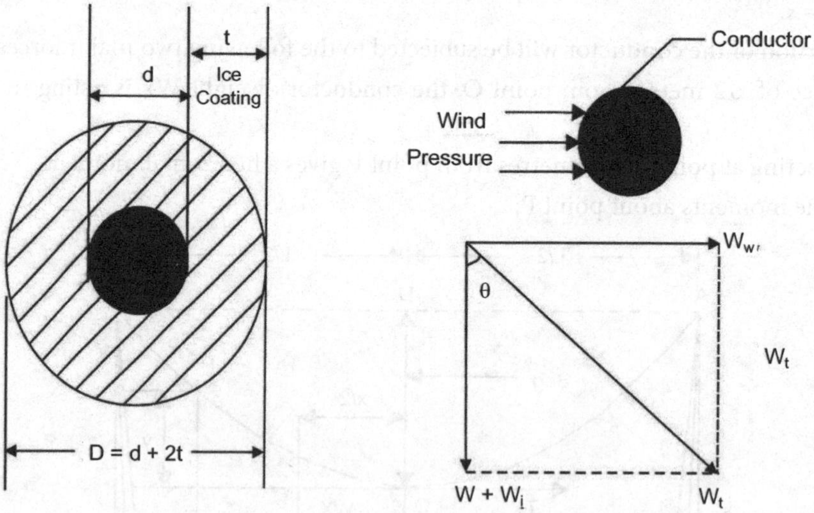

Fig. 5.16: Effect of ice and wind on Sag

The total weight of the conductor per unit Length is

$$W_t = \sqrt{(W+W_i)^2 + (W_w)^2}$$

W = conductor weight per unit of length

= (conductor material density) × (volume per unit length)

W_i = ice weight per unit length

= (density of ice) × (ice volume per unit length)

= (density of ice) × $[\frac{\Pi}{4}\{(d + 2t)^2 - d^2\} \times 1]$

(density of ice) × {π t (d+t)}

W_w = wind force per unit length

= (wind pressure per unit area) × (projected area per unit length)

= (wind pressure) × (d + 2t) × 1

When the conductor is subjected to ice and wind loads, the following issues should be considered:

(a) The conductor will position itself in the plane at an angle θ to the vertical.

$$\tan\theta = \frac{W_w}{W + W_i}$$

(b) The sag in the conductor is given by,

$$S = \frac{W_t . L^2}{8.T}$$

Here, "S" stands for the slant sag in the direction making an angle θ with the vertical. The formula above is used to determine slant sag when it is not specified in the given problem..

(c) Vertical sag is given by; $S_v = S . \cos\theta = S . \frac{W + W_i}{W_t}$

5.8 INDIAN ELECTRICITY RULES AS AMENDED TILL 1976

The Government of India has established several regulations to carry out all electrical work methodically and securely. These regulations are known as the 1956 Indian Electricity Rules. We should first analyze the need for the creation of these rules and regulations before we truly examine the Indian Electricity Rules (I.E. Rules) and other safety measures.

The Institution of Electrical Engineers has created rules and regulations to

- Safeguard consumers of electrical energy (users) from a shock.
- Minimize the risk of fire.
- To ensure as much as satisfactory operation of equipment and apparatus used.

5.9 INDIAN ELECTRICITY RULES PERTAINING TO CLEARANCE

The clearance of overhead lines from the ground and the building is explicitly stated in Indian Electricity Rules, 1956, as revised up till 1976, and is included in Rules Nos. 76, 77, 78, 79, and 80.

5.9.1 Rule No. 76 : Clearances Above the Ground of the Lowest Conductor

(a) Any conductor in an overhead line, including service lines, may not be installed across a street at a height lower than

(i) For medium to low voltage lines - 19 ft. (5.791 m)

(ii) For high voltage lines - 20 ft. (6.096 m)

(b) None of the conductors in the overhead line, including the service lines, shall be installed along any street or portion thereof at a height less than

(i) For medium and low voltage lines - 18 ft. (5.486 m)

(ii) For high voltage lines - 19 ft. (5.791 m)

(c) No overhead conductor, including service lines, shall be installed anywhere other than along or across any street, or at a height less than

(i) For low, medium & high voltage lines up to & including till 11kV, when bare - 15 ft. (4.572 m).

(ii) For low, medium & high voltage lines up to & including 11kV when insulated - 13 ft. (3.963 m)

(iii) For high voltage lines higher than 11kV volts - 17 ft. (5.182 m)

(d) Extra high voltage lines should have clearance above the ground of at least 17 feet (5.182 meters) and an additional 1 foot (0.3048 meters) for every 33,000 volts. As long as there is a minimum clearance of 20 feet along or across any street (6.096 m).

5.9.2 Rule No. 77: Clearance between the Conductors and the Trolley Wires

Any conductor crossing a tramway or trolley bus route that uses trolley wires shall have the following clearances above any trolley wire.

(i) Medium and low voltage lines: 4 ft (1.219 m), provided that there is a minimum space of 2 ft between the trolley wire and the insulated conductor that is hanging from bare wire (0.6096 m).

(ii) High voltage lines up to & including 11kV ...6 ft. (1.829 m)

(iii) High voltage lines above 11,000 volts...8 ft. (2.439 m)

(iv) Extra-high voltage lines.....10 ft. (3.048 m)

5.9.3 Rule No. 78: Clearances from the Buildings for the Medium and Low Voltage Lines and the Service Lines

(a) Depending on the maximum sag, the following minimum clearances from any accessible point must be kept where the medium or low voltage overhead line crosses over, is near to, or terminates on the building:

(i) For open balcony, flat/verandah roof & lean to roof -

1. Where the line cross over a building, the overhead clearance from the highest point shall be of 8 feet (2.439 m)
2. The horizontal clearance from the closest point when the line runs adjacent to a building must be 4 feet. (1.219 m)

(ii) For pitched roof -

1. Where a line runs over the building the overhead clearance immediately below the lines shall be 8 feet (2.439 m)
2. The horizontal clearance from the closest point when the line runs adjacent to a building must be 4 feet. (1.219 m)

(b) Any specific conductor positioned in such a way as to have a clearance smaller than that specified in sub-rule (1) should be properly insulated and shall be connected to the bare earthed bearer wire with a breaking strength of at least 7.00 lbs (317.51 Kg) at appropriate intervals using metal clips.

(c) The horizontal distance should be calculated from the point where the line is most inclined from the vertical due to wind pressure.

5.9.4 Rule No. 79: Clearance for the Buildings for High and Extra High Voltage Lines

(a) Considering the maximum sag, the vertical clearance immediately over the tallest section of the building beneath such lines should be at least:
   (i) In case of a high voltage line up to & including 33kV. .12 ft. (3.658 m)
   (ii) In case of an extra-high voltage line. 12 ft. (3.658 m) plus 1 foot (0.3048 m) for every extra 33, 000 volts or any part there of.

(b) The horizontal distance between the nearest conductor and any part of the building depending upon the maximum deflection because of the wind pressure should not be less than:
   (i) In case of high voltage lines up to & including 11kV...4 ft. (1.219 m)
   (ii) In case of high voltage line above 11kV & up to & including 33kV...6 ft. (1.829 m)
   (iii) In case of extra-high voltage lines: 6 ft. (1.829 m) plus 1 foot (0.3048 m) with each addition of 33kV, or the part thereof.

5.9.5 Rule No. 80: Conductors at Different Voltages on the Same Supports

In this case, the same supports are used to install conductors as a component of the system operating at different voltages. Adequate precautions should be taken to prevent the risk that lines and others equipment working at low voltages might not be exposed to leakage or contact with a higher voltage system that could charge the lower voltage system over its usual working voltage.

5.10 UNDERGROUND CABLES

Even though, the underground system is more costly than the overhead method for distributing electricity, large cities are increasingly using it due to the following benefits:

(a) It secures uninterrupted continuity of the supply
(b) Less maintenance.
(c) Longer life span.
(d) Good appearance.
(e) It eliminates hazards of electrocution because of the breakage in overhead conductors.

An underground electrical distribution system uses cables with one or more than one conductor cores covered with suitable insulating material & surrounded by a protective cover. Underground cable is used for transmission and distribution in cities when using an overhead system is not possible or unsafe. The underground cables must meet the following requirements:

(a) High-conductivity tinned copper or aluminum must be utilized as the conductor material in cables. Stranded conductors are used to make the cables more flexible.

(b) The size of the conductor should be such that it can carry the required load without overheating and should not cause a voltage drop that is more than the permitted limits.

(c) The cable should have adequate insulation thickness to offer a high degree of safety and dependability at the specified voltage.

(d) The materials used to make the cables should be chemically and physically stable.

(e) Every cable must be mechanically shielded to survive the rough handling during installation.

5.11 CLASSIFICATION OF CABLES

Underground cables are typically categorized according to the voltage for which they are designed. Depending on the voltage, these are categorized as:

(a) L.T. (Low-tension) cables	-	used up to 1kV
(b) H.T. (High-tension) cables	-	used up to 11kV
(c) S.T. (Super-tension) cables	-	from 22kV to 33 kV
(d) E.H.T (Extra-high tension) cables	-	from 33 kV to 66 kV
(e) Extra super voltage cables	-	beyond 132 kV

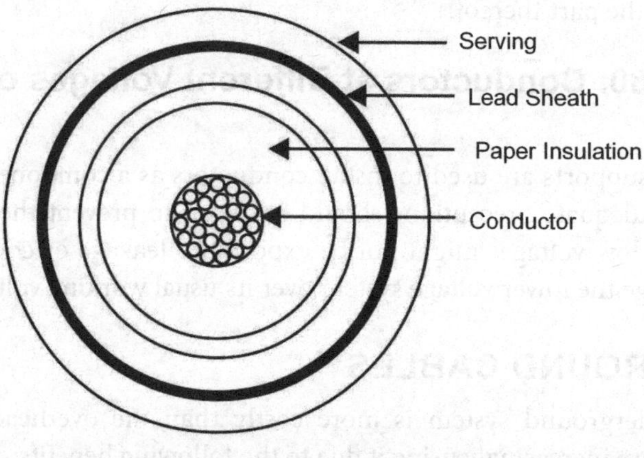

Fig. 5.17: High tension cable

5.11.1 Low-tension (L.T.) Cables

Low tension cables are used up to 1000 V. Typically, these cables are used for distribution at roughly 400 V. Depending on the service, these cables may contain one or multiple cores. Three single-core cables or three-core cables can be used for a three-phase three-wire supply.

Low-tension cables have no particular type of construction since the stresses occurring in the cable at low voltages are minor and thermal conductivity is not of much relevance. In this type of cables, conductors are insulated with rubber or PVC (polyvinyl chloride) and have a lead sheath cover over them to keep moisture out of the cable's core. A composited fibrous substance protects the lead sheath. To minimise excessive loss within the armour, single-core cables are often not armoured.

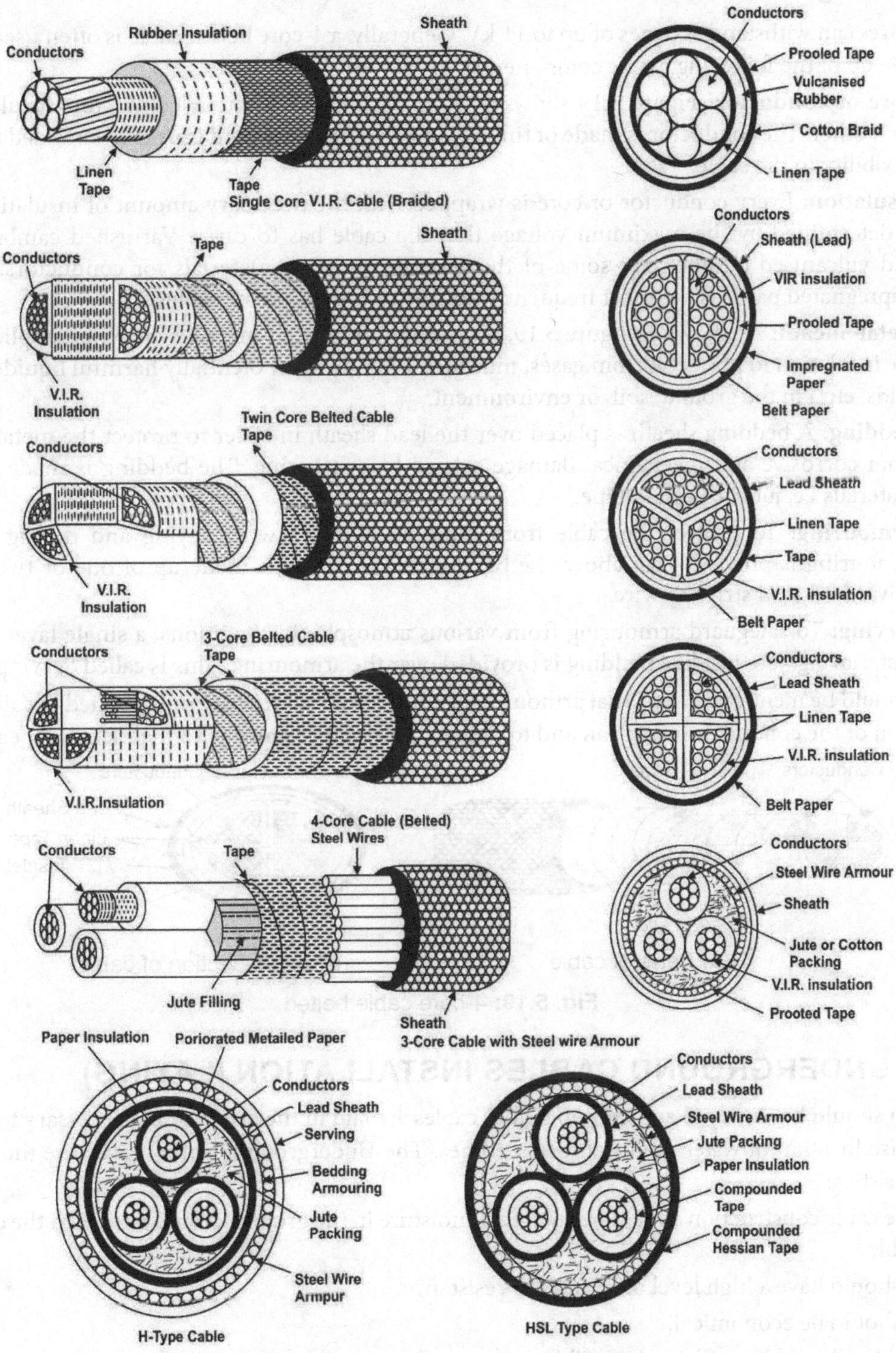

Fig. 5.18: Classification of cables

5.11.2 High Tension (H.T.) Cables

These wires can withstand voltages of up to 11 kV. Generally, a 4-core belted cable is often used at 11 kV. It is made up of the following major components:

(a) **Core or conductor:** Figure 5.19 shows a 4-core cable having four conductors insulated from each other. The conductor is made of tinned copper/aluminium and is usually stranded to provide flexibility to the cable.

(b) **Insulation:** Every conductor or core is wrapped with the necessary amount of insulation, which is determined by the maximum voltage that the cable has to carry. Varnished cambric, paper, and vulcanised bitumen are some of the several insulating materials for conductors, although impregnated paper is the most frequently utilised as insulation for cables.

(c) **Metal Sheath:** As shown in figure 5.19, an aluminium or lead metallic sheath is supplied around the insulation to protect it from gases, moisture, or any other potentially harmful liquids (alkalies, acids, etc.) in the ground, soil, or environment.

(d) **Bedding:** A bedding sheath is placed over the lead sheath in order to protect the metallic sheath from corrosive and mechanical damage caused by armouring. The bedding is made of fibrous materials i.e. jute or hessian tape.

(e) **Armouring:** To protect the cable from mechanical stress when laying and during handling, armouring is provided just above the bedding. Typically, it is made up of one or two layers of galvanised steel strips or wire.

(f) **Serving:** To safeguard armouring from various atmospheric conditions, a single layer of fibrous material e.g. jute just like bedding is provided over the armouring. This is called Serving.

It should be mentioned here, that armouring, bedding, and serving are only applied to cables for the protection of the conductor insulation and to prevent mechanical damage to the metallic sheath.

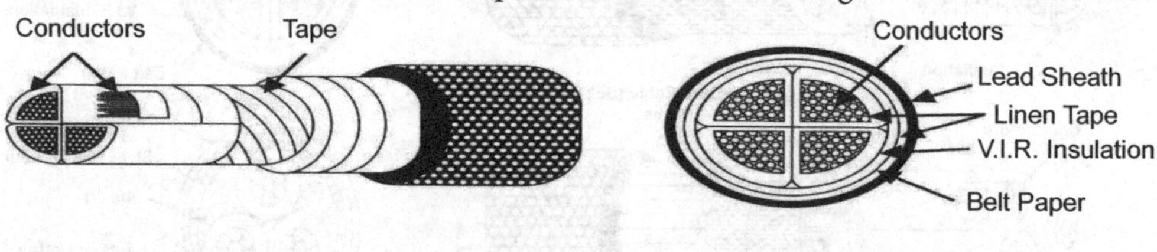

(a) Parts of cable

(b) Cross section of cable

Fig. 5.19: 4-core cable belted

5.12 UNDERGROUND CABLES INSTALLATION (LAYING)

The path should be surveyed and chosen before cables are laid in the ground. It is necessary to ascertain the precise location of water mains and sewer lines. The Underground cables must have the following characteristics:

(a) The cable construction should be such that moisture in the ground should not reach the core of the cable.

(b) It should have a high level of insulation resistance.

(c) It should be economical.

(d) Cables should be sufficiently flexible.

(e) Cables should not be very bulky.

(f) It must be able to handle the heat produced due to the flow of load current.

(g) Armoured cables are used to avoid any damage to the cables during laying and operation.

The methods of laying underground cables are listed below:

(a) Laying the cables directly in the ground (Direct laying).

(b) Laying the cables in ducts (Draw-in-system).

(c) Solid system

5.12.1 Laying the Cables Directly in the Ground (Direct Laying)

The cables with steel tape/wire armoring are placed directly into the ground as shown in figure 5.20. Armoring provides excellent protection from mechanical injuries. This method is simple, inexpensive, and widely used. In this method, a trench about 1.5 m deep and 45 cm wide is dug along the route of the cable. This trench is covered by a layer of fine sand (approximately 10 cm thick), and the cable is laid over the sand bed.

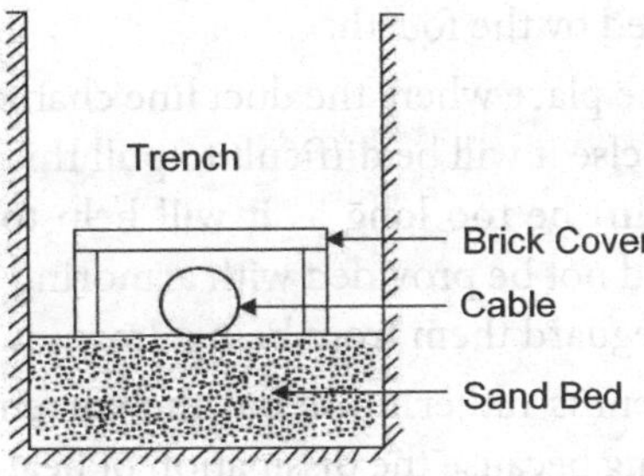

Fig. 5.20: Direct laying of cables in the ground

Sand serves the purpose of preventing moisture from penetrating in the cable core from the ground and protecting the cable from deterioration. After the cable has been installed in the trench, the second layer of sand, about 10 cm thick, is placed over it to ensure that no sharp stone comes into direct contact with the cable. A single layer of bricks or tiles is then added to protect the cable from mechanical damage. Concrete or wooden slabs can also be used to protect the cable as well. To reduce the effect of mutual heating and to ensure that a fault developing in one cable doesn't affect the neighbouring cable, a horizontal/vertical inter-axial distance of at least 30 cm is made when more than one cable is to be put in the same trench. To provide safety against corrosion and electrolysis, cables having a serving of bituminized paper and hessian tape are used.

5.12.2 Laying the Cables in Ducts (Draw-in-System)

This draw-in technology is usually employed in crowded areas where excavation is expensive and cumbersome. A trench is dug to lay a line of conduits, ducts, or tubes. Concrete or glazed stoneware cement is used to make the conduits/ducts. Cables are fixed into place from man-holes or brick pits spaced at regular intervals after conduits or ducts have been installed.

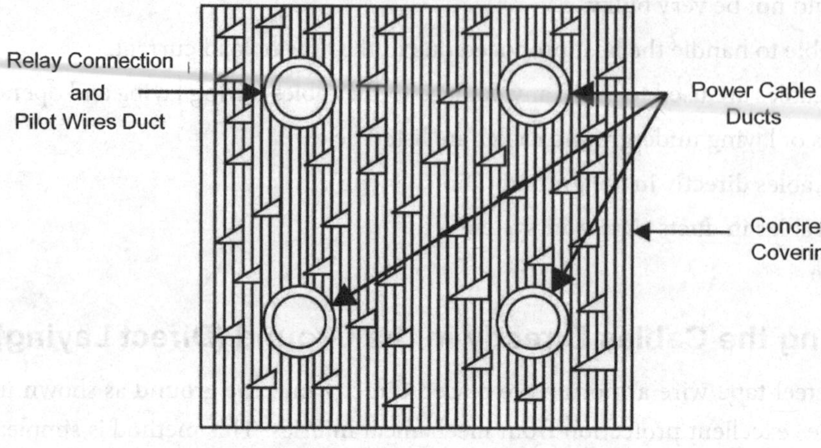

Fig. 5.21: 4-way underground duct line system

A section of a 4-way underground duct line system is shown in Figure (5.21).

Transmission or distribution cables are carried by three of these ducts, while a relay protection connection and pilot wires are carried by the fourth.

It is important to take care at the place where the duct line changes depths, direction, dips & offsets be made with a very long radius, or else it will be difficult to pull this large cable between the manholes. Distance between manholes shouldn't be too long as it will help to pull the cables easily. The cables intended for drawing into ducts need not be provided with armoring but these should be secured with a serving of hessian tape & jute to safeguard them from being drawn inside.

The initial amount of the system is rather more but the current carrying capacity of the cable is definitely decreased by close grouping because the dissipation of heat is restricted. Anyhow, if anywhere fault occurs, it can be repaired very easily.

5.12.3 Solid Laying System

In this method, underground cables are placed in open pipes or throughs excavated along the cable route. The throughings are generally made of treated wood, cast iron, stoneware, asphalt, or ceramic and filled with a bituminous or asphaltic after laying the cables. Un armored cables are used in this method as the cable is protected from breakdown due to corrosion and electrolysis. The disadvantages are that this method of cable lying is costlier than the direct laying method. The requirement for skilled labour and favourable weather is another drawback of this method. The current caring capacity of the cable is reduced due to poor heat dissipation capability. Due to these drawbacks, underground cable installation using this method is no longer often employed.

5.13 OVERHEAD VERSUS UNDERGROUND SYSTEM

Electrical power can be transmitted/distributed via the following methods:

(a) Over-head system
(b) Under-ground system

5.13.1 Over-head System

In this design, the line support (poles or towers) are placed at suitable distances and overhead bare conductors made of either copper or aluminum are mounted on the cross arms of the line supports with insulators. one end of the insulator is connected to the cross-arm and the conductor is supported on the other end.

5.13.2 Underground System

In this method, power cables laid in the pipelines, ducts, and trenches that are located below the earth's surface are used to transmit or distribute electrical power. As compared to an overhead system this method is comparatively more expensive, on the other hand, it is also significantly safer and more dependable. This system is preferred in densely populated regions, at road and bridge intersections, as well as in significant communities. The following is a comparison of the two systems.

5.14 COMPARISON BETWEEN THE OVERHEAD AND THE UNDERGROUND SYSTEM

The table gives the comparison between the overhead system and underground system.

Table 5.1: Comparison between the Overhead and the Underground System

Sr. No.	Overhead System	Underground System
1.	Less safe as compared to the underground system for operational staff and public	Safer
2.	Economical system	Capital cost is high
3.	More prone to faults	Less prone to faults
4.	Since all the installation is visible so not give a good appearance.	Since all the installation is underground hence gives a Good appearance.
5.	More flexible system	Less flexible system
6.	Fault detection and repairs can be done easily	Difficult to detect and repair faults
7.	Can be used at very high voltage levels	Difficult to use beyond 66kV due to insulation problems
8.	The effect of weather conditions such as lightning is high.	Less affected by weather conditions
9.	Interference with communication lines is high.	The underground system has no interference with communication lines
10.	Insulation cost is less	Insulation cost is higher
11.	Used for long-distance transmission of electrical power,	Mostly used for the distribution of electrical power in congested areas

5.15 INSULATION RESISTANCE

Insulation Resistance of the cable is the term used to describe the resistance offered by the cable insulation to leakage current. Through the insulation, the leakage current travels in a radial pattern. The cable insulation resistance should be quite high for the successful functioning of the system.

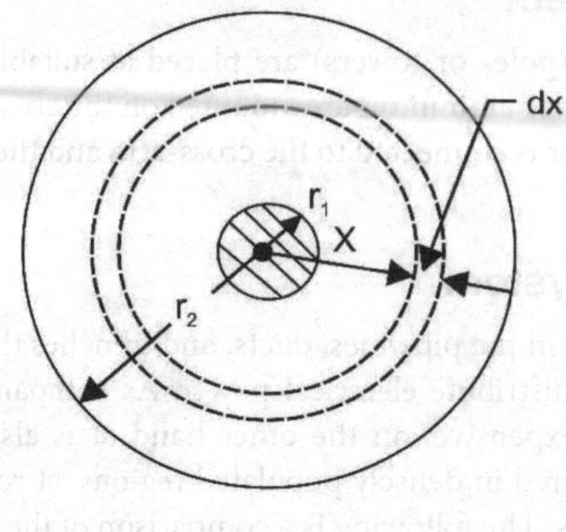

Fig. 5.22: Insulation resistance calculation of single -core cable

Insulation resistance calculation of single -core cable :

Assume that r_1 represents the diameter of the conductor in a single-core cable and r_2 represents the internal diameter of the sheath as shown in figure (5.22).

Assume that the insulation resistivity is ρ and the length of the cable is *l*. Consider a very small thickness of insulation dx at a distance x from the centre. The length of the path for the flow of leakage current leakage current is 'dx' and is the cross-sectional area offered to this flow is ($2\pi xl$).

Thus, insulation resistance of the small thickness of cable insulation $= \rho.\dfrac{dx}{2.\pi.x.l}$

Therefore,

$$\text{The resistance of the cable (R)} = \int_{r_1}^{r_2} \rho \frac{dx}{2\pi xl} = \frac{\rho}{2\pi l}\int_{r_1}^{r_2}\frac{dx}{x}$$

or $$R = \frac{\rho}{2.\pi.l}.\log e^{(r_2/r_1)}$$

The above equation shows that the insulation resistance of single-core cables is inversely proportional to its length. The insulating resistance decreases as cable length increases and vice versa.

UNIT SUMMARY

The key transmission and distribution line components are thoroughly covered in this unit. An in-depth discussion is given regarding the main elements of an overhead transmission line, such as insulators and conductor material line supports (poles and towers). The characteristics of the various materials used to produce these components and how they ought to be correctly assembled are given to the readers. Overhead line insulators are critical components for the safe and efficient operation of transmission and distribution lines. The major causes of the failure of insulators, the concept of string efficiency, and methods of improving string efficiency are presented to the readers. The underground system using cables is discussed. The classification, construction, and methods of laying cables are presented and a comparison with the overhead system is presented.

UNIT Highlights

1. Overhead transmission lines: These are lines that are meant for transmitting bulk electrical power from generating stations to load centres.
2. Various overhead transmission lines components: The major overhead transmission line components are:

   (a) Line supports (b) Conductors
   (c) Insulators (d) Cross Arms
   (e) Phase plates (f) Lightning arrestors
   (g) Barbed wire (h) Bird guards
   (i) Earth wire (j) Fuses and switches
   (k) Miscellaneous item
3. Line supports: These are also known as poles and towers. Poles are used for L. T. lines and towers are used for H. T. lines. These can be of the following types:
   (a) Wooden poles: These are used in rural areas for LT. lines. These are preferred due to their low cost and their natural insulating properties.
   (b) Steel poles: These are used in urban areas for the distribution of electrical power. These are of different shapes : (l) Tubular (ii) Rail Poles (iii) Steel joists.
   (c) R.C.C. poles: These are also used in urban areas. These have the advantage of longer shelf life without getting affected by insects & various atmospheric effects. They have a good appearance and less maintenance.
   (d) Steel towers: These are used to transmit bulk power at higher voltages. They have much more mechanical strength, long shelf life & can bear harsh atmospheric conditions.
4. Conductor: The most frequently used material for conductors in overhead lines are: (a) Copper(Cu) (b) Aluminium(Al) (c) Aluminium conductor steel reinforced(ACSR)
   (a) Copper(Cu): This is the ideal conductor material for power transmission & power distribution. Due to its high cost & non-available in abundance, it has limited applications.
   (b) Aluminium: This conductor material is next to copper. It is cheaper than copper and is used where straight lines are required, due to its non-flexibility.
   (c) A.C.S.R.: These are used nowadays, These conductors have a central core of galvanised steel whereas aluminium conductors form the outer layer. They are mechanically strong and tighter in weight. Therefore these can be used for longer spans.
5. Insulators: Generally Porcelain is used in the manufacturing of insulators, Insulators help in insulation the line conductors from supports.

   These are of the following types:

   (a) Pin type Insulator
   (b) Suspension type
   (c) Strain insulator
   (d) Shackle insulator
   (e) Egg or stay insulation

6. Potential Power Distribution over the string of insulators: When transmission of power is done at 33 kV or above, a string of suspension-type insulators are used. In the string, each insulator is placed in between two metal links and forms a capacitor, so that the potential is distributed along these insulators. The potential across the disc which is nearest to the transmission line conductor will be highest and will be lowering as we proceed towards the cross-arm.
7. Methods of enhancing string efficiency: The string efficiency can be enhanced by various methods:
   (a) By putting in use long cross-arms (b) By grading insulators (c) By use of guard-ring
8. Sag: The difference in the level between the point of support and the conductor's lowest point is called the sag. Sag has few effects on the design of overhead lines. It tells about the tension in the conductor and the height of the tower.
9. The factors which affect the sag are:
   (a) Weight of the conductor
   (b) Length of the span.
   (c) Working tensile strength.
   (d) Temperature
10. Calculations for sag formula:

$$\text{Sag, S} = \frac{WL^2}{8T}$$

If the effect of ice and wind pressure is considered:

Then, the total weight, $W_t = \sqrt{(W+W_i)^2 + (W_w)^2}$

The vertical sag is $S_v = S \cdot \cos\phi = S \cdot \dfrac{W+W_i}{W_t}$

11. Underground cables: These are the cables, which consist of either one or more than one conductors which are covered in the insulating material surrounded by a protective cover and are placed under the ground. These underground cables are utilized in distribution of the electrical power.
12. Classification of the cables: These are classified depending upon the voltage for which they are manufactured:
    LT (Low-Tension) cables.
    HT (High-Tension) cables.
    ST (Super-Tension) cables.
    EHT (Extra-High-Tension) cables.
    Extra-power voltage cables.
13. Construction of H.T. cables: The main components are:
    (a) Core or conductor (b) Insulation
    (c) Metallic sheath (d) Bedding
    (e) Armouring (f) Serving
14. Laying of underground cable: The various methods are:
    (a) Direct-laying

(b) Draw-in-system

(c) Solid-system

15. Insulation resistance of single core cable:

$$R = \frac{\rho}{2.\pi.l} .\log e^{(r_2/r_1)}$$

EXERCISES

1. What are the various materials that are commonly used for overhead line insulators?
2. What is a strain insulator and where is it used?
3. What is the operating voltage of glass insulators?
4. What is the need for stranding the conductors?
5. Explain why pin type insulators are not used in EHV lines?
6. What do you know about sag in the overhead lines? Explain.
7. What is meant by «insulator string» ?
8. What do you mean by ‹line supports›? Name the different types of line supports.
9. Why have Indian Electricity Rules been framed?
10. List the properties of overhead line supports.
11. Name the different types of lire supports used for overhead lines. Discuss in detail, lattice steel tower in detail with a neat sketch.
12. Summerise the various types of insulators employed in the transmission lines & their applications.
13. Explain strain and shackle insulators.
14. Mention appropriate locations where you would use the following insulators type:
    - Pin
    - Suspension
    - Strain
    - Shackle
    - Egg
15. Enumerate the various components in overhead transmission lines.
16. Explain the process of electrical breakdown that can occur in the insulator?
17. Define & describe string efficiency. Can the value of string efficiency be 100%?
18. Enumerate the different methods for enhancing string efficiency. Explain.
19. List the merits and demerits of ACSR conductors over copper conductors for use in overhead transmission lines.
20. Explain the term 'Sag' in overhead transmission lines? For a transmission line having a very small or very large sag, discuss its advantages.
21. Describe the merits & demerits of Pin and Suspension type insulators.
22. Derive an expression for the sag in the overhead line, given, supports are kept at equal levels.
23. Compare overhead and underground distribution systems.

24. When and where the underground distribution system is beneficial.
25. With a neat sketch/ diagram explain the basic construction of an underground cable.
26. Classify the underground cables according to insulation used, voltage rating and a number of cores.
27. For the single core metal sheathed cable, derive an expression for the insulation resistance.
28. What are the requirements of the underground cables?
29. Compare various merits & demerits for the direct draw in & solid systems of laying underground cables.
30. Label the parts of the high voltage single-core cable with the help of a neat sketch.
31. Enumerate and explain different methods for laying the underground cables.
32. Write the merits & demerits of each method of cable laying?
33. Draw a neat cross-sectional diagram of the following cable:
    - 3-core belted
    - High-tension
    - Super-tension

Multiple Choice Questions

1. Pin-type insulators can be utilized for supporting transmission conductors up to
   (a) 6600 volts (b) 11000 volts
   (c) 33000 volts (d) 66000 volts
2. The depth of a pole supporting overhead lines planted in the ground should be
   (a) 1/2 of pole length (b) 1/4 of pole length
   (c) 1/6 of pole length (d) 1/8 of pole length
3. As per Indian Electricity Rules, the voltage should be at the consumer›s end maintained within
   (a) $\pm$ 3% (b) $\pm$ 5%
   (c) $\pm$ 6% (d) $\pm$ 1%
4. Power loss on high voltage lines due to corona is known as
   (a) dielectric loss (b) ionization energy loss
   (c) corona power loss (d) loss of electrostatic energy
5. At high voltage power transmission lines, the conductors are suspended across towers to
   (a) provide increased ground clearance
   (b) provide reduced ground clearance
   (c) take care of the the increase in length
   (d) decrease the wind & snow effect
6. Wooden poles are used as line supports for voltages up to
   (a) 11000 Volts (b) 22000 Volts
   (c) 66000 Volts (d) 400,000 Volts
7. Which of the following support in overhead transmission has the minimum life?
   (a) Wooden poles (b) Fabricated steel structure
   (c) R.C.C. poles (d) Steel poles

8. The conductors utilized in the high tension overhead line are
   (a) Stranded (b) Solid
   (c) both solid and stranded (d) neither stranded nor solid
9. In ACSR conductor, the steel core used is mostly of
   (a) alloy-steel (b) galvanized-steel
   (c) stainless-steel (d) high-speed steel
10. The sag for the transmission line conductor in the summers is
   (a) less than that in the winter (b) more than that in the winter
   (c) same as in the winter
11. Sag the in a power transmission line depends on
   (a) span length (b) conductor tension
   (c) conductor weight per unit length (d) all of the above
12. The spacing between the phase conductors is around ________in an extra high voltage (400kV) transmission line.
   (a) Eight meter (b) Eleven meter
   (c) Fourteen meters (d) Seventeen meters
13. In an 11 kV transmission line the top conductor is
   (a) R-phase (b) Y-phase
   (c) B-phase (d) Earth-conductor
14. Insulators used in EHT transmission lines are composed of
   (a) PVC (b) Porcelain
   (c) Glass (d) Steatite
15. For a string of suspension insulators the string efficiency depends on
   (a) insulators size (b) Number of discs in the string
   (c) tower size
16. The potential drop in a suspension insulator is ____________disc
   (a) larger across the lowest (b) larger across the topmost
   (c) distributed uniformly over
17. Improvement in String efficiency can be done by using
   (a) long cross-arms
   (b) guard ring
   (c) grading the insulators
   (d) long cross-arm, guard ring, and grading the insulators
18. The insulators used in guy cables are
   (a) egg or stay insulator (b) shackle insulator
   (c) pin type insulator (d) disc type insulator
19. Conduit pipe is generally employed for the protection of ________ cables.
   (a) Unsheathed (b) Armoured
   (c) PVC sheathed (d) unsheathed or armoured or PVC sheathed

20. The material commonly used for sheaths of underground cable is
    (a) Copper (b) Lead
    (c) Steel (d) Rubber
21. The bedding consists of ___________ on a cable
    (a) Jute strands
    (b) Hessian tape
    (c) paper tape compounded with a fibrous material
    (d) Jute strands, hessian and paper tape compounded with a fibrous material
22. Material used for armouring of an underground cable is/are
    (a) galvanized steel wire (b) steel tape
    (c) aluminum (d) either (a) or (b)
23. Against mechanical injury, ___________ protects the underground cables.
    (a) Armouring (b) Bedding
    (c) Sheath
24. In cables, _________ is the insulating material(s) normally required.
    (a) Rubber (b) Butter paper
    (c) Polyvinyl chloride(PVC) (d) Glass wool
25. In power cables conductor size depend on
    (a) operated voltage (b) power-factor(cos-ϕ)
    (c) carried current (d) both (a) and (c)
26. Multi-core cables normally require ___________ conductors.
    (a) oval-shaped (b) sector-shaped
    (c) square (d) either (a) or (b)

ANSWERS

1.	(c)	2.	(c)	3.	(c)	4.	(c)	5.	(a)	6.	(b)	7.	(a)	8.	(a)
9.	(b)	10.	(b)	11.	(d)	12.	(a)	13.	(d)	14.	(b)	15.	(b)	16.	(a)
17.	(d)	18.	(a)	19.	(b)	20.	(b)	21.	(d)	22.	(a)	23.	(a)	24.	(b)
25.	(c)	26.	(d)												

Fill in The Blanks

1. Tension in the overhead transmission line ___________, when there is increase in sag.
2. For a transmission line, ac resistance is _____ than dc resistance.
3. ________ is extensively used material for manufacturing overhead line insulators.
4. In a conductor, due to ________, ac resistance is _______ than dc resistance.
5. ________ types of insulator are used for a transmission line where the direction is changed.
6. If 0.915 gm/c.c is the ice density, the weight of 1 cubic metre of ice shall be _____.
7. For a transmission line, cross-sectional conductor area _______ with the increase in voltage.
8. ________ type insulators are used on extra high voltage.
9. For a 200 m span, the sag is 10 m of a power line. If 20% is increased in the height, its sag shall be

_______.

10. For 220 kV power transmission lines, _______ type of insulators are used.
11. Due to ________ capacitance p.d. is varied across the several discs of the suspension string.
12. If 100% is the efficiency of string, it is called ________ .
13. String efficiency is ______ while using a guard ring.
14. For 220 kV lines, we use _________ type of insulators.
15. If string efficiency is given by the relation V/n . Vn, then ‹n› is the ________.
16. For larger sag __________ towers are required.
17. __________ the string efficiency for long cross arms.
18. Wind pressure acts __________ to the weight of the conductor.
19. Cross-arms is to provide __________ to the insulator for poles or towers.
20. An ACSR conductor with specifications 48/7 contains ________ number of aluminium strands.
21. For an equivalent overhead transmission system, an underground system is ______ costly.
22. Belted cable are normally used up to ___________ kV
23. Overhead line system, can be used generally upto _________ .
24. Underground cable system, can not be used above __________ due to insulation.
25. The rated load of an underground cable is always _________ its natural load.
26. For an overhead transmission line, the economical load is _________ than the natural load.
27. The multicore cables for use upto 11000 V are of _________ type.

ANSWERS							
1.	decreases	2.	more	3.	porcelain	4.	more, skin effect
5.	strain	6.	915 kg	7.	decreases	8.	suspension
9.	the same	10.	suspension	11.	shunt	12.	potential across each disc
13.	increased	14.	suspension	15.	number of units in a string	16.	taller
17.	greater	18.	perpendicular	19.	support	20.	7
21.	more	22.	11	23.	400 kV	24.	66 kV
25.	higher than	26.	greater	27.	belted		

True or False

1. The line support cost reduces with the increase in voltage of the transmission line.
2. With the increase in voltage of transmission, longer cross arms and higher towers are used.
3. ACSR conductors being lighter in weight and having high tensile-strength produces longer spans with small sag.
4. Composite conductors are principally used for shorter spans, not exceeding 100 metres.
5. Gay wires are generally galvanised.

6. Support for conductors may have unequal heights in hilly areas.
7. Heavier the conductor, smaller will be the sag.
8. The square of length of span is directly proportional to sag.
9. Maximum sag occurs for transmission line conductors, when there is no wind pressure and having maximum temperature.
10. For voltage upto 33 kV pin insulators can be used for supporting transmission lines.
11. Suspension insulators are required on E.H.T. transmission lines.
12. String efficiency decreases by using graded insulators.
13. Due to smaller life and more maintenance, wooden poles are rarely used in overhead lines.
14. The value of $V_{(CD)}$(disruptive-critical-voltage) is considerably increased during bad atmospheric conditions such as fog, sleet, rain and snow storms.
15. In short transmission lines, series impedance is a lumped parameter and the shunt capacitance is totally neglected.
16. The charging current of a 400 kV transmission line is more than that of a 220 kV line of the same length.
17. For reducing the capacitance around the insulation, metallic sheath of lead(pb) or aluminum(Al) is provided in an underground cable.
18. The operating voltage for low tension cable is upto 400 V.
19. For voltage upto 6600V, electrostatic stresses developed in cable are very small.
20. The operating voltage for extra super tension power cables is beyond 66 kV.
21. The sheath loss in open circuited sheath is about 2% of the total loss.
22. Direct laying of underground cables is rarely used because of its high maintenance cost.
23. When a cable is to cross a road, it should be laid in conduits, ducts or tubes made up of iron, glazed stoneware, clay or cement concrete.
24. A single core cable, copper used, is tinned stranded.
25. Multicore cables are used upto 11 kV.

ANSWERS									
1.	**False**	2.	**True**	3.	**True**	4.	**False**	5.	**True**
6.	**True**	7.	**False**	8.	**True**	9.	**True**	10.	**True**
11.	**True**	12.	**False**	13.	**True**	14.	**False**	15.	**True**
16.	**True**	17.	**False**	18.	**False**	19.	**True**	20.	**False**
21.	**True**	22.	**False**	23.	**True**	24.	**True**	25.	**True**

Short and Long Answer Type Questions

1. Explain the advantages and disadvantages for suspension type insulators over pin insulators.

Ans. The suspension insulators have following advantages:

(a) Suspension insulators are economical for transmission using voltage beyond 33kV voltage level.

(b) Voltage rating of the string can be increased by adding number more number of insulating discs.

(c) Whole string does not become useless when the insulator gets damaged, i.e. only damaged insulators can be replaced.

(d) By raising the line voltage increased demand can be met by adding one or two more discs.

(e) Suspension type insulators placed on steel towers as the conductors run below the earthed cross-arm which protect the line conductors partly from lightning.

Disadvantages:

(a) Due to the large amplitude of the swing, more spacing between conductors is required in case of suspension than with pin type insulators.

(b) It is costlier than a pin type insulator, so it is not used below 33 kV transmission voltage.

2. What is an ACSR conductor? For overhead lines, why are they preferred over copper(Cu) conductors?

Ans. ACSR conductors means Aluminium Conductor Steel Reinforced. Now-a-days in overhead transmission lines ACSR conductors are widely used due to their high mechanical strength and lightweight. They are also preferred because chances of sag are less. Therefore, ACSR conductors can be used for a long span. The centre core of ACSR conductor is a galvanised steel wire which provides mechanical strength to it. Around the steel core, there are aluminium strands which carry most of the current through it. Thus ACSR conductors are a unique combination of strength (steel wire) and good conductivity (Aluminium strands) and this is the main reason why ACSR conductors are fast replacing copper transmission and distribution lines.

3. What is meant by string efficiency consisting of a number of units of suspension type insulators? What causes the string efficiency to be less than 100 %? Describe any one method of improving the efficiency of string.

Ans. Across the disc in the string, it's the ratio of voltage across the entire string to the product of the number of discs and voltage across disc nearest to the conductor is known as String efficiency.

$$\text{String efficiency} = \frac{\text{Voltage across the string}}{n \times \text{voltage across disc nearest to conductor}}$$

It decides the potential distribution among strings. Steady the distributed voltage means greater will be the value of efficiency along the string. String efficiency is 100%, if voltage across each disc is uniform, but because of the presence of shunt capacitance it is not possible to have 100% efficiency. By using a larger cross-arm string efficiency can be improved.

4. Name at least two conductor materials required for over-head transmission lines and mention some mechanical and electrical properties.

Ans. The conductor materials most commonly used are copper(Cu) and aluminium(Al) in transmission lines. But due to the heavy cost of copper, the next conductor material widely used is ACSR conductor.

Copper: Due to higher tensile strength and electrical conductivity copper is an ideal conductor material for overhead transmission lines. The main characteristics of copper are:

(a) The conductivity of copper conductors is best as compared to other metals.

(b) Copper has high current density. It has two merits:

(i) small area of cross section is required

(ii) conductor to wind load area reduced.

(c) It has low specific resistance.

(d) Copper does not corrode in normal atmosphere.

(e) High scrap value and durable.

Aluminium: Aluminium conductors are much in use now-a-days due its lower cost than copper:

(a) It is light in weight.

(b) Conductivity of aluminium is lower than that of copper i.e. 60.6% that of copper for any power transmission thus a larger area of cross-section is required.

(c) For same ohmic resistance, aluminum is around 1.27 times of copper in case of conductor diameter.

(d) They are light in weight. Therefore, liable to greater swing, so larger cross arms are required.

(e) The melting point of aluminium is low.

(f) Jointing of aluminium is more difficult than copper.

5. Discuss the factors which effect the sag of an overhead line?

Ans. Please refer to article no. 5.7.1

6. Mention the various types of line supports and discuss the type of lines for which each of them is suitable.

Ans. Please refer to article no. 5.3

7. Explain the importance of sag and how you will calculate it?

Ans. Please refer to article no. 5.7 and 5.7.1

8. Draw a cross-section of a 4-core cable used in an underground distribution system. Discuss the function of different parts.

Ans. Figure (5.23) shows the cross-sectional view of 4 core cable, 3 cores are meant for phases and 4th core is for neutral. The size of the neutral wire core can be of the same size as that of the phases or it can be 1/2 of that of the phases. The main parts of a 4-core cable are cores or conductors, armauring, insulation, metallic sheath, bedding and serving. For more details about the function of components, please refer to article no. 5.11.2.

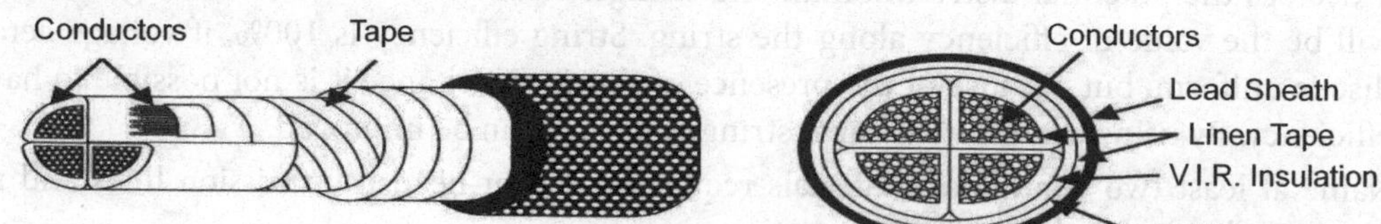

Fig. 5.23: 4-Core cable belted

9. In terms of sheath diameters, core diameter and specific resistance of dielectric for a single core cable, write an expression for the insulation resistance.

Ans. Cable having single core, the insulation resistance is

$$R = \frac{\rho}{2.\pi.l} . \log e^{(r_2/r1)}$$

For more detail please see article no.5.15

10. For laying of underground cables, compare the merits, demerits of direct, draw-in and solid systems.

Ans. Methods for cable laying, please see article no. 5.12

11. When, where and why underground distribution systems should be preferred?

Ans. The underground distribution system is preferred when:

(a) We want uninterrupted supply.

(b) We want elimination of breakage of overhead conductors due to electro-cution.

These under-ground distribution systems are used in urban areas. These underground distribution systems are preferred because they provide much safety and their appearance is also good.

12. Compare overhead and underground distribution systems.

Ans. Please refer to article no. 5.14

Numerical Problems

1. For one meter length of conductor, 0.7 Kg is the weight of a line conductor. Find the maximum sag in the transmission line, if 1400 Kg is the maximum allowable tension for a 200 meters span of overhead transmission line.
   (Ans.: 2.5m)
2. For a 132 kV transmission line, find the height for the conductor to be suspended above ground level. When weight of the conductor is 0.680 × 10^3 kg/km, span length(L) is 0.26 × 10^3 meter and ultimate-strength is 3100 kilogram. Given that the 10 meter is the ground clearance and take safety factor(f) equal to 2. (Ans.: 13.7 m)
3. Calculate the sag for wind a pressure of 0.3685 Kg/m for a 150 meter span between two supports of an overhead transmission line. The weight of the conductor is 0.62 Kg/m and permissible tension in the conductor is 586kg. (Ans.: 3.46 m)
4. Find the factor of safety for a 300 meters span of a transmission line. If total sag is 8.484 meters and breaking stress 5000 Kg/cm^2, X-sectional area is 1 cm^2, Weight of conductor 0.65 Kg/meter, wind pressure 1 Kg per meter, ice loading 0.35 Kg/meter. (Ans.: 3.03)
5. Explore the percentage voltage distribution across different units of the string by analyzing the self-capacitance of four insulators, which is equivalent to five times the pin-to-earth capacitance. Additionally, determine the string efficiency. (Ans. : 16%, 19.2%, 26.3%, 38.5%, 64.86%)
6. Consider a string of 3 insulator units in a transmission line with a mutual capacitance between the unit and the earthed framework that is ten times greater than the shunt capacitance. Calculate both the voltage distribution across the string and the string efficiency for this system operating at 33kV. (Ans.: V_1= 5.587 kV, V_2 = 6.146 kV, V_3 =7.319 kV, string efficiency = 86.77%)
7. Given a string of six insulator units in a transmission line operating at 33 kV, determine the voltage distribution from top to bottom across each disc of the string and calculate the string efficiency. Given the self-capacitance of each insulator is 10 times the capacitance among each earth and insulator pin.
   (Ans.: 9.904%, 10.894%, 12.974%, 16.351%, 21.346%, 28.512% String efficiency = 58.45%)
8. Calculate the inter-disc voltage in a suspension-type insulator configuration with four discs in a string, suspending from the cross arm a 3-ϕ overhead power transmission line. The voltage across the second unit is 13.2 kV, and the voltage across the third unit is 18 kV. Determine the voltage between the conductors in this setup. (Ans.: 70 kV)

9. Find the insulation resistance (R) for a 3 kilometer long single core cable having insulation thickness of 4 mm and radius of conductor is 6mm. The specific resistivity () of the insulating material is 5×10^{14} ohm-m. (Ans.: $135.5 \times 10^{16}\ \Omega$)
10. The insulation resistance of a single-core cable is measured to be 4×10^5 ohm-meter. The cable has a core diameter of 20 mm and an overall cable diameter, including the insulation is 50 mm. Determine the resistivity (ρ) of the insulating material used in the cable, considering it is 5 km long. (Ans: $=13.72 \times 10^9\ \Omega$ m)
11. The insulation resistance of a single-core cable of length 3m is measured to be 1820×10^6 ohm-meter. The cable has a core diameter of 15 mm and an overall cable diameter, including the insulation, is 50 mm. To determine the resistivity (ρ) of the insulating material used in the cable. (Ans.: $28.6 \times 10^{12}\ \Omega$m)
12. Given the insulation resistance of a single-core cable as 495 MΩ/Km and the resistivity of the insulation material (ρ) as 4.5×10^{14} ohm-cm, calculate the thickness (t) of the insulation. The diameter of the core is provided as 2.5 cm. (Ans.: 1.25 cm)

Solved Numerical

1. In an overhead 33 kV power transmission line, the self-capacitance between each insulator pin and the earth is 12%. To determine the distributed voltage across three insulators and the string efficiency for a three-unit string of insulators.

Ans. Given:

Number of string of insulator of units, n=3

Thus, the ratio of $\frac{\text{shunt - capacitance}}{\text{self - capacitance}}$ i.e. $K = \frac{C_1}{C} = 0.12$

String voltage(V) = $33/\sqrt{3}$ =19.0525kV

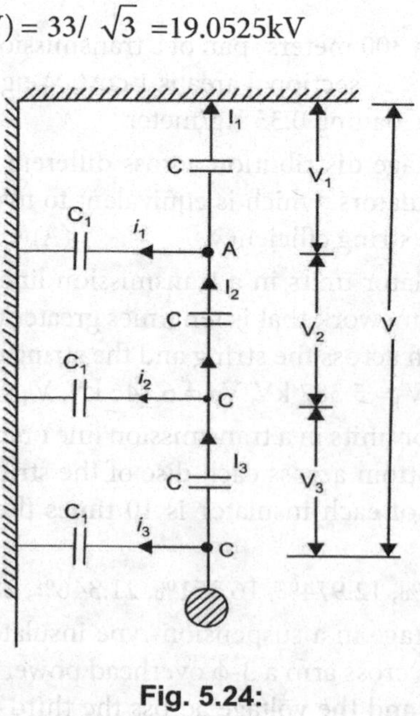

Fig. 5.24:

At node 'A' apply KCL,

$$I_{(2)} = i_{(1)} + I_{(1)}$$
$$V_{(2)}\omega C = V_{(1)}\omega KC + V_{(1)}\omega C$$
$$V_{(2)} = V_{(1)}(K+1)$$
$$= V_{(1)}(0.12+1)$$
$$V_{(2)} = 1.12V_{(1)}$$

At node 'B' apply KCL,

$$I_{(3)} = i_{(2)} + I_{(2)}$$
$$V_{(3)}C = (V_{(1)} + V_{(2)}).(KC) + V_{(2)}C$$
$$V_{(3)} = (V_1+V_2).K + V_2$$
$$= (V_{(1)} + 1.12V_{(1)}).(0.12) + 1.12V_{(1)}$$
$$\therefore \quad V_{(3)} = 1.3744V_{(1)}$$

(i) Across the insulator string, Voltage(V)=$V_{(1)}+V_{(2)}+V_{(3)}$

$$= V_{(1)}+1.12V_{(1)}+1.3744V_{(1)}$$
$$19.0525 = 3.4944V_{(1)}$$

Therefore, Across top-unit, Voltage($V_{(1)}$) = $\frac{19.0525}{3.4944}$

$$= \mathbf{5.4523\ kV}$$

Across second-unit, Voltage($V_{(2)}$) = 1.12 × 5.4523 = **6.107 kV**

Across bottom-unit, Voltage($V_{(3)}$) = 1.3744 × 5.4523 = **7.494kV**

(ii) percentage String-efficiency = $\frac{\text{Voltage across the string}}{\text{n} \times \text{voltage across disc nearest to conductor}} \times 100$

$$= \frac{19.0525}{3 \times 7.494} = \mathbf{84.75\%} \ \textbf{(Ans.)}$$

2. At the top unit of the insulator string, the potential is 9 kV, and at the middle unit, the 3-Φ line has a potential of 13.2 kV, of a three-disc insulator string. Determine the ratio of potential across each unit, self-capacitance between the pin and earth, as well as find the line voltage and string efficiency

Ans. Given,

No. of units = 3

Unit across near to tower, Voltage(V_1) = 9 kV

Across middle unit, Voltage(V_2) = 13.2 kV

Figure (5.26) shows 3 units consisting of the equivalent circuit of a string insulator.

(i) Let 'K' is the ratio across each unit of self-capacitance between earth and pin, Therefore,

Between pin and earth, capacitance (C_1) = KC

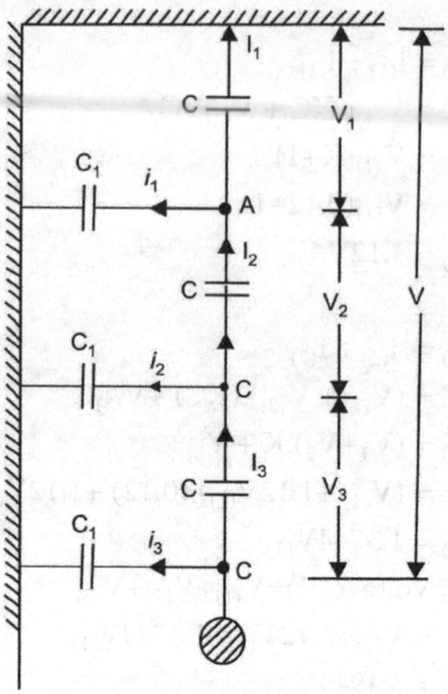

Fig. 5.25:

At node 'A' apply KCL,

$$I_{(2)} = i_{(1)} + I_{(1)}$$

$$V_{(2)}\omega C = V_{(1)}\,\omega KC + V_{(1)}\omega C$$

$$V_{(2)} = V_{(1)}\,(K + 1)$$

Therefore, $$K = \frac{V_2 - V_1}{V_1} = \frac{13.2 - 9}{9} = \mathbf{0.4667\ (Ans.)}$$

At node 'B' apply KCL,

$$I_{(3)} = i_{(2)} + I_{(2)}$$

$$V_{(3)}C = (V_{(1)} + V_{(2)})\,.\,(KC) + V_{(2)}C$$

$$V_{(3)} = (V_1 + V_2)\,.\,K + V_2$$

$$= (9 + 13.2)\,.\,0.4667 + 13.2$$

⊠ $$V_3 = 23.56\ \text{V}$$

Therefore, potential between earth and line, Voltage(V)= $V_{(1)} + V_{(2)} + V_{(3)}$

$$= 9 + 13.2 + 23.56$$

$$V = 45.76\ \text{kV}$$

Therefore, Line voltage = $\sqrt{3} \times 45.76 = 79.26$ kV

(ii) $$\text{String efficiency} = \frac{\text{Voltage across the string}}{\text{n} \times \text{voltage across disc nearest to conductor}}$$

$$= \frac{45.76}{3 \times 23.56} = \mathbf{64.74\%\ \ (Ans.)}$$

3. Calculate the maximum sag in the transmission line, given the weight of the line conductor as 612 kg for a 1000-meter length, and considering a maximum allowable tension of 1430 kg for a 250-meter span of the overhead transmission line.

Ans. Given,

Span having length (L) = 250 meter

Conductor having weight, (W)= 612 kilogram per 1000 meter

$$W = \frac{612}{1000} = 0.612 \text{ Kg/m}$$

Working tension, T = 1430 Kg

$$\text{Sag, S} = \frac{WL^2}{8T} = \frac{0.612 \times 250 \times 250}{8 \times 1430} = \mathbf{3.43 \text{ m (Ans.)}}$$

4. For a 132 kV transmission line, find the height for the conductor to be suspended above ground level. When conductor weight (W) is 612 Kg/km, span length (L) is 240 m and ultimate strength is 3000 kg. Given that the 10 metres is the ground clearance and safety factor (f) is 2.

Ans. Given,

Span having length (L) = 240 meters

$$\text{Conductor having weight (W)} = \frac{612}{1000} = 0.612 \text{ kilogram per meter}$$

$$\text{Working tension, T} = \frac{\text{Ultimate strength}}{\text{Factor of safety}}$$

$$= \frac{3000}{2} = 1500 \text{ Kg}$$

Therefore, $$\text{Sag , S} = \frac{WL^2}{8T} = \frac{0.612 \times 240 \times 240}{8 \times 1500} = 2.93 \text{ m}$$

Therefore, the height of supported conductor be

= 10 + 2.93 =**12.93m (Ans.)**

5. Determine the sag in the overhead transmission line for a 130-meter span between two level supports, given a wind pressure of 0.356 kilograms per meter length, a conductor weight of 0.63 kilograms per meter length, and a permissible tension of 580 kilograms.

Ans. Span having length (L) =130 meters

Conductor having weight (W) = 0.63 kilogram per meter

Wind pressure, W_w = 0.356 Kg/m

Working tension, T = 580 Kg

Total weight of conductor, $W_t = \sqrt{(W)^2 + (W_w)^2}$

Therefore, $W_t = \sqrt{(0.63)^2 + (0.356)^2}$

$W_t = 0.7236$ Kg/m

Therefore, Sag, $S = \dfrac{W_t L^2}{8T} = \dfrac{0.7236 \times 130 \times 130}{8 \times 580} =$ **2.63 m (Ans.)**

6. A 220 kV transmission line uses ACSR conductors whose data is given as under:

The diameter of Conductor, d = 20 mm.

Weight, W = 680 Kg/Km

Breaking stress, f_b = 5000 Kg/cm²

Factor of safety = 2

Length of span, L = 300 metres

When 7 meters is the ground clearance, calculate the sag and the height required for the conductor to be supported above ground level.

Ans. Conductor having area of cross-section,

$$a = \frac{\pi \times d^2}{4} = \frac{\pi \times 2^2}{4} = 3.14 \text{ cm}^2$$

Ultimate strength = Breaking stress × Cross section area

Ultimate strength = 5000 × 3.14 = 15700 Kg

Factor of safety, f = 2

Therefore, Allowable safe strength $= \dfrac{15700}{2} = 7850$ Kg

Weight of conductor, $W = \dfrac{680}{1000} = 0.68$ Kg/m

Length of span, L = 300 metres

$$\text{Sag, } S = \frac{WL^2}{8T} = \frac{0.68 \times 300 \times 300}{8 \times 7850} = 0.974 \text{ m}$$

Therefore, the height of the supported conductor be =7 + 0.974 = **7.974 m (Ans.)**

7. Find the allowable sag, if 4500 Kg/cm² tension is not exceeded to 1/3rd of ultimate strength, for the transmission line which is 150 metres single span in length. 1.5 Kg/m is the wind pressure and has an ice coating of 1 cm. 2.58 cm² is the cross-sectional area of the copper conductor. Assume that 0.915 gm/c.c. is the densities of ice and 8.89 gms/c.c. is the densities of copper. The supporting structure being of the same level.

Ans. Length of span, L = 150 metres

Conductor cross-sectional area (a) = 2.58cm²

Ultimate stress, f_b = 4500 Kg/cm²

Ultimate strength = 4500 × 2.58 = 11610 Kg

Working strength $= \dfrac{1}{3} \times$ Ultimate strength $= \dfrac{1}{3} \times 11610 = 3870$ Kg

Volume of conductor per metre= Area × Length

= 2:58 × 100 = 258 cm^3

Weight of conductor/m, W = Volume × Density

W = 258 × 8.89 = 2.294 Kg

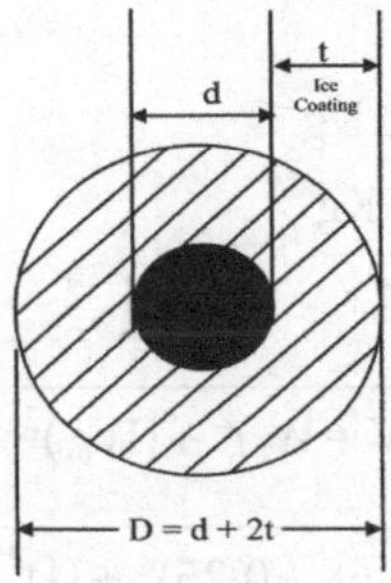

Fig. 5.26:

Therefore, Diameter of conductor, $d = \sqrt{\frac{4x\ a}{\pi}}$

$$d = \sqrt{\frac{4 \times 2.58}{3.14}} = 1.812\text{cm}$$

Thickness of ice coating = 1 cm

Therefore, outer diameter after ice coating,

Therefore, D = (d + 2t)

= (1.812 + 2 × 1) = 3.812 cm

Area of a cross-section of ice coating = [(d + 2t)^2 – d^2]

Therefore, Area of X-section of ice coating = [(3.812)^2 – (1.812)^2]

= 8.835 cm^2

Volume of ice coating/m = 8.835 × 100 = 883.5 cm^3

Weight of ice/m, W_i = volume of ice x density

$$= \frac{883.5 \times 0.915}{1000} = 0.808 \text{ Kg}$$

Total weight of conductor/meter length

$$W_t = \sqrt{(W + W_i)^2 + (W_w)^2}$$

$$W_t = \sqrt{(2.294 + 0.808)^2 + (1.5)^2}$$

$$W_t = \sqrt{(3.102)^2 + (1.5)^2} = 3.45 \text{ Kg}$$

Allowable Sag, $S = \frac{W_t L^2}{8T} = \frac{3.45 \times 150 \times 150}{8 \times 3870}$ = **2.50 m (Ans.)**

8. Calculate the factor of safety for a 200-meter span of a transmission line using the following information: total sag of 7.084 meters, breaking stress of 2500 Kg/cm², cross-sectional area of 1 cm², conductor weight of 0.68 Kg/meter, wind pressure of 1 Kg per meter, and ice loading of 0.25 Kg/meter.

Ans. Length of span L = 200m

Weight of conductor/m, W = 0.68 Kg

Weight of ice coating/m, W_i = 0.25Kg

Horizontal wind loading/m, W_w = 1 Kg

$$\text{Total weight/m, } W_t = \sqrt{(W+W_i)^2+(W_w)^2}$$

$$W_t = \sqrt{(0.68+0.25)^2+(1)^2}$$

$$W_t = \sqrt{(0.93)^2+(1)^2}$$

$$W_t = 1.37 \text{ Kg}$$

$$\text{Sag, } S = \frac{W_t L^2}{8T}$$

Therefore,

$$\text{Tension, } T = \frac{W_t L^2}{8S} = \frac{1.37\times200\times200}{8\times7.084} = 967 \text{ Kg}$$

$$\text{Allowable maximum stress} = \frac{\text{Allowable max. tension}}{\text{X – section area of conductor}}$$

$$= \frac{967}{1} = 967 \text{ Kg/cm}^2$$

$$\text{Factor of safety} = \frac{\text{Breaking stress}}{\text{Allowable max. stress}} = \frac{2500}{967} = \mathbf{2.58\ (Ans.)}$$

9. Determine the Sag and Vertical sag values for a transmission line with a cross-sectional area of 2 cm² and having a span of 150 meters between level supports. The given parameters include a wind pressure of 1.49 kg/m length, conductor tension of 2000 Kg, and a specific gravity of conductor material is 9.9 gm/c.c.

Ans. Span length (L) =150 meters

Area of cross section (a) = 2 cm²

Working tension, T = 2000 Kg

Per meter conductor material volume = 2 × 100 = 200 cm³

$$\text{Weight of conductor material/metre} = \frac{200\times9.9}{1000} = 1.98 \text{ Kg}$$

length of conductor per meter for Wind force (W_w) = 1.49 Kg

Therefore, for per meter length of the conductor, the total weight is:

$$W_{(t)} = \sqrt{(W)^2 + (W_w)^2}$$

Therefore, $$W_t = \sqrt{(1.98)^2 + (1.49)^2}$$

$$W_t = 2.478 \text{ Kg/m}$$

Therefore, $$\text{Sag, } S = \frac{W_t L^2}{8T} = \frac{2.478 \times 150 \times 150}{8 \times 2000} = 3.4875 \text{ m}$$

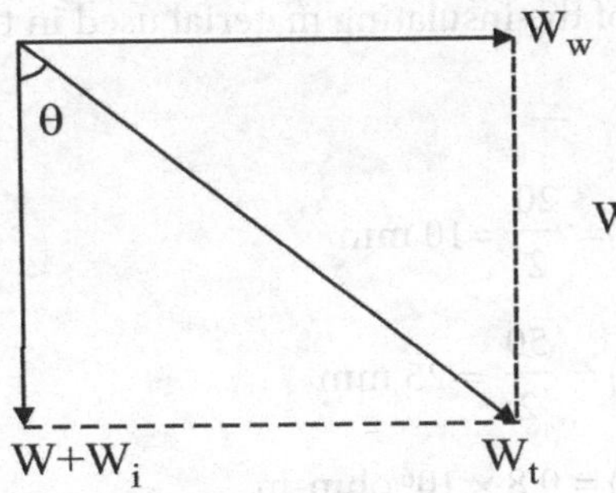

Fig. 5.27:

Thus with vertical direction slant sag is making an angle θ.

Referring figure 5.27, the value of theta (θ) is:

$$\tan\theta = \frac{W_w}{W}$$

$$= \frac{1.5}{1.98}$$

$$\tan\theta = 0.757$$

$$\theta = \tan^{-1} 0.757 = 37.125^\circ$$

Thus $$(S_v) \text{ Vertical Sag} = S \cdot \cos\theta$$

$$= 3.4875 \times \cos(37.125^\circ) = \mathbf{2.7807 \text{ m (Ans.)}}$$

10. Find the insulation resistance (R) for a 3 kilometer long single core cable having an insulation thickness of 10 mm and a radius of the conductor is 12.5mm. The specific resistivity () of the insulating material is 5×10^{12} ohm-m.

Ans. Given,

Radius of conductor, $r_1 = 12.5$ mm

Thickness of insulation =10 mm

Sheath internal radius(r_2) = 12.5 + 10 = 22.5 mm

Length of the cable, = 3 km = 3000 m

$$\log e^{(r_2 / r1)} = \log e^{(22.5 / 12.5)} = 0.5878$$

Therefore, Insulation Resistance,

$$R = \frac{\rho}{2.\pi.l} . \log e^{(r_2/r1)}$$

$$= \frac{5\times10^{12}}{2.\pi.3000} . 0.5878$$

R = 156 M-ohms (Ans.)

11. The insulation resistance of a single-core cable is measured to be 8 x 10^5 ohm-meter. The cable has a core diameter of 20 mm and an overall cable diameter, including the insulation, is 50 mm. Determine the resistivity (ρ) of the insulating material used in the cable, considering cable length to be 5 kilometer long.

Ans. Given,

Radius of the conductor, $r_1 = \frac{20}{2} = 10$ mm

sheath internal radius(r_2) = $\frac{50}{2}$ = 25 mm

Insulation Resistance (R) = 0.8 × 10^6 ohm-m

Cable having length, = 5 kilometer = 5000 meter

$\log e^{(r_2/r1)} = \log e^{(25/10)}$

Therefore, Insulation Resistance,

$$R = \frac{\rho}{2.\pi.l} . \log e^{(r_2/r1)}$$

$$0.8 \times 10^6 = \frac{\rho}{2.\pi.3000} . \log e^{(25/10)}$$

= 13.878 × 10^9 ohm-m (Ans.)

12. For a single-core cable, the insulation resistance is 480 Mega ohm/ kilometer. Calculate the thickness (t) of the insulation, if the resistivity of insulation () is 4.8 x 10^{14} ohm centimeter and the diameter of the core is 2 cm.

Ans. Given,

Insulation Resistance, R = 480 × 10^6 ohm

Cable having length, = 1 kilometer = 1000 meter

Radius of conductor, $r_1 = \frac{2}{2} = 1$ cm

Let the internal sheath radius be 'r_2'.

Therefore, the cable having insulation resistance of

$$R = \frac{\rho}{2.\pi.l} . \log e^{(r_2/r1)}$$

Or $$\log_e (r_2/r_1) = \frac{R.2.\pi.l}{\rho} = \frac{480 \times 10^{(6)} \times 2 \times 3.14 \times 1000}{4.8 \times 10^{14}}$$

$$= 0.6283$$

$$= \text{antilog } e^{0.6283} = 1.8745$$

Therefore, Outer radius, $r_2 = 1.8745 \times r_1$

$$= 1.8745 \times 1$$

$$r_2 = 1.8745 \text{ cm}$$

Insulation Thickness, $t = (r_2 - r_1) = 1.8745 - 1$

$$\mathbf{t = 0.8745 \text{ cm (Ans.)}}$$

PRACTICAL

Collect different samples of Overhead Conductors, Underground Cables, Line supports, and Line Insulators.

KNOW MORE

Students are advised to visit the following websites to understand the transmission and distribution system in India and the latest developments going on more deeply:

- Ministry of power, Govt of India - https://powermin.gov.in/
- Central Electricity Authority, Govt of India - https://cea.nic.in/?lang=en
- Ministry of new and renewable energy -https://mnre.gov.in/
- Any state electrical transmission utility.

REFERENCES AND SUGGESTED READINGS

- https://nptel.ac.in/courses/108102047
- https://nptel.ac.in/courses/108107112
- https://nptel.ac.in/courses/108105104

❑❑

CO AND PO ATTAINMENT TABLE

Course outcomes (COs) for this course can be mapped with the programme outcomes (POs) after the completion of the course and a correlation can be made for the attainment of POs to analyze the gap. After proper analysis of the gap in the attainment of POs necessary measures can be taken to overcome the gaps.

Table for CO and PO attainment

Course Outcomes	Expected Mapping with Programme Outcomes (1- Weak Correlation; 2- Medium Correlation; 3- Strong Correlation)						
	PO-1	PO-2	PO-3	PO-4	PO-5	PO-6	PO-7
CO-1	-	-	-	-	-	-	-
CO-2	-	-	-	-	-	-	-
CO-3	-	-	-	-	-	-	-
CO-4	-	-	-	-	-	-	-
CO-5	-	-	-	-	-	-	-

The data filled in the above table can be used for gap analysis.